TOTAL
CAT MOJO

TOTAL CAT MOJO

The Ultimate Guide to Life with Your Cat

JACKSON GALAXY

with Mikel Delgado and Bobby Rock

A TarcherPerigee Book

tarcherperigee

An imprint of Penguin Random House LLC
375 Hudson Street
New York, New York 10014

Copyright © 2017 by Jackson Galaxy

Illustration credits can be found on page 352

TarcherPerigee with tp colophon is a registered trademark of Penguin Random House LLC.

Most TarcherPerigee books are available at special quantity discounts for bulk purchase for sales promotions, premiums, fund-raising, and educational needs. Special books or book excerpts also can be created to fit specific needs. For details, write: SpecialMarkets@ penguinrandomhouse.com.

LIBRARY OF CONGRESS CATALOGING-IN-PUBLICATION DATA
Names: Galaxy, Jackson, author.
Title: Total cat mojo: the ultimate guide to life with your cat / Jackson Galaxy.
Description: New York, New York: TarcherPerigee Book, [2017]
Identifiers: LCCN 2017026753 (print) | LCCN 2017030305 (ebook) | ISBN 9781524705268 | ISBN 9780143131618 (paperback)
Subjects: LCSH: Cats. | Cats—Health. | BISAC: PETS / Cats / General. | PETS / Reference.
Classification: LCC SF447 (ebook) | LCC SF447 .G23 2017 (print) | DDC 636.8—dc23
LC record available at https://lccn.loc.gov/2017026753

Printed in the United States of America
10 9 8 7 6 5 4 3 2 1

BOOK DESIGN BY KATY RIEGEL

This book is dedicated to Barry:

Teacher, empath, healer, comic genius, exception to the rules

First-time cat, full-time friend to all beings

Loved and missed beyond comprehension or expression.

May your travels through time bring you back to us.

Contents

SECTION THREE

The Cat Mojo Toolbox

SECTION FOUR

The Cat Mojo Cookbook—Cat Daddy Solutions
for Industrial Strength Issues

Acknowledgments

I CLEARLY REMEMBER APPROACHING Mikel Delgado, a very busy person in her own right (working both as a private consultant and on completing her PhD), to help on my new book by saying that it was simply about curating and editing—just gather together all of what I've said, filmed, recorded, written, etc., about cats and their world through the years and put it in one place—really, how hard could that be? I spend my free time these days on a new hobby, finding new and novel ways to beg her forgiveness. *Total Cat Mojo* became a true labor of love and an all-consuming affair that spanned nearly eighteen months—and that affair was happening at the same time I was working on two different TV shows, getting the Jackson Galaxy Foundation through its nail-biting first year, and surviving a year of profound personal tragedies.

Clearly, wrangling the Catzilla could never have been done alone. I'd like to acknowledge the following people, some of whom worked on the book, some who actively supported it, and some who just gave me the space to go stark-raving cat for a spell. As individuals, they remind me that devotion to animals is something worth working for, above and beyond what might be expected. And the sum of the parts became the glue in the binding and the ink on the page. "Thank you" will *never* be enough—but, hey, it's a start:

FIRST AND FOREMOST, to Team Cat Mojo—Mikel Delgado, Bobby Rock, and Jessica Marttila: One of the many lessons learned during this epic journey is that a vision takes you only to the foot of the mountain; belief, sheer will, and surrender to said mountain takes you the rest of the way. Together, we pushed our base camp slowly upward on the daily. Whether pulling all-nighters like college freshmen (while being rudely reminded physically and mentally that we are definitely *not* college freshmen anymore), poring over every word, every image, crafting an arc and refusing to let it crumble under the weight of time, the doubts of others, and my lofty ambitions (and sometimes logic)—no task was spared.

Your unflinching willingness to go the distance trumped the quit that was ever the monster under my bed. It's safe to say that you are the reason this ever saw the light of day. Your talents are formidable, your dedication to this vision humbling, and your passion for the animals we serve will stand the test of time.

To Joy Tutela, from the beginning, you saw me not as crazy cat guy/ musician/TV personality, but as a writer who you believed in, first and foremost. Four books later, I'm glad you (and David Black) still believe— especially after this doozy. For every moment you had to put out fires, prop up my depleted spirit, and offer reassurances that these are words that will help cats and their humans, I will keep my solemn promise: the next time I say, "I've got a book for you," you can first take a Louisville Slugger to my kneecaps. And then we'll do it again . . . right?

To the team at TarcherPerigee and Penguin Random House—Joanna Ng, Brianna Yamashita, Sabrina Bowers, and Katy Riegel: from introduction to conclusion, the amazing design work and the way in which the world learns about Cat Mojo—I'm always honored to put my words in your hands. To Sara Carder—I know this was a nail-biter and a true test for us both. Thank you for standing by me, as you've always done.

To our wonderful team of artists spread around the globe—Osnat Feitelson, Emi Lenox, Franzi Paetzold, Sayako Itoh, Omaka Schultz, Brandon Page, Kyle Puttkammer, and Scott Bradley. Thank you for taking the plunge and putting your individual gifts on display to create a coherent, collective portrait of our cat Mojo and his Mojo-fied world.

To Lori Fusaro, your photos have always captured our lives at their most vulnerable and our relationships with our animals at their most precious. No matter how many times I see it, your photo of Velouria and me will remain a testament to a lasting love long after we both are gone. I haven't the words to thank you enough.

To Minoo, for what you always have been, the love of this and many lives, the guardian of my heart and sanity, believer and partner in a shared mission and for standing by me even when I'm not there. Also . . . the bat I'm giving Joy? The next time I say I want to write a book, you get a few swings, too.

To my brother Marc, for coming onboard in a time of unimaginable loss to steer the Good Ship Mojo—just in time to survive some thirty-odd rogue waves. My gratitude for lashing yourself to the deck while continuing to chart a course, and my love for believing in me and protecting me from the storm.

To my animal family—Mooshka, Audrey, Pasha, Velouria, Caroline, Pishi, Lily, Gabby, Sammy, Eddie, Ernie, Oliver, Sophie (not in any order, kids!), for a daily reminder of why we do it and for the daily dose of pure love that fills my tank.

To my father and my entire extended human family, thank you for loving me in my seemingly never-ending absence. The light you never fail to send is the soft landing I always feel.

To Stephanie Rasband, for keeping me right-sized and right here, right now.

To RDJ and The Fam, for reminding me that the steering wheel is not mine and for loving me, the helpless and wild-eyed passenger.

To my Discovery/Animal Planet family, for your continued support and desire to put a megaphone to the mojo, my continued, heartfelt thanks.

To Sandy Monterose, Christie Rogero, and our growing team of staff and volunteers at the Jackson Galaxy Foundation, for your dedication to bring the mojo to every cat who needs it and every human who needs and helps that cat.

To Ivo Fischer, Carolyn Conrad, Josephine Tan, and their teams at WME Entertainment, Schreck, Rose, Dapello & Adams, and Tan Management, for, as always, keeping the wheels on and the barbarians from the gates.

To Siena Lee-Tajiri and Toast Tajiri, for who you are and what you've always brought to our company, our vision, and to me.

Additional thanks to the wonderful and expanding team at Jackson Galaxy Enterprises, for your enthusiasm for and commitment to the mojo vision; to Susie Kaufman, for her transcriptionary brilliance; and to Julie Hecht, for her thoughtful, dog-centric feedback.

THE FIRST THING I usually do at this very moment is to call my mom and read this list to her. Whether something done out of habit or superstition, even if I know it is complete and ready to be submitted, the book is unfinished without her explicit seal of approval (always given) and the added bonus of asking me if I realize how lucky I am and telling me that I deserve all of these wonderful people surrounding me.

Yes, I am learning—that you are always there if I listen, that the universe lovingly provides, and that I should be grateful for that. I'm learning how to cope with your physical loss. Learning how to keep my heart from breaking day after day. But these lessons won't be learned tonight, and my book will just remain eternally unfinished. And I'll learn to be okay with that, too.

I miss you, love you, and thank you for everything I am.

Introduction

¿Que Es Mojo?

I AM IN FRONT of a large and very enthusiastic audience in Buenos Aires, while on a tour of Latin America. Over the course of the year, I've adjusted to speaking with a translator in places like Malaysia and Indonesia, and I had just been in Bogotá and Mexico City. If you can have simultaneous translation, with the audience wearing headphones, it is a blessing beyond belief, because the audience is with you—the laughing, gasping, and applauding happens (one hopes) just a second or three later than with an English-speaking crowd. In the big scheme of things, it's a minor inconvenience.

But, when you and your translator switch off (you finish a full thought before he begins), well . . . it's just a massive headache at best, an absolute kamikaze mission at worst. My translator would stand next to me, a ghost dodging my physical outbursts and stream-of-consciousness rants. The more excited I get, however, the less I remember to heed the presence or the needs of my "ghost." Some translators, the ones who pride themselves as practitioners of a linguistic art form, allow me to get an entire paragraph out of my mouth before tapping me on the shoulder or giving me that sideways glance, in order to succinctly and with equal fervor catch the audience up.

On this night in Buenos Aires, my translator isn't that person. She is actually a newscaster who happens to be bilingual. It is not the most graceful dance, that's for sure. There is much in the way of toe stepping on both of our parts.

Improvisation aside, I always introduce the concept of Cat Mojo early in the show. It's the linchpin of my entire presentational spiel. That introduction, on this night, is firing on all cylinders; I'm feeling it for sure, as I attempt to occupy the space between cat guy and Pentecostal revivalist. I'm breathlessly demonstrating what a Mojo-fied cat looks like, shamelessly preening, modeling the tail and ear postures, the overall gait of confidence. This all culminates at that moment when I say, "And what do we call this? Man, we call this Cat Mojo. Your cat. Has . . . MOJO." I allow that statement to reverberate. And it reverberates for entirely too long, going from a drama-filled beat to an awkward silence. I give my translator that sideways glance. Nothing comes out of her mouth, and her eyes betray a slight panic.

At once, she allows her newscasterly character to fall away. She leans in close to me and whispers, "Qué es mojo?" And I respond, in hindsight maybe a bit too loud, "What do you mean, 'What is mojo?' You don't know what mojo means?" We're having a conversation on this stage, and with every passing reverberant second, I'm losing my grip on this audience. Incredulous, I turn to them with equal measures of validation seeking and creeping dread, and say in full sideshow-barker voice, "Hey, folks, you know what mojo means, right? 'You've got your mojo on,' 'You've got your mojo workin'.' How many people here know what the word 'mojo' means?"

Cue the crickets. That feeling of creeping dread is now a full-on, flop-sweat-inducing nightmare. For the first time since I was twelve years old, holding a guitar with a broken string at a YMCA talent show, I am about to flame out before a live audience, and I couldn't think of a single way out of it.

I THINK BACK to 2002, when I was sitting at my desk in Boulder, Colorado. The desk consisted of a big chunk of particleboard resting on two sawhorses. I was inspired at the time to turn what I knew into a manifesto of sorts—well, less inspired and more motivated. After a few years as an independent behavior consultant, I found myself trying entirely too hard to boil my knowledge base about all cats down to a relatable info-nugget for my clients, so we could more readily get to the part where they apply that knowledge to getting to know *their* cats. As is the case today, but much more so back then, cats are dismissed as being inscrutable—so far outside the behavioral and experiential realm of humans that we have no anchor point to hang a relationship on. I was determined to find that *hook*.

Finding the hook was not about convenience, either. Remember, I had worked for ten years in an animal shelter and was more than a little invested. Far too many cats—millions a year—were (and still are) being killed in these shelters. Time and time again I would witness a question mark-shaped barrier of communication becoming a barbed-wire fence that led to the fracturing of very tender and tenuous relationships. It was the "mystery" of cats' behavior—their inscrutable nature being fed through the human gumball machine called ego and emerging as a perceived insult—that compelled those frustrated humans to surrender them to the shelter or even turn them loose into the street. I was trying to, at the very least, take the barbed wire off the fence, so that the human and the animal could meet there safely and begin the process of deepening, instead of destroying, their bond.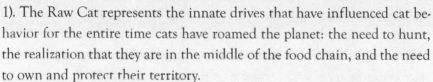

One hook that I had already started employing with my students and clients was the concept of "the Raw Cat"—the idea that the cat in your lap is, in an evolutionary way, millimeters removed from his ancestors (more on this in chapter 1). The Raw Cat represents the innate drives that have influenced cat behavior for the entire time cats have roamed the planet: the need to hunt, the realization that they are in the middle of the food chain, and the need to own and protect their territory.

As such, I came to believe that many, if not most, of the problems that my cat clients were experiencing (with the exception of undiagnosed physical issues), could be boiled down to territorial anxiety. The Raw Cat, content most of the time to stay in a place in the back of your cat's mind, comes screaming to the fore when confronted with a threat to territorial security. Whether that threat is real or perceived matters little. The fact is, if they feel it, they will almost *have to* act upon it. It's not enough to address the symptoms that become hair-pulling annoyances to us. Rather, we must find the opposite of that anxiety and coax that Raw Cat quality out to the point where it dominates and eventually extinguishes the anxiety.

Back to my makeshift desk: It was very late at night, and I was trying to push through that insistent, hallucinogenic moment when sleep would come whether I liked it or not. The risk of going face-first into the keyboard was fifty-fifty at best. I would type, realize I was in zombie mode, go back over it, erase almost everything, and start again.

I was about to pass out, so I got to my feet and started to concentrate on what confidence *looks like* instead of trying to explain it. Pacing my office, I decided that it was a strut. It was tail up in the backward question mark position, ears relaxed, eyes not dilated, whiskers neutral. No threat in sight, no fight-or-flight mechanism enacted. Neither the weaponry nor radar was needed. No need to take the feline alert system to DEFCON 1 and unlock the box that had the red button in it, because there was a deep, abiding sense that all was well in the world. This strut was not artificial in any way; it was not a product of how cats want the world to perceive them. In other words, it didn't come from a place of cockiness. It was confidence that could only come from a deep sense of knowing that they own their place in the world. They could go about their day without eyes in the back of their heads, without wondering whether what they owned would be ripped from underneath them. This instinct was so grounded that it was beyond skeletal. It was coming from the vibration of history—a quantum communication—connecting cats to each other through the ages. The hook I was searching for, the thing I wanted humans to relate to, was what it felt like to experience the essence of *confident ownership of territory.*

I thought that if guardians could recognize and massage this present state of confidence, as simplistic as it may seem, it could help them head off most of the "symptoms" they complain so bitterly about, including cases of aggression and inappropriate litterbox behaviors. As I paced around the room, trying to humanize this strut, this confident swagger, the first vocal manifestation of the physicality came out of my mouth—the gusto-filled refrain from one of my musical heroes, Muddy Waters: "I got my mojo workin'!"

The hook had come, and I was not about to let it slip away. I had to wake myself up. I splashed water on my face. I slapped myself on the back of my neck, something I think a friend of mine taught me in high school to keep me awake during class. I even stepped outside my apartment into the Colorado winter in the dead of night, in nothing but my robe, partly to keep *my* mojo working and partly just to be aware of the moment, because I was so sure that it would be one I'd want to remember. And I was right; as time has gone on, it's not an exaggeration to say that almost everything I have built in the name of helping cats revolves around humans understanding Cat Mojo.

NOW, WE'RE BACK in Buenos Aires, back to the moment of crickets and creeping dread. I'm on that stage, asking the audience a simple question: "How many people here know what the word 'mojo' means?" Two, maybe three people—out of five hundred—raise their hands. I had built my career on a word that was falling on not just deaf ears, but on *very* confused ears.

Because of the language barrier (and because I am completely panicking and without words, English or otherwise), I have no choice but to *demonstrate*. I am forced back to that night in Boulder, forced to find and deliver that hook again; I need to find something that (a) my audience can relate to, and (b) my translator can translate. And all I can think of is *Saturday Night Fever*. And that scares me.

I have no time to consider whether this would be a *really* bad, evening-sinking choice . . . so away I go, painting a picture, faithful to my teenage memories, of the opening frames of the movie:

The Bee Gee's "Stayin' Alive" is pounding. The camera captures the sidewalk of Brooklyn, tracking upward from '70s fabulous-looking shoes. It starts to pan up from hem to belt of flared-out and equally fabulous pants, past the silky, open-to-the-chest shirt, finally rising to reveal John Travolta, a.k.a. Tony Manero. He is carrying a can of paint in one hand and a slice of pizza in the other. And we discover, from shoes to perfect hair, the definition of swagger; Muddy Waters must surely be nodding his head in vigorous affirmation from somewhere in the great blues beyond—Tony has his mojo workin'.

I pause a beat to gauge response. Between the increasingly frenetic tempo and tone of my interpreter, and the steady outbreak of knowing smiles throughout the theater, I know the audience is getting it. So I begin to imitate the Manero strut.

Tony knows things. In the spirit of mojo, he doesn't know these things as a way of convincing himself of his status. He. Just. *Knows*. The girls want to be with him, and the guys want to *be* him. Most important, Tony knows that Tony owns Brooklyn. Or at least this couple of blocks of Brooklyn. And that is understood wordlessly, spoken through the Mojo-fied language of swagger. The Manero strut is not a walk of demonstra-tion, of proving. It is simply the outer manifestation of a grounded inner sense of ownership and belonging. The pizza grease dripping off his chin, the cans of paint that signify his lack of status, even the unresponsiveness of the numerous women he is catcalling along the way—none of it matters.

Doing the Manero strut back and forth across the expansive stage has me winded. With my hands on my knees, I look up and am met with ex-cited murmurs and head nodding, telling me that I just dodged a bullet for sure. Having my feet held to the fire by a language barrier is the best thing that could have happened. That night in Buenos Aires marks a mat-uration of the concept of Cat Mojo, not only because I can define it in a way that I never thought I had to, but because I now know that I can show anyone, regardless of cultural differences, what mojo is, and that their mojo comes from the exact same place as Cat Mojo.

FROM MY LATE-NIGHT epiphany in Boulder to the night in Buenos Aires seven-teen years later, to every live performance, every in-home consultation, every class I've taught, and every episode of *My Cat from Hell*—it all leads us here, to this book: *Total Cat Mojo*. My primary occupation through these years ac-tually has not been about solving cat issues, but about teaching you how to find, cultivate, and hold on to mojo. Am I referring to you or your cat right now? Well, both, really. Because if you got your mojo workin', it's a heck of a lot easier to bring it out of your cat. And if your cat has his mojo workin', it's enough to make any human smile with envy . . . even Tony Manero.

Section

ONE

The History of the Mojo-fied World—
From Raw Cat to Your Cat

Cat Daddy Dictionary: Cat Mojo

For cats, Mojo is all about confidence. Mojo is proactive, rather than reactive. Cats' source of Mojo is unquestioned ownership of their territory and having an important job to do within that territory. That job is a biological imperative that cats inherited from their wildcat ancestors, and I call it: Hunt, Catch, Kill, Eat, Groom, Sleep. When we create a rhythm that mirrors that of the Raw Cat—the ancestor—we're there. When cats are at home inside their bodies, they can make the space outside their bodies their home as well.

1

Who Is the Raw Cat?

T HERE IS ANOTHER cat living inside your cat. Strip away the "creature comforts"—the cat beds, the mouse-shaped toys, a life spent
looking out the window, or lying peacefully on the couch. You
might see a glimpse of that other cat when she
wakes you up in the middle of the night hunting
your toes under the blanket—and there you'll find
that "other" whom I call the Raw Cat. In essence,
the Raw Cat is your cat's ancestral twin. These
twins, separated by eons, are nonetheless in very
close contact, as if there were a tin-can-and-string
telephone connecting them through their DNA
strands. Through that straight and unadulterated

Hi! I'm Mojo!
I'll be your guide to the Raw Cat.

line, the Raw Cat sends constant transmissions to your companion about
the urgency of securing territory, hunting, killing, eating, and staying ever
alert, because just as cats hunt, they are also being hunted.

From Big to Small

11 million years ago (mya)—The family Felidae split
into the two categories of existing cat species, the
Pantherinae (seven species of big cats: tigers,
lions, jaguars, and four species of leopards) and the Felinae, which
is mostly small cats, including the ones who live in our homes. (For
perspective, humans split from our closest relatives much later,
between 5 and 7 million years ago!)

9.4 mya—The first bay cats
(*Catopuma*) form a separate
lineage from the ancestors of all
the remaining members of the
Felinae subfamily.

11 million years ago

9.4 mya

Everything about our cats, from their territorial identification and nutritional requirements to the ways they play and behave, are linked back to their raw twin. These characteristics all represent a shared prime objective, passed down with minor dilution, over tens of thousands of years. In fact, when you take into consideration how many traits—both physical and behavioral—that your cat has retained from the Raw Cat, it's safe to say that from an evolutionary standpoint, these twins are almost identical.

Throughout this book, I'll be asking you to tune into your cat's *rawness* because that's where Mojo lives. You'll start to recognize when she's tapping into her Raw Cat, and you'll learn the importance of knowing how and where that happens. But I also want you to have a true 360-degree perspective of her moment-to-moment actions, and that only reveals itself once we understand *why* the pulse of the Raw Cat beats so close to the surface.

8.5 mya—The Caracal lineage (servals [*Serval*], caracals [*Leptailurus*], African golden cats) diverges.

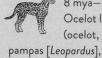 8 mya—The Ocelot lineage (ocelot, margay, pampas [*Leopardus*], Geoffroy's cats) diverges.

 7.2 mya—The Lynx lineage (lynx and bobcat [*Lynx*]) diverges.

9.4 mya

RAW CAT ROOTS

Once upon a time—a really long time ago—the first inkling of cat-ness happened when carnivores appeared on earth. Carnivores evolved from smaller mammals around 42 million years ago. Members of this order (which includes cats, dogs, bears, raccoons, and many other species) are defined by the structure of their teeth—which are designed to shear meat—and not by their diet. (Some members of the order Carnivora are omnivorous or even vegetarians.)

The Carnivora (evolutionarily speaking) split into two groups, or "suborders": the doglike animals—called the Caniformia, and the catlike animals—called the Feliformia. And what exactly helped define them as "catlike"? Well, what would you call a group of ambush hunters who tended to be more carnivorous than other members of Carnivora? I'd call that the very Rawest Cat!

Cat Daddy Fact

The genomes of tigers and domestic cats are over 96 percent similar—meaning the proteins that make the cat "blueprint" are organized similarly in many cat species.

6.7 mya—The Cheetah lineage (pumas and cheetahs [*Acinonyx*]) splits off from the remaining small cats.

6.2 mya—The genus *Felis* (the European wildcat, the Southern African wildcat, the Central Asian wildcat, Chinese desert cat, and Near Eastern wildcat), which includes our own domestic cats, form a separate lineage from the other small cats (Asian leopard cats, fishing cats, and the Pallas's cat).

A BEAUTIFUL MUTATION IS BORN!
HOW NEW SPECIES COME ABOUT

As we're looking at our evolutionary cat timeline, you might be asking, "What's with all of these splits and divergences?" They mark periods when there was an ancestral species—the grandparent of all those cats, so to speak—and from that grandparent, a separate family branched off to do its own cat thing.

Specifically, new species form when genetic changes occur over time and cause populations to mutate. These changes often happen when a group of animals becomes isolated from other members of the same spe-

Cat Nerd Corner

Far East, Far Out:
The Origins of the Siamese Cat

When cats spread to the Far East around 2,000 years ago, there were no local wildcats for these newcomers to interbreed with. This genetic isolation led to some mutations related to appearance, which led to several of the distinct features of the Oriental breeds—including the Siamese, Tonkinese, and Birmans. Recent DNA studies suggest about 700 years of independent breeding from other breeds, and while still the same species as other domestic cats, have a genetic profile that suggests they have a unique ancestor with origins in Southeast Asia.

130,000 years ago (ya)—Near Eastern wildcats, our cats' closest relatives, split from other *Felis*. A 2009 genetic study of 979 cats (domestic, feral, and wild) demonstrated that all domestic cats are descendants of *Felis sylvestris lybica*, the Near Eastern wildcat, and that the Near East was the origin of domestication.

cies. This can be due to changes in the environment—perhaps an area becomes more or less protected, or prey abundance shifts—leading some animals to move to a different territory. There can be proximity barriers, such as when islands form or a new river emerges, creating separation between groups. And there can be behavioral factors—for example, when nocturnal animals are less likely to mate with animals who are active during the day.

These genetic changes are usually physical (if the two species have different features) or reproductive (when two species cannot interbreed) in nature. But the lines can get a little blurry—as demonstrated by the ability of humans to produce several kinds of hybrid cats. Nonetheless, the faster the animals can reproduce, the quicker these changes can take effect (in evolutionary time, of course) and lead to new species.

THE SMALL CATS

Small cats can be further classified as either Old World (from Africa, Asia, or Europe) or New World (from Central and South America). Old World cats include domestic cats, wild cats, fishing cats, lynx, bobcat, caracal, serval, and cheetah. New World cats include ocelots, Geoffroy's cat, and pumas.

There is not as clear a division between the New and Old World cats as there is within other species of animals, mainly because all cats are evolutionarily pretty tightly knit. However, there are a few behavioral differences. For example:

Domestication Time
The timeline, like cats, is a little fuzzy

12,000 ya—The earliest human grain stores of the Middle Eastern Fertile Crescent created a high concentration of rodents, which would have attracted small carnivores.

9,500 ya—Archaeologists found evidence in Cyprus that a cat was buried with a human, along with various decorations, in a grave that was dated at almost 10,000 years old. Wildcats were not native to this island, meaning they would have been introduced by humans in some way. This individual cat may have been *tamed*, even if cats were not fully domesticated yet.

12,000 ya

9,500 ya

Old World   *New World*

- Old World cats lie with their paws tucked under the body (in the "meatloaf position"), while New World cats do not.
- Old World cats are less likely to pluck the feathers from their small bird prey, while New World cats are inclined to thoroughly pluck before eating their birds.
- Old World cats bury their poop, while New World cats do not. (Imagine how different our litterbox situation might have played out had our beloved house cats descended from the New World, rather than the Old!)

Cat Daddy Fact

All big cats roar (except for snow leopards), but they don't typically purr (except for cheetahs). Small cats purr, but can't roar. This is due, in part, to a small bone in the neck called the hyoid. In big cats, this bone is flexible, but in small cats, it is rigid. The big cats also have flat, square vocal cords, and a longer vocal tract that allows them to make a louder, lower sound with less effort. In small cats, the hardened hyoid combined with vocal folds are believed to create the purring sound.

5,000 ya—Evidence of cat domestication in China, where the first domesticated species was the Asian leopard cat (*Prionailurus bengalensis*): this was a short-lived relationship, perhaps because Asian leopard cats are notoriously more difficult to tame than *F. s. lybica*, which frequently live in close proximity to humans. (Today, all domesticated cats in China are descendants of *Felis sylvestris lybica*.)

Roaring may give big cats another way to control their turf without fighting or engaging in face-to-face conflict. Its sheer volume is a long-distance message—"I'm here, keep your distance please." (For more on purring, see chapter 4.)

With all of this talk about what separates Old and New World, big and small cats, and small from one another, we might forget the most remarkable, undeniably raw fact: *all* existing cat species (currently estimated at forty-one) share a common ancestor. That means that *all* felines are obligate carnivores, with large eyes and ears, powerful jaws, and a body built to kill. *All* cats walk quietly on their toes, with protractible claws, which supports their silent stalk-and-rush hunting style. And, last but not least, perhaps the most unifying (and definitely the most Mojo-rific) force connecting all felines, from lions to tabbies, is the drive to claim and own territory.

THE ROAD TO LESS WILD:
THE "DOMESTICATION" STORY

It is difficult for scientists to form a really clear timeline of the recent domestication of cats, because genetically, physically, and behaviorally they are so similar to their closest wild relatives (so much so that there's been a lot of interbreeding among domestic cats and other wildcat species). In fact, the word "domestic," when applied to cats, has always struck me as fundamentally . . . well, just wrong. I don't believe cats have ever been fully domesticated. This speaks to my insistence at seeing the rawness in your cat at all times. To me, in each moment that you identify the Raw

4,000 ya—Evidence of domestication in Egypt: remains of F. s. are found in tombs, and paintings and sculptures depict cats as existing side by side with humans, and with collars.

2,500 ya—Despite a ban on exporting cats from Egypt, they moved to India, and by 2,500 ya, cats had spread to Greece, the Far East, Eurasia, and Africa.

2,500 ya

Cat in your cat, you are disproving the very notion of domestication. That said, as we continue with our story here, let's take a look at what we do know about how the Raw Cat gradually transformed into what we now call the "house cat."

For thousands of years, cats lived with and around people, but were never completely dependent on them. *F. s. lybica*—the ancestral species—appears to be one of the more tameable of all the closely related wildcats, suggesting a predisposition for living with humans. Ultimately, though, the pathway to evolution was laid by the benefits that cats and humans mutually provided for each other. As agriculture began to flourish in our earliest human settlements, the rodent population drastically increased. This made proximity to humans attractive to cats, and the natural pest control they provided attractive to humans. This would prove to be a recurring "win/win" theme throughout history.

GODS AND MUMMIES

The downside of any long-term relationship between humans and animals is that it's not an equitable one. Humans, through the centuries, unfortunately always held the cards and could be very harsh in how they dealt those cards out. In general, cats seemed to be revered in proportion to how much a cat's pest control prowess was needed. That said, the true human/ cat roller coaster ride began in earnest as humans were left to simply appreciate cats for their unique personalities and brand of companionship. As the ride heated up, gaining momentum and speed through history, our feline friends often found themselves reviled . . . to the extreme.

We've all heard stories of cat worship in Egypt. But it's important to note that the Egyptian economy was highly dependent on grains . . .

2,000 ya—The Romans expanded their empire, and cats tagged along.

1,200 ya—Domestic cats spread into Northern Europe.

which means agriculture . . . which means rodents . . . which means, once again, cats playing their welcomed role as "nature's exterminator." This likely set the stage for the elevated status that would come to them in Egyptian society. (Contrast this, for example, with the many parts of Europe where weasels were already playing this exterminator role, so cats were not of particular use.)

Still, the Egyptians revered cats, perhaps like no other culture. Cats were depicted throughout Egyptian artwork, lived in religious temples, and were kept as pets. The intentional harming of a cat brought serious penalties, and if a cat passed of natural causes, the human family would shave their eyebrows to mourn. This feline worship/devotion is documented through the mummification of cats, who were often prepared for a life in the afterworld with mummified mice to accompany them.

500 ya—Domestic cats spread into the Americas and Australia. Cats were probably passengers on the *Mayflower* to serve as pest control.

But even in the cat-loving environs of Egypt, the aforementioned roller coaster would take a few unfortunate plunges. Not all mummified cats were cherished pets. They were also used as offerings to deities, and the demand for these offerings led to cat "breeding mills," so cats could be deliberately killed and mummified.

The prophet Muhammad was another cat lover, and in Islamic cultures, cats have always been appreciated for more than just their extermination skills. According to one of the most well-known stories about Muhammad's reverence for his beloved cats, when he was called to prayer and his favorite cat, Muezza, was sleeping on the sleeve of his prayer robe,

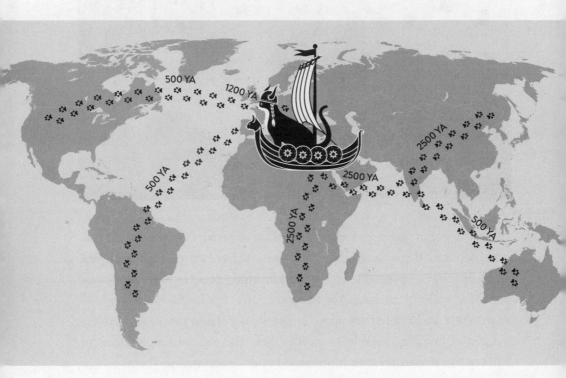

Today, cats live on every continent except Antarctica.
They are perhaps the most successful species on the planet
in their ability to adapt—second only to humans.

500 ya   *Today*

Muhammad cut off the sleeve of the robe rather than disturb Muezza. (Sound familiar? How many of you have forgone getting off the couch because you had a cat asleep on your lap?)

In other parts of the world where cats were worshipped—particularly in pagan cultures—cats' hallowed status became tainted as the persecution of non-Christians increased. In fact, things got really bad for our cat friends during the Middle Ages, when they were associated with cults and declared unholy. It is believed that millions of cats were sentenced to death and burned in witch trials or thrown into bonfires. And if cat owners tried to protect their pets, they would face inquisition themselves.

The sad irony is that during this time, the Black Death spread and killed thousands of people. Rats (or rather the fleas they carried) were known carriers of the plague, and killing massive numbers of cats would have certainly contributed to the proliferation of rats. Granted, archaeologists have more recently called the relationship between rats and the spread of the plague into question, suggesting that the plague spread so quickly due to close contact between humans, not between *rats* and humans. Regardless, killing thousands of cats could not have helped matters.

Even today, superstition and stigma continues to color folks' perceptions of cats. We've all heard "Don't let a black cat cross your path," or that cats can "steal a baby's breath." And even though cats are more popular than ever, we still kill them in mass numbers in shelters every year, and there has even been a widespread call to eradicate feral cats from the outdoors. Hopefully, these ideologies will soon become part of our past as well.

The Victorian Tipping Point

D ESPITE ALL OF the ups and downs our Raw Cat has experienced through the centuries, nothing would impact her experience quite as much as her moving indoors. Come to think of it, the same could be said for *our* experience, as well. This is where the evolutionary timeline starts zigging and zagging, and the human/cat relationship begins to define and redefine itself in rapid succession based on a new close-quarters living arrangement. But considering we were all doing just fine with the "you stay outdoors and we'll stay indoors" agreement that we'd always had with cats, how and why did this ever happen? And . . . how have things progressed in the human/cat dynamic since?

Bringing the Outdoors In

Here's a quick overview of the modern cat's rising rank in society, once the indoor cat model was popularized:

1871—First cat show in the United Kingdom

1876—First manufacturer of cat food in the UK (Spratt)

1870

MOVING ON UP . . .

Around 150 years ago, humans decided to bring cats into their homes. Many credit Queen Victoria for popularizing the idea of "I like cats, and I want them in my house."

Queen Victoria was known as a bit of a loner, and also as a huge animal lover. She advanced the cause of animal welfare and, with her patronage, assigned the term "royal" to the SPCA, making it the Royal SPCA. In addition to her many dogs, horses, goats, etc., she had two beloved Persian cats. Her last cat, White Heather, lived out her life at Buckingham Palace, long after the queen herself had died.

During this time (Victorian era, nineteenth-century England), the practice of pet keeping increased. The humane treatment of other animals was growing, and pets were both a status symbol and a way for the genteel to demonstrate their power over nature. The fastidiousness of cats may have made them a perfect "wild but still clean" species for humans to get close to. Also, many writers and artists expressed their love for the cat, and people began having funerals for their beloved felines.

1895—Spratt brings cat food to the United States ●

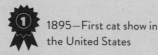
1895—First cat show in the United States

1930s—U.S. production of canned cat food ●

. . . TO A DELUXE APARTMENT IN THE SKY

Clearly, much has changed since the Rawest of Raw Cats roamed the earth, both from their relationship to humans and, to a lesser degree, their genetic makeup. While both cats and dogs have been famously successful at coexisting with humans, our relationship with cats (in stark contrast to dogs) has blossomed without us really asking them to change. The cat we had around to protect our grains from rodents is essentially the same cat we share a bed with today.

The biggest shift in human/cat relations has occurred because of the demographic shift of cat "ownership" from a rural model to a more urban model. As previously mentioned, the role of cats in the rural model was more about being farmhand exterminators than about being part of the family unit . . . even to the extent that they might be let indoors. In contrast, the urban model has spawned a more affectionate, family-member type of relationship between cat and guardian. There are a number of reasons for this.

First, urbanism typically means that more people live singly, rather than in groups, and with fewer relatives nearby. Combine this with more divorce and fewer children, and you can begin to see how the human/cat relationship occupies a more central role in the guardian's life. Also, people in cities tend to live in smaller spaces and work longer hours. This has created a tendency to adopt smaller companion animals, like cats, as a matter of practicality. Oh yeah, and let's not forget my favorite reason for cats' popularity in urban settings: they are often portrayed as a "low-maintenance" pet! Of course, if that were the case, I wouldn't have a job, right?

Still, this rural-to-urban, outdoor-to-indoor paradigm shift is not a done deal—not even close. It is in progress; we are still very much *shift-*

1930s—Spaying and neutering of cats and dogs introduced

1940s—Meat shortage
+ Limited meat rations in the 1940s leads to the development of dry food, which made use of livestock scraps and fish.
+ Dry food eventually becomes the majority of cat food produced and purchased.

1930

ing. For one thing, there are still many places around the world where cats are perceived as pests or vermin. And in cultures (like ours) where they are loved and revered, many still see cats in the classic "born free" model of their free-roaming ancestors and consider it cruel, an act of hostage taking, to keep them indoors. As we've seen throughout the story of the Raw Cat and his human companions, the happily ever after is an elusive goal.

TURBOCHARGED EVOLUTION: HOW HAS LIVING WITH HUMANS CHANGED CATS?

Approximately 96 percent of cats still choose their own mates these days. This has made for a relatively unaltered and organic genetic through line in the majority of our modern cats. But that doesn't mean cats haven't changed simply by living with us. In a sense, cats have self-selected: friendlier cats, who are more tolerant of humans, may be more likely to be fed and sheltered by them, and more likely to mate with cats who have similar friendly/tolerant genes. So, while there's been an absence of strong intentional selection for specific physical or behavioral characteristics among cats, it has actually been our relationship with them that has led to the most significant genetic changes.

1947—Invention of kitty litter by Ed Lowe. Before that, people used ashes, dirt, or sand, but most people let their cats "go" outside.

1940s and 1950s—Spay/neuter continues, but is not common
+ General anesthesia is recommended, but not required!
+ Somehow the idea spreads that it is "humanitarian" to allow females to have one litter.

Cat Nerd Corner

What Has Changed with Today's Cat?

In 2014, scientists collected cheek swabs for DNA analysis of twenty-two domestic cats of several breeds (Maine Coon, Norwegian Forest, Birman, Japanese Bobtail, Turkish Van, Egyptian Mau, and Abyssinian), as well as the Near Eastern and European wildcats. From this information, they were able to determine some of the key genetic changes that occurred in domesticated cats.

Genetic changes that are associated with:

- Better ability to form memories
- Better ability to make associations between a stimulus and a reward (such as humans offering them food)
- Less rapid fear conditioning—meaning today's cat is not as quick to go into fight-or-flight mode

Physical characteristics:

- Smaller body
- Shorter jaw
- Smaller brain
- Smaller adrenals, which control fight-or-flight instinct
- Lengthened intestines, for adaptation to scavenging human food
- All cats have long canine teeth that allow them to kill with a bite to the neck. Domestic cats' teeth are more narrowly spaced than those

1969—First low-cost spay/neuter clinic opens in Los Angeles. Before that, euthanasia numbers were *off the charts.*

1950s—Explosion of cat food brands

1950

of other cats, because they are adapted to catching smaller rodents—most domestic cats' preferred prey.

What Has Not Changed with Today's Cat?

- Skull shape—the shape of the skull across all cat species is similar, and they have a specialized jaw designed to kill with a powerful bite. Our cats' skulls may be a lot smaller than lions' and tigers', but the structure is very similar.
- Behavior! (To a large extent . . .)
- Most cats choose their own mates, which keeps the gene pool diverse.
- Cats still (for the most part) can survive without us.

THE PUPPET MASTER ENTERS: PUREBRED CATS

Humans first got a decent grasp on the principles of genetics in the late 1800s, when Gregor Mendel published his famous work on the inheritance of dominant and recessive traits in pea plants. Before that era, people were breeding animals, including farm animals and, of course, dogs. At that time, breeding of most animals was for the purpose of ensuring a reliable source of food. Dogs, on the other hand, were bred for specific jobs—to aid with hunting by flushing out game, to retrieve, or to fight. But when it came to creating desired results for appearance or behaviors, success was anything but consistent, primarily because we had only a rudimentary understanding of how genetics worked.

But once we had that understanding, humans were able to "influence"

1972—ASPCA requires adopted animals to be spayed and neutered before going home.

1970s—Change to primarily indoor-only lifestyle (especially in United States)
- ✦ Recommended by many veterinary and humane organizations to protect cats from danger, to protect wildlife from their hunting, and because cats are increasingly accepted as family members.

1990

cat evolution via controlled breeding—that is, selecting cats' mates for them. However, the starting point for breeding cats was for aesthetic, rather than functional, purposes. We weren't asking them to change who they were, just how they looked.

As a result, by selecting and mating cats for certain physical features, the early breeds (such as the Persian) were born. In fact, the earliest cat breeding was often an attempt to achieve certain coat colors (with the misunderstanding that breeding a black cat with a white cat would produce gray kittens). The first Championship Cat Show in the United Kingdom in 1871 featured Persians, Russian Blues, Siamese, Angoras, and Abyssinians, in addition to Manxes and shorthaired cats of many colors.

And once there were particular breeds of cats, up sprang several clubs to celebrate these breeds, and the "cat fancy" was born: shows, judges, bows, and proud parents—like *Toddlers and Tiaras*. But instead of focusing on the perfect spray tan and tap-dancing routines, the fanciers developed standards that would define the preferred physical characteristics that a given breed should have, such as the shape of their eyes, ears, face, tail, and even their paws. Often, though, these differences were as simple as coat color. For example, Persians were initially defined by their long chinchilla-colored coat, not by having a flat face. Seal point coloration alone was what distinguished the Siamese from your average cat. These breeds were distinct, but not extremely different, in appearance from other domestic cats.

Today, breeding is an altogether different beast (so to speak), with organizations recognizing anywhere from forty-four to nearly sixty different breeds of cats. In the process, we have pushed cats' physical appearance to extremes, often without regard for the well-being of the cats being bred. We've made the Persian's face flatter and the Siamese face thinner and

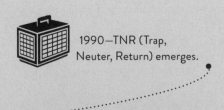

1990—TNR (Trap, Neuter, Return) emerges.

1994—First mobile spay/neuter truck is started in Houston, Texas, when it is recognized that people need the service, but cannot always travel to a vet clinic to get their pets spayed or neutered.

more pointed. Consequently, the changes we have imposed through breeding are in many ways detrimental to the Raw Cat.

By selecting Persians for the brachycephalic (short-nosed) appearance, we have actually made it harder for them to breathe, increased the chance of skin, dental, and eye disease, and made giving birth riskier and more difficult. Scottish Folds are used as a model for studying pain and arthritis because the mutations that cause the folds in their ears also lead to painful degeneration in their bones and cartilage. Manx cats are prone to back pain, constipation, and other elimination problems because of spinal cord deformities. Maine Coon cats are prone to heart disease, and Siamese cats have a higher likelihood of asthma and hyperesthesia.

These are just a few examples. When you limit the gene pool, you increase the chance of dangerous mutations and disease. There's no other way around it.

Humans may be pulling the strings when it comes to cats' exteriors, but are we making any progress in understanding their inner world?

FOR ALL THE progress we've made by bringing cats indoors, cat domestication has ushered in a new set of problems, at least from where I stand. It seems that no matter where the pendulum swings, it doesn't swing in full favor of the cat. Previously, their role as farmhands secured their survival but, as we've seen, not their status. Likewise, they are now too often seen as "family lite," more of a representation of what it is to parent another than actually occupying the true nature of that relationship.

Now, I'm not trying to hang humans out to dry; this period of massive adjustment cuts both ways, and it's asking a lot of both parties to change the way they live in order to accommodate another. I'm just asking you to

1999—The organization In Defense of Animals (IDA) begins the Guardian Campaign, seeking a change of language and legal status for companion animals by changing the term "pet owner" to "pet guardian."

2003—West Hollywood becomes first U.S. city to ban declawing.

think about this: in the less-than-150 years since Queen Victoria—which is an evolutionary blink of an eye—we now ask cats to pee in a box, sleep all night, sit on the couch, not traipse across our counters or our computer keyboards . . . and last but not least, to shrink their territory from a few hundred acres to a studio apartment. The upshot here is that the more that cats are seen as home accessories, the less they can achieve the ideal we've set for them, and the more slippery the slope that leads them back to social pariahs.

AND THERE YOU have it: forty-two million years of evolution, and a thorough introduction to the Raw Cat, all boiled down to a couple of short chapters. In section 2, we'll get into everything you always wanted to know about your cat—as he or she exists in the present—but were afraid to ask.

Section

TWO

A Crash Course in Cats

3

The Raw Cat Rhythm

BACK IN THE early days of my job, I just assumed my clients and students—along with cat guardians everywhere—were thirsty for knowledge about *all* cats. So I spent entirely too much time staying up at night trying to break my philosophy down into bite-sized pieces for them. It turned out that most of the cat people in my stratosphere were mainly interested in knowledge relating to *their* cats, because, understandably, those who hired me wanted to know how to make *their* cats stop acting out. As a result, they saw my impassioned attempts at connecting the cat dots as unnecessary icing on the cake. This led me to the revelation that, when it came to getting these folks on board the big-picture train, I had a very small window of opportunity before their eyes started glazing over.

And so, just as I did with the term "Cat Mojo," I needed to find that *hook*: a quick-fire way of reminding guardians that their cats' behavior was tied to the behaviors of the Raw Cat. In this case, I wanted them to understand the paramount importance of the "three Rs"—Routines, Rituals, and Rhythm—in their cat's life; the three Rs are based on the hunter's lifestyle of their ancestors. The Raw Cat, as we've established, *needed* to accomplish very specific tasks every single day in order to feel Mojo-fied.

The hook that I came up with—that mnemonic sticky note—was *Hunt,*

Catch, Kill, Eat, Groom, Sleep (HCKEGS). I would (and still do) have my clients repeat the words in rhythm and with gusto, as if we were cat cheerleaders, until it became a mantra. The mantra, once absorbed, serves as a constant reminder to the guardian that this Raw Cat Rhythm makes the world go 'round for your cat, and it is your job to "feed the rhythm." This reminds you to establish routines around playtime, rest time, and mealtime—even down to what your cat is eating. Every road leads to Mojo, and one of the major street signs along the route says, in neon letters, HCKEGS.

HUNT, CATCH, KILL, EAT

Historically, as we discussed in section 1, our goal for cats to serve as nature's pest control, and their goal for themselves as honorary exterminators, aligned perfectly. Hunt, Catch, Kill, Eat (HCKE)—the anchoring foundation of Raw Cat Rhythm, and the four-step process that cats engage in to procure and devour their food—served both parties well, and that's why our relationship with cats followed the same trajectory for so many years. It's really been in just the last 150 years that this thread has frayed, and a fork has appeared in the road to cat domesticity. Until then, it was a given that cats should be outside and that it was cruel to move them indoors.

That's what makes this moment in time so important for our future: what was a given for thousands of years suddenly is not anymore, as we continue to reconcile the safer, better quality of a life of indoor living with the cat's innate, biological drives. HCKE is not about providing a minimum of care for your cat. It's a reminder of the direct thread that connects your cat to her Raw Cat ancestor; it's that "tin can on both ends of a string" communication I keep talking about.

Still, so many people want to know "Is it okay if I don't play with my cat?" or "Can I get an automatic feeder and leave my cat alone for two days?" Instead of wagging my finger and saying "no," the goal is to show you, from the crucial starting point of HCKE, how obvious the answer is, to the point where you won't need to ask those types of questions. And if HCKE is our diving board, and Cat Mojo is the water we dive into, then understanding a cat's key physiological mechanics—particularly as they relate to hunting—well, that's the spring in the board.

HOW THE CAT EXPERIENCES THE WORLD AS A HUNTER

As natural-born hunters, cats rely on multiple senses to do their thing—primarily touch, vision, and hearing. This means that virtually every part of your cat's physiology has a function in the hunting process.

Touch

Cats are extremely sensitive to touch. This is, in part, because they have skin receptors that fire continuously as long as they are being touched—meaning these cells don't adapt to physical contact because the brain keeps getting a signal saying, "I am being touched." This is in contrast to humans, whose sensory receptors, for example, *do* adapt to touch, as evidenced by the fact that we don't consciously notice, moment by moment, that we are wearing clothes. The type of cells that cats have (Merkel cells) are ultrasensitive, more like those on your fingertips. Even their hair follicles are innervated, so having hairs out of place can be irritating for a cat.

Here are a few more interesting tidbits about cats and touch:

- Cats have some areas that are extra sensitive: the nose, toes, and the pads of their front feet all have even more receptors than other parts of their bodies. (Dr. John Bradshaw describes cat's feet as "sense organs.")
- Their nose pads can detect wind direction and temperature.
- Cats have hair receptors in their toes, which explains why long-haired cats in particular may be especially sensitive to things like the feel of litter on their paws, and being groomed.
- They have short, stiff hairs around the mouth and wrists to detect vibration.
- The base of the claws can sense displacement, which comes in handy, for example, when a mouse is wiggling in a cat's grasp.

Overstimulation, and possibly even some self-grooming and compulsive disorders, are often related to this exquisite sensitivity. So the next time you are petting or brushing your cat and he whips around to take a chunk out of your hand or brush, try not to take it personally! (More on this in section 3.)

At the same time, understand that all of this sensory perception is not just intended to accommodate their hunting activities. Cats are also prey for some animals (like coyotes and hawks). Being sensitive to touch means being sensitive to pain. Cats need to know if they are being attacked, to be extra cognizant of the warning signs of an attack, so their razor-sharp fight-or-flight mechanism can kick in.

By a Whisker!

 When it comes to touch, however, nothing comes close to the acute sensitivity of the whiskers. Compared to dogs, cats have a larger area of the brain dedicated to receiving signals from the muzzle area. Whiskers have receptors that communicate with the somatosensory cortex of their brain, giving them information about the ambient temperature, their balance, and the size of a space they are trying to move through. Whiskers can also detect movement and airflow, and send messages to the brain about how strong, what direction, and how quickly the air around them is moving, which could foretell potential movements of their kill.

Cats' up-close vision is not especially sharp, so they rely heavily on information from their whiskers when prey is in or near their mouth. When in hunting mode, the twelve whiskers on both sides of the nose are held forward to detect the prey's movement, so that the cat can make fine-tuned adjustments for the killing bite. These whiskers on their upper lip—combined with the whiskers on their cheeks, over the eyes, and on the chin, inner wrist, and back of the legs—all help cats "see" in 3-D.

Cat Daddy Fact

Wildcat species who are nighttime hunters have more prominent whiskers than daytime killers.

Vision

Everything about the anatomy and function of cats' eyes (and for that matter, every Raw Cat muscle, body part, and instinct) supports their existence as hunters. Cats have large eyes (in proportion to both body and head size) that face forward, which is common in predatory animals. Their visual field covers about 200 degrees, including their peripheral vision. Of that field, 90 degrees is "binocular"—in which both eyes work together for depth perception (such as determining how far away a bird is). Cats' eyes are also more responsive to fast movement, ideal for allowing our beloved hunters to catch a scurrying mouse.

However, their vision is not used so much for the up-close handling of prey, as their short-range vision is rather fuzzy and less detailed than ours. Instead, their optimal focal distance is between two and six meters—perfect for stalking a bird or mouse. If the prey is closer than a foot away, the cat's eyes don't even focus; at that point, the whiskers take over by pointing forward to pick up the details. That said, indoor cats are slightly nearsighted because the objects they focus on tend to be closer, while cats who go outside are usually farsighted, just like their Raw Cat ancestors.

The Eyes Have It: Comparing Cats' Eyes to Humans' Eyes

A cat's eye works in a way very similar to ours: light enters the pupil, or the opening in the center of the iris (the colored part of the eye), is focused by the lens and cornea, then is projected onto the retina at the back of the eye. The retina has two types of receptors: rods and cones. Rods are specialized for low light conditions, and cones are best for daylight color detection. Here's where a major difference between cat eyes and human eyes occurs: cats have three times the number of rods as the human eye, but they have fewer cones than we do. So, although they can detect some color in daylight, colors aren't nearly as prominent—or, apparently, important—to them. In dim light, they see only in black and white, but they can see much more clearly than we can. As always, everything boils down to "whatever helps the hunt." They will take clarity over color any day of the week!

Speaking of how evolution has helped the raw hunter, here are a few more key differences:

- Cats' pupils aren't round like ours. Instead, they have a vertical slit shape that allows them to respond faster to light, and open and close more and in all directions.
- Cat's eyes are slower to focus because the lens of the eye is stiff. And when the pupils are highly constricted—such as in bright daylight—it is actually more difficult for them to focus.
- Humans have a fovea, which is a tiny pit in the retina that is specialized for seeing details. Cats instead have a "visual streak," which serves a similar function but is densely packed with rods, giving cats better vision under low light conditions.
- Behind the retina, cats have reflective cells called tapetum lucidum. These cells are like a built-in flashlight, providing cats with a signal boost under low light conditions. Incidentally, they are also what make your cat's eyes "glow" when you take a picture of them with flash.

Hearing

As with their touch and vision, cats' hearing is also an important tool in their HCKE routine. Cats have the broadest hearing range of the carnivores—10.5 octaves. Cats and humans have a similar range at the low end of the scale, but cats can hear much higher pitched sounds (like mouse squeaks) than we can—about 1.6 octaves above the sounds we hear. Most aspects of a cat's hearing are related to detecting prey rather than communicating with other cats.

The cat's outer ear boosts frequencies and is shaped to literally funnel hard-to-detect sounds into the ear canal for better analysis. Their ability to move each ear separately allows cats to pinpoint the source of a sound—be it a prey animal, a predator, or a distressed kitten crying for Mom. They can also rotate each ear almost 180 degrees, allowing cats to be aware of anyone coming at them from behind.

Now, EQUIPPED WITH a better understanding of how cats' physiology and anatomy support them as master hunters, let's look at a few particulars about how and what they kill.

"Smaller Than a Pigeon": Killing in the Real World

 Cats will hunt anything that is smaller than them, but they tend to prefer prey that is smaller than a pigeon. Their favorite prey is small rodents, with birds as a close second. Cats may also hunt bugs, reptiles, and amphibians.

Recent studies have shown that domestic cats, like their cougar cousins, have individual preferences for prey. Most cats are specialists—they hunt just one or two prey types—but some cats are generalists with a wider range of prey preferences ("anything that moves").

Birds are a little harder for cats to catch, which is probably why the free-living cat diet is over 75 percent rodent. Prey preferences can be influenced by what's available, and even by what a mom cat brought to her kittens when they were young. The bottom line is that hunters must adapt; so if there are fewer mice available, cats must hunt birds . . . or go hungry.

This leads us to cats' preferred hunting styles, which are no doubt influenced by their food source of choice. Individual cats show different strategies for killing, some preferring to:

- ambush from an open clearing
- stalk-and-rush from behind cover
- wait for their prey to pop out of entrances to burrows and warrens

Don't forget, this applies to all cats, which means that your innocent indoor companion will have a preference in hunting style as well. It will be your job to discover this individual hunting "sweet spot" when we talk about cat play in chapter 7.

Going In for the Kill

Typically, cats grab prey with paws first, then dig in with their teeth, finishing the job with a "kill bite" to the nape of the neck, placed specifically to sever their prey's spinal cord. If they're unsure about the prey's ability to fight back, or they're not very experienced hunters, they may bite multiple times. They may also appear to be "playing with their food," as they bat at it or toss it about in a torturous fashion. But this isn't because the cat is being cruel; it is actually a strategy used to tire out a dangerous victim, making that final killing bite easier to deliver.

Until the bitter end, there is a method to their madness. In addition to the whiskers' role in the final sensory confirmation of a kill, cats also have nerves in their teeth that allow them to detect movement and make small adjustments while biting. All of these fine behavioral details are part of their DNA and allow for an efficient, thorough, and low-risk kill.

While all of these components serve to make cats one of nature's most perfect hunters, these are not just a random collection of attributes and talents; they are responses to specific environmental conditions. Likewise, understand that, as both predator and prey, cats have become uniquely adapted to both hunting and protecting themselves. What has made them successful is the fact that they can stay alive *and* kill with equal skill. For more on this unique blend of talents—and how it specifically influences their behavior and relationships with the other inhabitants of their home turf—check out "Cat Chess" in chapter 10.

NOW THAT WE have a better idea of how your cat's body, behavior, and astute hunting prowess have evolved to serve HCKE, it's easy to see how it is an indispensable part of Cat Mojo. Hunting is pleasurable to cats, and to the Raw Cat, experiencing pleasure and fulfilling their primary objective mean basically the same thing. Simply put, it is the primary end goal to every cat's day. The biggest favor you can do for your cat is to help the Raw Cat find a home for his daily superobjective within the relatively new and somewhat restrictive confines of *your* home by establishing a flow of Routines, Rituals, and Rhythm around HCKE. More on this in chapter 7.

Eating—Meat, the Whole Meat, and Nothing but the Meat

After the hunt—whether it be in the "real world" or via your faithful reenactment of one during a play session—it's time to eat. And after all that's been discussed so far, it should make perfect sense by now that your cat is not a vegan. No, cats are obligate carnivores: their digestive system is designed, specifically and exclusively, to process meat. Likewise, it should come as no surprise that cats, as opportunistic hunters, are not scavengers, and as such are not digestively built to graze.  That doesn't necessarily mean they are meant to eat huge meals, either. Opportunistic, by definition, means that whatever presents itself will do—whether a grasshopper enters the crosshairs, or a bird.

Generally, cats have a weak sense of taste, with fewer taste buds than humans. Their sense of smell is much more useful for them in hunting, and thus important for eating. That sense is so ingrained that congested cats often lose their appetite; it's as if with one frayed wire, the entire machine will go on the fritz. That said, cats can still detect salty, sweet, sour, and bitter, and tend to show dislike for sour and bitter (this is likely a response that evolved to prevent the ingestion of dangerous toxins). Additionally, cats have a taste receptor for adenosine triphosphate (ATP), a molecule that's a source of energy for all living cells. ATP is sometimes referred to as a signal for meat, and, interestingly, we can't "taste" it.

How Do Cats Eat?

- Cats are opportunistic and will adjust their activity based on food availability.
- Cats will eat more at one sitting when food is generally less available.
- One mouse provides about thirty calories, and a typical cat might hunt ten to thirty times a day in order to obtain around eight mice.
- Cats often carry their prey away from where they kill.
- Cats crouch when they eat, and if their kill is big enough, they may even lie down to eat.
- You may notice your cat eating with her head tilted. This is an ancestral behavior related to eating their prey from the ground, not from a bowl. Harder-to-chew items usually increase the degree of head tilting.
- Cats pick up a small amount of food and give a quick "shake" of the head. This is another ancestral behavior that helps loosen meat from bones, and removes feathers from a bird's body.
- Cats don't do much chewing; their teeth are designed to tear meat into small strips that can be swallowed.

GROOMING AND SLEEPING

Cats are naturally fastidious and typically clean from tip to tail, spending 30 to 50 percent of their waking hours grooming. They let their tongue—which is naturally abrasive—do most of the work, and use their paws to get at hard to reach areas.

What purpose does grooming serve in the wild? Grooming keeps the coat clean, prevents parasite infestation, and helps cats strengthen their own personal scent while ridding themselves of the smell from their kill, which would attract other predators.

As for sleeping, a cat's natural circadian rhythm shifts with day length and sunlight, much like ours. Cats usually sleep in several short bursts rather than in longer chunks, and like us they have cycles of deep and light sleep. During deep sleep, you may notice their limbs or whiskers twitching as some of their muscles contract during dreams.

But superdeep sleep is not something that is achieved every time they lie down. More typically, it's all about catnaps—sleeping lighter, for a shorter duration of time. That's life in the middle of the food chain, folks—sleeping with one eye open—both for finding sustenance and for preserving your own life. In the world of kill or be killed, the long and short of it is that a nice deep sleep isn't always the wisest option.

Do Cats Sleep All Day?

If I asked you what you think your cat is doing while you're at work, I bet you would say one thing: sleeping. People assume cats sleep all day, but a 2009 study that placed cameras on cats' collars showed that when cats were home alone, they slept only around 6 percent of the time. In contrast, they spent over 20 percent of their time looking out the window. (If this doesn't impress upon you the importance of "Cat TV," I don't know what will! More on Cat TV in section 3.)

50% grooming

21.6% looking out windows

1.7% in the sink

6.1% sleeping

How do your cats **spend their day?**

11.8% hanging out with other animals

4% eating/drinking

5% playing with toys

6.1% looking at computer

- Feral cats are active both at day and night, but travel farther at night

- Their biggest threats are cars and coyotes

- Older males may be part of a colony, but younger males may be loners

- Spend 15 percent of their day hunting. They make 20-30 hunting attempts a day but only around 30 percent are successful

How do feral cats spend their day?

- They use rubbing, scratching, and spraying to mark twigs, stumps, and fences along commonly traveled paths and the edges of their range

- They have sunning locations— ferals use the Cat Sundial too

- During the day, they mostly stay under cover, stay close to shrubs, fences, tall grass for protection from heat, predators, and humans

Are Cats Nocturnal?

It has been widely stated and assumed (most likely by those who are kept up by their hyperactive cats in the middle of the night), that cats are nocturnal animals. Cats are more active at night than we are, but they are not truly nocturnal. Rather, they are crepuscular. Their natural rhythm, devoid of other influences, is to be active at dawn and dusk, just like rodents, their primary prey animal.

As YOU CAN tell by now, the ancestral cat is absolutely alive and well in every cat, informing each and every aspect of the HCKEGS daily rhythm. That's not where it ends, though—not by a long shot. If you've ever said to yourself, "I wish my cat could tell me what she's thinking," well, she can, and does. You just have to have your ears to the Raw Cat in order to hear what your cat has to say.

4

Communication

Cat Code Cracking

THE CONSISTENT FEEDBACK (or rather, the absolute teeth-clenching, neck-vein-popping, eye-rolling frustration) that I've encountered over the years from adopters, clients, *My Cat from Hell* viewers, and, hell, just strangers on the street—is that **cats are inscrutable**. There is a pretty volatile combination at play when it comes to the cat/guardian relationship. When we don't understand what cats are trying to communicate through their behaviors, we try to figure it out and are met with a blank stare. That look becomes a blank canvas for all kinds of projections from humans. Let's say you are sitting in the living room, watching TV. Your cat comes into the room and, without hesitation, walks up to your gym bag—and pees in it. I mean, talk about a potentially explosive moment! What immediately makes a bad situation worse is you, executing a slow boil and assuming that you know what he is trying to tell you ("I hate my dinner," "I hate the fact that you left me for twelve boring hours today, and you do it every single day," "I hate your new girlfriend," or, if you are circling this particular drain, that last big blast of projection, "I hate *you*.").

Depending on how crappy your day has been up to that point, and perhaps how many times your cat has executed such blood pressure–spiking actions in the past, the speed at which your relationship deteriorates can be dizzying—and dangerous. I've seen a bond that was already a bit shaky crumble in that moment like a house of cards. And once that house comes down, well, your cat already has a paw out the door. It has been a fundamental part of my job since the beginning to interrupt this downward spiral before it gets to that irreversible point. Don't forget, I began counseling guardians while working at an animal shelter, on the phone as they were asking me how much we charged to take back their cat. I know all too well where that downward spiral leads: to a homeless cat in a cage.

Part of the issue is that we, perhaps subconsciously, look at cats through dog-colored glasses; that is to say, we expect them to communicate with us

Through Dog-Colored Glasses

in a way that we can instantly recognize. As you can guess by now, that expectation goes against the entire history of our relationship to cats. We've molded dogs over thousands of years to be recognizable, to reflect humanness back at us. We've bred in attributes that benefit us because, to boil it down, one of our main desires is companionship. That was never the priority in our relationship to and with cats. Remember that it was all about what was mutually beneficial when cats acted as hunters who protected our food supply. So to suddenly expect your cat to change his fundamental communication style after all this time is foolhardy at best.

Between the two worlds of humans and cats, the two languages, there is a fence. We must meet *at that fence*. Dogs will gladly jump the fence and run to our side in order to communicate; cats simply won't, because that has never, until this point in our relationship, been part of our arrangement.

That said, the language of cats is just as eloquent as that of any other species on Earth. You just have to commit to meeting at the communicative fence. From cat-specific vocalizations to body language to behaviors like, yes, peeing—it all adds up to form a linguistic whole that, once learned, will make for a much more fulfilling relationship—and one not fraught with resentment.

So let's dig in and start with how cats "talk."

MORE THAN MEOWS: THE TALKATIVE CAT

Chirrups. Trills. Purrs. Yowls. Snarls. And of course, meows. Your cat can make up to a hundred different sounds, which is more than most carnivores (including dogs). Of course, if you have a "Chatty Catty," that might seem like a lowball estimate. Why do cats have so much to say? Vocalizations can be ferocious or friendly; they might say "stay away" or "come closer." Calls can provide information from a greater distance than just body language can, and may even tell the listener how big and strong the sender is.

Let's consider three facts: feral cats are typically quieter than their domestic counterparts; many vocalizations are directed toward humans; and there is a wide range of individuality when it comes to how talkative a cat is. Genetics may play a part, as some breeds—namely, Siamese, Oriental, and Abyssinian—tend to be more vocal than your average cat. But we can assume that we humans have played a large role in how verbose our cats are. After all, meows get attention, which often leads to food, petting, or getting a door opened. It's interesting to note that cats rarely meow at each other, with the key exception being the cry of kittens in distress for their mom.

Cats use *other* sounds to communicate with each other. Some of these sounds, like the meow, start with an open mouth that closes during the sound, such as howls and sexual calls. The less friendly calls are made with the mouth held open—those yowls, growls, snarls, hisses, and shrieks that are heard during fighting or are a response to pain.

Perhaps the cutest and friendliest sounds that cats make don't require them to open their mouths at all. Purrs, chirrups, and trills are reserved for greetings and personal contact.

WHAT'S UP WITH THE PURR?

Purring is one of those Mojo Mysteries that we still don't totally understand. It is usually a positive response, but sometimes cats purr when they are stressed, in pain, or even dying. Either way, we're pretty sure that the purr is not under the cat's conscious control, but is more like a reflex. The brain sends a signal to the muscles in the larynx, or what we call the voice box. These muscles move the vocal cords at a rate of approximately twenty-five times per second while cats inhale and exhale, which produces that distinctive rumble we call a purr.

Purrs help the Raw Mom Cat keep kittens nearby—the kittens' purrs tell Mom they are nearby, and the purr helps with bonding by releasing self-soothing endorphins and lulling the kittens to sleep.

Purrs might have healing powers; they are in a similar range (20 to 140 Hz) to sound frequencies that help with both healing injuries and improving bone density (at least for cats, anyway; to date, the evidence on healing human bones is inconclusive). This may help explain why cats who are wounded or sick will often be purring.

I've heard speculation that a cat's purrs during the killing bite can aid in lulling the prey into a catatonic state. But they might manipulate us as well. A 2009 study by Dr. Karen McComb and colleagues demonstrated that humans could tell the difference between a purr that a cat was making while soliciting food—which they labeled an "urgent" purr—from a nonurgent purr. The urgent purrs included a high-frequency component that indicated some level of excitement that we pick up on, and probably respond to with attention or food.

Cat Daddy Fact

The Guinness World Record for loudest purr is held by Smokey, a British cat who could purr at 67.7 dB (about as loud as conversation in a typical restaurant).

THE TOOTH CHATTER

It's a common sight: Your cat is staring at a bird through the window, locked in with complete focus. Then this crazy chattering, quacking sound comes out of your cat's mouth. What the heck?

Many cats chatter their teeth when they see prey that they can't get to. Some will even chatter at other cats. One idea is that your cat is expressing frustration that they can't get to that delicious bird. Some think the tooth movement is your cat practicing their "killer bite."

The theory with perhaps the most weight is that cats are mimicking the sounds of their prey. Margays, Amazonian wildcats, mimic the sounds of tamarin monkeys to lure them within pouncing distance. A 2013 Swedish study showed overlap between the types of sounds birds make and the sounds emitted by cats during the chatter, including chirps, tweets, and tweedles. Makes sense, doesn't it? The Raw Cat, more than most predators, will find a novel way to secure its kill. Wolf in sheep's clothing? Try the Raw Cat in bird's clothing. Anyhow, for now, we'll have to chalk this one up to Mojo Mysteries, but it might be another example of how vocalizations have evolved to help cats get what they need.

BODY LANGUAGE

Cats tell us a lot through their bodies. While all cats will have subtle differences in how they communicate what they are feeling—whether confident, relaxed, fearful, defensive, or ready to attack—there are some general signals they use, with both humans and other cats. Many of these signals are inherited from their Raw Cat ancestor, which, as you will see, sometimes creates challenges for the modern cat.

The Tail

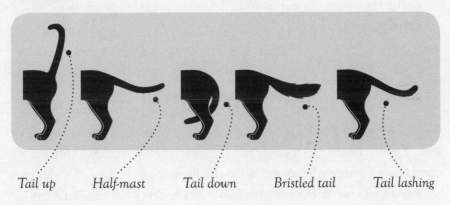

Tail up   Half-mast   Tail down   Bristled tail   Tail lashing

A cat's tail serves many purposes. It helps with jumping and balance, and can even provide warmth and protection. But when a cat is sitting, or walking slowly, the tail is free to communicate. The cat's tail can send several different messages because the tip can move independently from the rest of the tail.

In the Raw Cat's ancestral environment (grasslands), the tail was likely a good long-distance signal of a cat's emotional state. Strutting by with the tail in the air is a Mojo moment. The "tail up" with a curve at the tip is a classic friendly or playful greeting that says "hello," or "right this way, follow me."

As the tail lowers, the message might change a little. An ambivalent tail is slightly lowered, at more of a 45-degree angle.

The tail at "half-mast," or horizontal to the ground, can be neutral, friendly, or even tentatively exploratory, and requires more contextual information for interpretation.

A "tail down" can serve a few different functions. Cats slightly lower the tail while stalking prey. But a cat might also be trying to make himself smaller by lowering the tail, assuming either a defensive or fearful posture. In extreme cases, the lower tail is accompanied by the "army crawl," or walking away from a potential threat quickly and as low to the ground as they can get.

The tail between the legs is the most extreme expression of fear.

A bristled tail generally signifies DEFCON 1. It can be offensive or defensive, but it is often a response to something alarming in the environment.

A quivering tail (sometimes referred to as "mock spraying" since that's exactly what it looks like) is usually a sign of positive excitement. In my experience, I've noticed the "mock spray" directed either at or near a person the cat is fond of. I can only guess that this signifies ownership with a posture that walks the tightrope between confident (body scent marking, rubbing, etc.) and unconfident (urine marking) cat language. Either way, I've learned to take it as a pretty high compliment!

Tail lashing is often an indicator of impending aggression or defensiveness, while smaller, subtle twitching movements can indicate frustration or irritation. (See "The Energetic Balloon" in chapter 7 for more on this.)

Cat Nerd Corner

The Tail-Up Studies

In a 2009 study of a feral colony in Italy, cats were observed for eight months. Researchers noted combative behavior between cats, which included biting, staring, chasing, and fighting. They also noted avoidance behaviors such as crouching, retreating, and hissing; and friendly behaviors, which included sniffing, rubbing, and presenting the tail up.

The "tail up" was most often directed toward aggressive cats by nonaggressive cats, suggesting it might be a message that says "I come in peace" and could also inhibit aggression in another cat.

To further demonstrate that the tail up served the function of expressing "Hey, I'm friendly," John Bradshaw and Charlotte Cameron-Beaumont studied how cats responded to just silhouettes of other cats with different tail positions. This would rule out the possibility that the cats in the study were responding to other things aside from the tail up (like pheromones, vocalizations, or other aspects of an in-person interaction). The result? Cats would approach the image faster and raise their own tails in response to a "tail up" silhouette. When they saw the "tail down" silhouette, cats tended to respond with tail twitching, or by putting their own tails down.

The Ears

Upright ears   Flattened ears   Flattened and sideways   Information gathering

The ears can move subtly, quickly, and independently, which is why they are often the most telling aspect of a cat's body language. They can be the first indicator of a cat's emotional state. More than twenty muscles control the movement of the ears, and they are always ready to spring into action, even when your cat is resting.

Upright ears allow cats to take in and respond to auditory information in the environment. For a relaxed cat, the ears will be upright, but slightly rotated to the side. When the ears are more forward facing, your cat is on alert, or maybe even frustrated.

Flattened ears can mean different things. If the ears are sideways and down, your cat is fearful, but also still trying to get information. The flatter the ears, the more fearful the cat. Complete backward rotation of the ears is getting them out of harm's way in anticipation of an attack.

When each ear is doing something different, the interpretation is more ambiguous . . . and in that moment, so is your cat's emotional state.

The Eyes

Avoiding eye contact   *Dilated pupils*   *Constricted pupils*   *Relaxed eyes*   *Blinking*

Pupils dilate under low light levels, but they also dilate during the fight-or-flight response. Dilated pupils let in more light and information about the environment (when cats are assessing danger, for instance, more information means securing multiple escape routes). The more dilated the pupils are, the more defensive the cat is probably feeling. On the other hand, a cat with constricted pupils is likely confident and relaxed.

However, it's not just about what the eyes are doing; it's also about how exactly they're being used. A stare is usually a challenge, but a cat's degree of focus and distractibility while staring will usually tell you how much of a "challenge" it really is.

A cat who is avoiding eye contact with another cat is typically doing so for a reason—usually to minimize the likelihood of a confrontation.

Blinking slowly is a sign of contentment and relaxation . . . which is why we try to evoke the Slow Blink when greeting or communicating with a cat. (More on this in the "Cat Greetings/Slow Blink" section in chapter 11.)

The Whiskers

The main function of whiskers is to provide tactile information to a cat. But they also provide us with some information about how relaxed or aroused a cat is.

Soft whiskers

Forward-pointing whiskers

A relaxed cat usually has soft whiskers that are pointing out to the side, while a fearful or defensive cat might flatten the whiskers against the sides of the face as another way of becoming "small."

Forward-pointing whiskers indicate a cat is trying to get more information, since those whiskers will detect air movements and objects. The more forward facing the whiskers are, the more attentive the cat is. Forward whiskers could indicate that a cat is about to attack, perceives a threat, or is just plain interested, so, as always, context is important.

No single behavior or posture happens in a vacuum, so remember to consider the big picture as you evaluate your cat's state: Is she relaxed on the couch? Staring out the window at another cat? Crouched under your bed? You also have to look at the whole enchilada—of course, that entails what's coming from the body, tail, eyes, ears, and whiskers, along with vocalizations, but also what's coming from the territory, the other inhabitants, even the time of day. If there's one thing I've learned in translating cat language, it's the importance of context.

Body Postures

Unlike some animals, cats don't have clear appeasement signals, or submissive body language that says "please forgive me." (Probably because such a thought would never occur to them!) But this communicative limitation impacts a cat's ability to engage in conflict resolution. How can cats function in this way?

Go back to the timeline and look at how recently cats have been social—not just with humans but with each other. The ancestor cat was not a social species, and these days, domestic cats often resolve conflict through avoidance and defensive behavior, and maintain bonds through a group scent and signals like the tail up. But understanding the communicative challenges will help you understand why cats sometimes have difficulties with each other.

Cats who are upset usually take one of two routes. They can go bigger, with hair on end and an expanded posture—i.e., the classic "Halloween cat." These cats are on full alert and may be willing to defend themselves if necessary. Straight legs, a puffed tail, and an elevated butt is a cat who is purely on the offense, essentially saying "Bring it on, I'm ready."

Cats who make themselves smaller, on the other hand, are trying to appear unthreatening. Their ears are back, their

shoulders are hunched, and they are crouching: everything is tucked in. If they get backed into a corner they will attack if they must, but that would be a last resort.

Lest you think cats are always defensive around each other, let's be clear—cats do have friendly full-body gestures, namely rolling and rubbing. Body rolls happen when a female is in heat, but male cats roll, too. Many cats roll in response to catnip, but they also roll in the presence of other (usually older) cats. Much like the tail up signal, rolling seems to be a way to signal "I'm friendly and unthreatening." Rolling is rarely seen during antagonistic encounters between cats.

Belly up is a play solicitation in kittens, although in adults, it could serve as a defensive posture, as their teeth and all four paws are readily available for protection in this position. Those belly-up adults are generally not interested in starting trouble, but it can indicate a willingness to defend themselves, if necessary. See the "Cat Hug" later in this chapter for more about belly-up cats.

Yawning and stretching are good signs that your cat is feeling mellow. A relaxed cat will often lay with all paws folded under the body, in what is often referred to as the Meatloaf position. All of the cat's weapons are tucked away, and there's no immediate intention to run or defend.

The Sphynx is another relaxed pose, where the front legs are extended

in front of the body. A truly content cat will be in one of these poses with very "drowsy" eyes.

Both of these poses must be distinguished from crouching—a tense position, where a cat might be hunched over or partially propped up on the front legs. Often you will see tension in the face, or tight blinking of the eyes. In cats, this is usually a sign of pain. Because cats hide pain so well, it is important to pay attention to these subtle behaviors.

Is Your Cat Annoyed?

Many guardians think that their cat bites "apropos of nothing," but most cats give many warnings, although these warnings may be subtle. Some cats may walk away or turn their back to you, and that is their way of removing themselves from an interaction. Or maybe you're seeing some tail swishing, or back twitching. A paw swipe is also a warning, as if to say: "I don't like this and you need to respect that. Next time there might be teeth or claws."

See "Overstimulation" in section 4 for more on warning signs of irritation.

Cat Daddy Dictionary: The Cat Hug

When a cat goes belly up for you, we call this the Cat Hug, because often it's the closest you will get to a cat actually hugging you. To fully appreciate this, you must understand the genetic experience of being a prey animal. By exposing their belly to you, they are essentially saying:

"I am 100 percent vulnerable to you right now. You could take your claw and eviscerate me down this line from my throat to my groin and essentially tear me open. It is the most vulnerable part of my body, and I am flipping over and showing it to you." Just like the body roll, it is a message of trust.

Now, is this an invitation to put your hands on your cat's belly? No! Again, if you respect their protective instinct as a prey animal, and understand what every bone in their body is telling them, then you will appreciate the Cat Hug from a safe distance (unless you've already established a clear and comfortable relationship with your cat that would include belly rubs). Also, as mentioned, because this position is sometimes used as a defensive one, it's very easy for cats to suddenly bite or scratch if they perceive your hand near their belly as a threat.

HOW THE CAT COMMUNICATES AS A SOCIAL ANIMAL: OLFACTION AND PHEROMONES

As stalk-and-rush hunters, cats don't use their sense of smell much for hunting. In contrast to dogs, who might track prey for long distances, cats follow prey only a short distance.

But smell is critical to how cats relate to each other. Their sense of smell is approximately fourteen times as strong as ours, and it's important to remember that olfactory information talks straight to the part of the brain that is key to emotions and motivations, such as anxiety and aggression.

Cats can also detect pheromones with their vomeronasal organ (VNO—also called the Jacobson's organ). Pheromones are special chemical signals that reveal information about sex, reproductive status, and individual identity. You might have seen your cat make an "open mouth sniff" or grimace, which is called the Flehmen response. This behavior is a sign that a cat is taking in those pheromones (usually via the urine of other cats). From that Flehmen response, they know *who* has been around, *when* they've been around, and possibly even their emotional state. Are they a familiar cat? Are they an intruder? A female in heat? An intact male? Are they stressed out? This information can be used to help cats avoid contact and conflict with other cats.

Urine spray elicits a lot of sniffing in cats, especially if it is the urine of an unfamiliar cat. But strange urine doesn't necessarily cause cats to avoid an area—it's not necessarily a "keep out" sign.

Pheromones

Cats can leave pheromone messages through glands on their cheeks, forehead, lips, chin, tail, feet, whiskers, pads, ears, flanks, and mammary glands. Rubbing these glands against objects or individuals leaves the cat's scent behind. The functions of all of the different pheromones are still Mojo Mysteries, but researchers have identified the functions of three facial pheromones.

One pheromone (F2) is a message from tomcats saying "I'm ready to mate." The pheromone F3 is released during cheek or chin rubbing on objects, and helps cats claim ownership of their territory. Finally, F4 is a social pheromone to mark familiar individuals—human, cat, or other. F4 reduces the likelihood of aggression between cats and facilitates the recognition of other individuals.

How cats rub to mark can tell you a little bit about their emotional state. Cheek rubbing is generally a sign of confidence, and "head bonking" against you is a sign of "cat love."

Scratching is another way for cats to mark their turf, but sometimes cats will also release alarm pheromones when scratching.

Urine marking is both a sexual behavior and a response to territorial changes (such as new animals or objects). While urine marking is a completely normal feline behavior, in some ways, it is the antithesis of facial marking; it's the Napoleonic response to territorial anxiety.

WHAT MAKES CATS Raw is what unites them all; the ties that bind, however, only tell half the story. As we complete our exploration of all cats, it's time to start digging deeper to discover what it is that makes *your* cat one of a kind. Now, let's get to know your companion better. Much, much better.

5

The Mojo Archetypes and the Confident Where

A T THIS POINT I hope I've painted a good picture of cats as a whole. All cats. How they—in the context of their Raw life, outside, free from the confines of your home—use the tools that evolution has graced them with to accomplish their daily objectives. The almost reflexive pursuit of these goals creates a cat springboard of sorts into the deep pool of Cat Mojo. Now it's time to start thinking about how we can take this all-cat info and bring it to *our cats*—whether that means using the Raw Cat to bring out the best in our companion cats, or finding out how our home territory can maximize their mojo and improve our daily relationship with *our* cats.

THE MOJO ARCHETYPES

Truth be told, I was never a big fan of "types," of reducing anyone to a handful of characteristics. As a matter of fact, that's why I've ditched the term "cat behaviorist" after my name. Talk about reductive! It makes it seem as if all I do is look at a four-legged bag of symptoms and arrange the puzzle pieces so that "it" becomes a perfect, connect-the-dots collection of "behaviors." Wouldn't you be just a little peeved if your therapist referred to herself as a "human behaviorist"? Feels more than a little cold, right?

That said, I unfortunately don't have the time to get to know every cat to the degree that I would like. In the span of a few hours, I have to get through the handshake, the observations of environmental and family dynamics, challenge line exercises, diagnosis, homework assignments, and wrap-up. With Cat Mojo as the end result I want to promise every animal and human client, I've found that underneath every individual cat I meet, there is a claim that he or she has staked along the mojo spectrum. Without pigeon-holing, I have found that guardians and I both benefit from identifying where their cat is and where they want to get to on that spectrum.

Cat Mojo begins with confident ownership of territory; but by the time we've done our work to raise their mojo bar, it's not just about *ownership*, but *pride*; and it's not about *territory*, but *home*. Knowing where your cat falls on the mojo spectrum gives us a clearer sense of what our goal looks like. And so I created the Mojo Archetypes. Allow me to introduce you to the Mojito Cat, the Napoleon Cat, and the Wallflower.

The Mojito Cat

You've got new neighbors, and a couple of weeks after they move in, they invite you to come over—a bit of a housewarming, get-to-know-you type of thing.

You knock on their door and you are immediately met by a level of exuberance that knocks you off your feet a bit. Your new neighbor greets you with a huge smile, welcoming you by name and offering a warm hug as if you've known each other for years. You are being hugged with one arm because, you notice, the other hand is holding a tray of drinks.

"Mojito?" she asks. "We've got a few different flavors here. This one is more lime-y, that one has a little more cucumber. These have salt on the rim and those don't."

You pause, still somewhat in a state of shock. She laughs, seeing that you are a bit quiet—but she just hands you one of the drinks and leads you gently by the elbow inside.

"Let me show you around. . . ."

Your first stop is the fireplace, where you're shown pictures on the mantel of vacations, birthdays, weddings. Your hostess stops to pick up an antique picture, lovingly running her fingers over it as she talks about the bond she had with her grandmother. She cries a few tears, wipes them away . . . and the tour continues.

You are taken through every nook and cranny. And, incredibly, there seems to be history in every one of them, and through this show and tell, you find yourself invested in this unfolding story.

Wait a minute . . . you stop in your tracks . . . these people *just* moved in here? It looks—and *feels*—like they've been here for years. And it's not just the arrangement of things—the mementos, the furniture, even magnets and to-do lists on the fridge—it goes deeper than that. . . . It's a *vibe*. You are just awestruck that two weeks ago, the moving trucks left this house, and today . . . it's a home.

Your hostess with the mostest, you notice, is not running around, trying to impress, nervously throwing coasters under your mojito. You realize that this sense of ease comes from the fact that she's not here to impress. She's not interested in the status that would come from being "perfect." She just wants to know you, and she wants you to know her. There is no artifice in this home. And the escape plan that you had in your back pocket? It stays there. Why? Because *you* want to stay *here*.

Now—imagine if this human were a cat.

Then, as soon as you walk into the home, this cat walks right down the center of the room, tail held high, chest up. Ears are forward to explore, but not flicking in all directions as if trying to pick up clues about this incoming being. Eyes are also forward, but to greet, not to check the periphery for escape routes. Instead of presenting a tray of drinks, the Mojito Cat begins to do figure eights between your legs, and those of anyone else who crosses his path. You reach a hand down to say hi. He takes your outstretched fingers and pushes them to his forehead, his cheeks. Simultaneously he is inviting contact with a stranger, allowing pleasure from that contact, and marking you in a confident way, turning you into his human scent soaker. As you walk into the family room, he climbs to the third level of the cat tree that stands near the door, showing you how he surveys the domain, displaying pride in what is his. You walk into the kitchen, he scoots ahead of you and digs into his dinner as you settle into a conversation. The scratching post in the living room gets a workout when you and the Mojito Cat pass through again. And with every stop on this "tour," you are head butted and cheek marked . . . and finally, as you settle on the couch for conversation, he falls asleep—either on or next to you.

The Mojito Cat lies at the center of our Mojo-meter. He is a true north of confidence. He has nothing to prove; he is Tony Manero strutting through Brooklyn. His love for, pride in, and unquestioned ownership of his territory are what makes it his home. The Mojito Cat is marked by this characteristic: he loves his environment so much that he just wants to *share it*. This is evidenced by his actions in his surroundings and with the beings who populate that environment. And that, folks, is what true Cat Mojo looks like.

The Mojito Cat occupies the center; he gives us a target to aim for, and a planet for our other two archetypes to orbit around. While Mojito is so confident he wants to show off his home to you, offering to share its riches, our other two cats are marked by their deep insecurities. Instead of exhibiting grounded ownership, our other cat archetypes are either petrified that you're going to take away what they have, or feel that they aren't worthy to have ever owned anything in the first place. Enter our second archetype.

The Napoleon Cat (a.k.a. the Overowner)

I grew up in New York City during a time when gang activity was so rampant that it felt normal. My parents taught me where I would be safe to travel and where I would not be.

After falling asleep on a bus one day, I found myself overshooting home by about twenty blocks. I cautiously got off the bus and went to cross Broadway to wait for the next bus heading back toward home. As I crossed to the downtown side of the street, I was stopped by . . . a kid; I mean he couldn't have been older than I was at the time, around thirteen. I don't remember the name of the gang he was a part of, but I knew he was a member. Why? Well, to begin with, he wore a denim vest, frayed at the shoulders, with the name of the gang on it, both on the front and the back. He put himself squarely in my path, puffing out his chest and folding his arms.

"You know where you are?" he said, his face inches from mine. "Let me tell you. . . ." And he motioned to a huge "tag," the name of his gang in white paint on the side of a brick building.

I remember being profoundly confused as to what he actually wanted from me. I assumed he had some kind of weapon on him because I was taught to believe that, but he never brandished it. He just stood in front of me, eyes narrowed to slits and his entire being ready to take action.

This kid clearly didn't want to kill me, but with every passing second he was, at the very least, growing more and more impatient with my lack of recognition. He wasn't trying to bar entry onto their turf (unless, of course, I was a member of a rival gang)—he just wanted me to acknowledge that this belonged to "them." It struck me, through my vaguely adrenalized state, how young yet intimidating he was. His arms-folded posture, his "bowed up" torso, and all of the elements of gang wardrobe—

together, they created a uniform of fear that had been mastered by so many kids back then.

And there were so many gangs to house all of the disenfranchised kids who needed a family to feel a part of. One of those gangs could easily land on that particular corner later on in the week and tag over this kid's gang tag with their own. Then this kid would come back to "his" corner and tag again—they *needed* to tell competing gangs (and the world at large) that this wall, this block, this neighborhood belonged to them . . . and don't you forget it.

I wanted to answer his question, I really did . . . but I couldn't. I was, instead, readying myself for violence. Every muscle in my body tightened. I tried to return a somewhat tough glare, but I was definitely a fish out of water in that respect. I tried to walk around him, and he slid in front of me. I went the other direction, and he shifted back. I'm not sure what I did next, but my body posture must have been such a clear sign of surrender that this kid actually laughed at me. Full-throated, head back—laughed. That cackle served as the final nail in the coffin of my pride; having snuffed me out like a cigarette under his shoe, his pride sated and his territory unquestionably safe, he finally let me pass.

In a sense, he needed to bolster his sense of ownership through intimidation and humiliation. He had to make sure I was completely beaten before he could wear his own crown. This instinct was the nature of gangs; what this one kid did to me, the gangs did to entire neighborhoods. The collective mojo of these communities suffered under the weight of the muggings, the endless tagging, the warfare that had blocks divvied up by a violent few in the name of ownership.

Although the Napoleon complex is not a recognized condition, the term has been used throughout the ages to describe an *overowner*, like my gang member. Because deep down they have absolutely no faith in their ownership, the goal becomes lost in the pursuit. They need to see another person's loss to reassure themselves of the space they occupy. We see Napoleons on a global scale—fundamentalists who destroy ancient artifacts, leaders who conduct a scorched-Earth policy when they sense their power slipping. . . . In the world of the Napoleon, if he can't own it, nobody can.

And yes, all of this applies to the ultimate practitioner of *anti-Mojo*, the Napoleon Cat. When you encounter a Napoleon Cat in his territory, you will be greeted with his ears forward, his eyes zeroed in on you just a little, and perhaps a crouching, even aggressive, posture. His initial thought is "Who are you, and what are you here to steal?" True to the complex that is his namesake, he is paranoid about the prospects of takeover and overcompensates accordingly. And in this cat's home, he will ambush others when they least expect it, even when those people (and animals) have already abdicated their position day after day.

If a cat could fold his arms, the Napoleon would find a way. Instead of greeting you at the door with a tray of mojitos, the Napoleon will stand across the doorway or right in the center of the foot traffic, just like the gang member from my youth. But in the Napoleon Cat's world, graffiti is sprayed not with paint but with urine. We see that lack of mojo on display when he paints the perimeter of your home—under windows and on doors—as if to say, "If I want to protect this castle, I should damn well build a moat!"

It's interesting that, in the years of one-on-one work I've done since defining the archetypes, I've noticed that the Napoleon Cat gets very little love, very little empathy. If we want our Napoleon to inch his way toward the center, toward his best Mojito self, empathy is what it takes. We can't save all of our parental protection skills for our final archetype.

The Wallflower (a.k.a. the Victim)

Although the Wallflower is a pretty self-explanatory archetype, knowing you have one is usually confirmed by someone visiting your home; they will ask, "You have another cat? I thought you had only one!" The Wallflower is a closet cat, an under-the-bed cat, someone whose primary objective is to remain unnoticed, safe from scrutiny.

She is the one who politely hopes you won't notice her as she sneaks by. While the overowner is lying across the doorway, and the Mojito Cat is walking around shouting, "Hey! How you doin'?" the Wallflower is hanging back against the wall (hence her moniker), never once daring to walk across the middle of the floor. The Wallflower is saying, "I don't own this. I assume you must be the owner . . . which is totally fine, but if it wouldn't be too much trouble, I'm just going to the litterbox over there. I'm not looking at you, just leaving. Don't mind me. Good-bye." And she leaves with a blink-and-you-miss-her, tail-tucked run, or the Wallflower special, the army-crawl exit stage left.

Ironically, it is the Wallflower's display of anti-Mojo—slinking around the periphery, avoiding confrontation at all costs, deferring, and often being overly fearful and shy—that leads to her role as the victim in multi-cat homes, a role often referred to as "the pariah." In such homes, you find her "caving" in the closet or under the bed, or sometimes cornering herself on a shelf or on top of the fridge. In extreme circumstances, our Wallflowers feel unable to come down from those "safe zones," to the point where they even poop and pee in those zones.

Like the Napoleon Cat at the other end of the confidence pendulum, the Wallflower cat is also anti-Mojo because hiding is reactive, not active. It doesn't matter whether the threat is real or imagined—it still requires her full attention and prompt action.

We want all cats to be their version of Mojito Cats—in other words, not

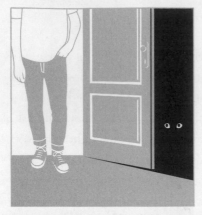

expecting them to conform to what we think confidence should look like, but acknowledging their tendencies and easing their anxieties to make them the best Mojito Cat they can be. What tends to be a hindrance in getting both Napoleon and Wallflower toward Mojitoland is our ingrained feelings about them. The Napoleon tends to get our scorn, and the Wallflower, our pity. The Napoleon gets locked away in a room where she can't beat anyone up, while the Wallflower gets special treatment in her "safe zones," which could mean a dish on top of the fridge or under the bed, or a cushy bed inside the closet. As the old saying goes, "The road to ruin is paved with good intentions." The only road to Mojitoland goes right through the challenge line.

AT HOME WITH THE RAW CAT

In the wild, a cat's territory isn't defined by walls, doors, or windows. Cats create their own maps and establish their own boundaries. Most cats have a core area that they identify as home. The size of their territory beyond that core may depend on whether they are male or female, how much prey is in the area where they live, what type of predators are around, the availability of mates, and how much direct competition there is.

In the absence of doors and walls, cats mark the space they occupy with territorial markers. But if we were to zoom in on what unites all felines, from lions to our cats, it's not just that they are territorial. It's *how* they express that territoriality. All cats use markers, or **signposts**—by urine marking, scratching, rubbing their cheeks and other areas that have scent glands, and perhaps even by pooping—to delineate their turf.

The Raw Cat uses scratch marks to define frequently traveled pathways, and will cheek rub on fences or fallen branches. Urine is used to mark the loose boundaries of a cat's range on prominent objects like tree stumps. As mentioned in the last chapter, marking behaviors say "I live here," not necessarily "keep out." Urine marks transmit information about how recently the cat was here and what his or her reproductive status is; spraying ramps up during mating season.

But the whole point of all these signposts is to allow cats to coexist without fighting. It's like leaving the message "Hey, I'd like to reserve this space from 2:00 to 4:00 p.m.—cool?" It folds into the feline style of avoiding conflict, securing resources (food) alone, and time-sharing as need be. Of course, we all know that sometimes cats don't agree—and that's when fights break out. But signposts help cats identify where and when they exist, and that's why they are so important to your cat—especially because *we* define their boundaries by keeping them indoors.

THE CONFIDENT WHERE

We've already established that cats see territory in a three-dimensional way that other species (including humans) don't. For instance, when we bipeds walk into a room, we take in its assets based on what's sitting on the floor—we scope out the most comfortable chair or couch, the best seat in proximity to a window or the TV, even the best place to drop our wallet and keys. Let's face it, we are very much terrestrial.

Cats, on the other hand, take in every square inch from floor to ceiling, assessing possible rest spots, advantageous perches where they can survey the comings and goings of other beings who share their turf, and spots where they can camouflage themselves to prey/play or just disappear from the world.

Mojo's swagger is partially based, as I've mentioned before, on that feeling of being "home." A baseball player's mojo is derived not only from his daily three Rs (which in his case might be batting practice, physical therapy, how he puts his uniform on, etc.), but also from where those rituals take place—at the ballpark. If we took Tony Manero out of his Brooklyn neighborhood and deposited him on Staten Island, would he still possess his mojo? Most likely not.

Similarly, a cat's Mojo is not strictly about her ability to hunt, to complete each step of the Raw Cat Rhythm; cats also create confidence based on where in the territory they tend to be most successful. Your cat will find various territorial sweet spots somewhere on the vertical axis, and claim them. Each cat has a preferred vantage point in the vertical world, or what I call the **Confident Where**. Our job is to discover and encourage their relationship to these places, which allows them to step into their greatness, full of mojo, and prepare themselves to take on the world. All we have to do is observe. When your cat walks into a room, where is he looking? Many cats will walk in, head high, looking straight up, as if to say, "That! I want that!" Identifying, with mojo, a specific area along the vertical axis is what I call *dwelling*. Discovering what kind of a dweller your cat is will go a long way toward creating a long-lasting Mojo-fied territory and an equally Mojo-fied cat!

CONSIDER THE FOLLOWING THREE CATEGORIES:

Types of Dwellers

Bush Dwellers are the cats waiting under the coffee table or behind a plant. They are often in the "Raw Cat" mind-set, waiting to hunt or to pounce. Bush Dwellers like to have all four feet on the ground.

Tree Dwellers can be found anywhere off the ground. These cats get their confidence from being up high and seeing what's going on. They're not necessarily up in the rafters, but they might be on a chair or on top of the couch. They demonstrate their confidence off the floor.

Beach Dwellers like all four feet touching terra firma, but rather than waiting under a coffee table, they let it all hang out. Beach Dwellers like being out in the open. This is the cat you trip over every day. They're sending a message to you and everyone else in the home: "You have to walk around me."

But before you label your cat a Beach, Tree, or Bush Dweller, you need to know the difference between dwelling and hiding. You can tell if cats are dwelling by their body language. Their ears are forward, and they are surveying the landscape, but they are not vigilant.

Hiding is notably different; it's about being small and invisible. It's what we call the **Unconfident Where**. Crouching down is not about comfort, and seeking safety is not about confidence. If your cat hides all the time, or spends most of his time under the bed, he is not a confident Bush Dweller. Similarly, your cat is not likely a Tree Dweller just because he lives on top of the refrigerator. Which brings us to . . .

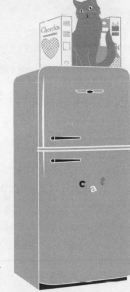

Fridging is when a cat lives on the fridge—up high, but still fearful. Although this behavior pulls on every one of our heart strings, this is a living situation that you simply shouldn't allow to persist. If your cat shows you that he doesn't just *prefer* to be up there but *needs to*, and you're feeding him there, you're not addressing the situation at hand: he is trying to get away from something, usually other animals or people. He only feels safe there, because there is something on the floor that is like broken glass to him.

In addition, **caves** are places where cats go to hide, and when they're hiding out in a cave out of

fear, we call it "caving." We tend to encourage caving by giving cats everything they need in their cave—we feed them under the bed or bring their
litterbox to them, in a misguided attempt to help them feel safe. But caving doesn't make cats feel safe; it just makes them small.

Cats often hide in what we call **the Unders**. This could be the furthest
corner under the bed, in the box spring of a mattress, deep in the back of
a closet, or even in a hole in a wall (I've seen it all). The Unders represent
the ultimate in caves. Eventually, all of the Unders need to be removed or
made inaccessible to your cat by blocking them off. But we're not going to
just rip away your cat's sense of safety.

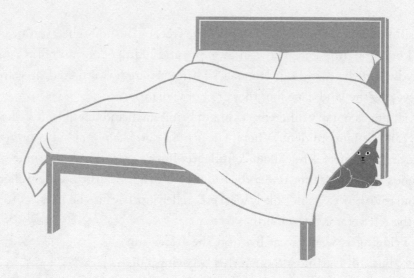

Cat Daddy Dictionary: Caves and Cocoons

A cave is a place where a cat goes to hide, a cocoon is a safe place where
a cat goes to transform.

We know that cats need safe spaces to spend time in to prevent stress. But we need an element of control over those safe spaces. That's where **cocoons** come in. A cocoon is a hideaway that you provide, with the objective to challenge and transform, not simply accommodate. It might be a tent-style cat bed, or a tunnel, or even a cat carrier that's been decked out with a soft blanket. A cocoon offers your cat safety while allowing her to gain confidence and be part of the household activity, because cocoons are eventually placed in socially significant areas. Cocoons allow your cat to feel safe without disappearing. Like their namesake, cocoons are built for metamorphosis; they allow your cat to grow and transform into their fully Mojo-fied self.

In chapter 8, we address all things territory and talk about turning Hiders into Dwellers.

ALPHA AND DOMINANCE: FACT OR FICTION IN CATLAND?

I'm not a big believer in alpha cats—the idea that one cat establishes and enforces dominance over a colony or household of other cats. The terms "alpha" and "dominance" get thrown around a lot—and in ways that can be harmful—when it comes to dogs and cats.

There's actually little evidence that cat groups form a strict hierarchy, where one cat is always on top. Instead, I believe that cats who live together settle into various "occupations" rather than certain rankings on some hierarchal totem pole. There's time-sharing that happens in different favorite spots, and there is that one cat who sort of goes around and keeps things in check like a benevolent dictator . . . a sort of a territorial corrections officer. In my house, it's Pishi who plays this role. He'll walk up, for example, sniff my other cat Caroline's butt, and she'll get the message.

"Lights out. Move along."

I think a lot of people would describe Pishi as an alpha. But there's a difference between roles that define any society and this sledgehammer label that is "alpha." Granted, the only thing that prevents any society from becoming a complete anarchy is role-playing. But alpha denotes dominance, and dominance is not a personality trait. It might describe a pattern of interactions between two animals, but there's really no good evidence for "wolfpack" behavior in dogs, much less cats. Research has also shown that a lot of the "dominant" or aggressive behaviors we think we see are probably more about age and familiarity between the cats. Bottom line: *there's no such thing as a truly alpha cat.*

A big problem with calling a cat "alpha" or "dominant" is that it doesn't actually help us understand his behavior. It doesn't fix anything. It just causes you to view your cat through an adversarial lens, where you interpret everything as aggression. And then, as a result, your response is to try to dominate *him.*

THE CAT ARCHETYPES CONNECTION

As discussed earlier, a Mojito Cat is sort of a social magnet. The world tends to revolve a bit around the Mojito, because she is confident—and not so tied up in self-preservation. Wallflowers and Napoleons, on the other hand, are so obsessed with taking care of their own stuff (and being anxious about it) all day long that they forget about the greater good of the household or colony. This anxiety can serve as a proverbial target on their back in the eyes of other cats.

But the Mojito is above that, so she can deal with the general structure of her world much easier. Does that make the Mojito "dominant"? No—because if you watch your cats carefully, you will see that it's flexibility and time-sharing that defines the majority of cat relationships. (More on this in section 3.)

Section

THREE

The Cat Mojo Toolbox

6

~~~

Welcome to the Toolbox

C AT WITH A capital "C"; Ubercat; Everycat; the Raw Cat. The cat throughout history, the (sometimes hard) transition as they learned to live among humans, the (even harder) acclimation to living indoors, and all that we've come to learn about them—that journey ends here. And this is where *we* begin. We've talked about the human influence on cats throughout history, but what about the here and now? I'm not talking about the epic story of humans and cats. I'm talking about the very individual story, which plays out day after day, year after year. We humans aren't just guardians of territory or providers of resources. We are participants in a relationship and have the opportunity to help guide our companions into their brightest light.

IN THE CHAPTERS ahead, you will be acquiring a lot of knowledge in the form of tools: time-tested, real-world suggestions and practices that will improve the quality of life for your cat and, by extension, you. But the tools—that is to say, the raw knowledge—are not the most important part of this section. The most important takeaway of this section is understanding that you are in a relationship with your cat.

Imagine this: You have a fifteen-year-old son who is friendly, outgoing, and generous—he is not one to ever give you or anyone else much trouble.

One afternoon, you receive a call from the school principal. She tells you that, for no discernable reason, he started a fight with another student, broke the kid's nose, and sent him to the hospital. Your son would have to be suspended until the whole thing is sorted out, and he's now in the principal's office, waiting for you to come pick him up.

You hang up the phone, overtaken by shock. You struggle to understand the underlying reason why your son might have done this, as a five-alarm level of parental concern kicks in. From the moment you grab your car keys to the moment you pull up to his school, you experience a dizzying array of extreme emotions—from anger to frustration to fear, with a dash of humiliation thrown in for good measure. At the eye of your inner storm, though, you envision him sitting there waiting for you, feeling scared, ashamed, maybe even still full of rage. In any case, you know beyond a shadow of a doubt that he is surely suffering, and because of that, so are you. He is your kid, and *you just want to know what's wrong* so you can help.

Now imagine *this*: You come home from a tough day at work, open your front door, and get hit with the stinging ammonia blast of cat pee. You've heard of this kind of thing happening, but your cat has never done anything like this in his life. Immediately, you begin the search, cursing at yourself and the cat because this day couldn't get much worse . . . and then it does: right on the center cushion of your brand new vanilla cream couch, you see the sizeable sunset-orange/yellow splatter.

Shock gives way to something just this side of rage as you grab the cleaning spray and get to work on the cushion. No matter what you do with the endless spraying and blotting, it's beginning to sink in that the cushion is toast. The stain can fade, but it'll always be there, along with that smell. Your temperature continues to rise along with the recurring thought that your cat acted out this way because of something *you did*. Clearly, this is a spiteful gesture, and no matter why he might feel the way he does, you know that you've done nothing wrong. You notice him sitting at the entrance to the kitchen, as he does every night, waiting for dinner. A few hours ago he decided that he hates you, and now it's business as usual? That's not going to fly. Debating the consequences, you shake your head because you realize that your cat will simply never know how much damage and suffering he has inflicted on you.

So, let's compare and contrast:

In each of these scenarios, both kid and cat signaled that something was definitely *not okay*. In the case of your child, the focus went immediately to your child. The *big why* dominated your thoughts—as in *why* did he feel he needed to resort to violence and *why* didn't you see the signs beforehand? This was followed by the *big how*, as in, *how* are you going to help him and *how* will you get through this as a family? In the case of your cat, the *big why* centered on *why* your cat would do something like this to you, and the *big how* was about *how* you were ever going to get the pee out of the cushion. You didn't struggle to understand what new issues might have arisen in the household to cause him to do this, nor did the "five-alarm level of parental concern" likely have you running him to the vet the next morning to see if he had an infection or some other health issue that could've factored into the equation.

Bottom line: in the first scenario, your reaction was centered on your concern for your kid; in the second scenario, your reaction was centered on your concern for your couch.

And there's the rub.

In the sanctified realm of our home among our family members, true empathy shouldn't be reserved for one and not the other, for some and not all. As enlightened as we may fancy ourselves, as long as there is even a splinter of treating our animal family members as things we own as opposed to those we love, that splinter will infect the body of our family. That splinter has a name: ownership. The way forward also has a name: relationship.

IT'S NOT WHAT YOU OWN, IT'S WHO YOU LOVE

If you took the species part out from the equation and just saw your cat as another member of your family, you'd be left with relationship. At the core of this relationship are fundamental elements that dictate your ability to successfully navigate that relationship, like:

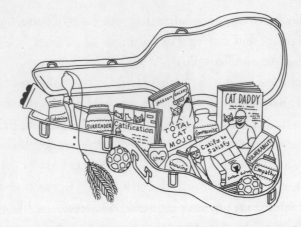

- *Knowing*—Likes and dislikes, fears, aversions, how their history dictates their present behavior.
- *Listening*—When they are soliciting something from you, whether it is affection, protection, or just your time, you bring your attention to them, even if there is nothing you can offer in that moment.
- *Compromising*—In any relationship you come to the realization that it isn't all about you and your needs. You bend to others when in reality it's the last thing you want to do.
- *Vulnerability*—The nature of the relational two-way street is remaining present with the other being, admitting you don't know everything, admitting that you don't control the outcome of each and every moment of that relationship. You don't have ownership over others' reactions, the way they handle the world around them. You can learn from others just as readily as they can learn from you. In other words, you dare to make yourself available to another, without relying on a safety net of your design and under your control.
- And of course, the magic ingredient in all of this is *loving*—a deep knowledge that your life together is better than your life apart, which makes you embrace all of the above conditions (even if you don't always joyfully do so) not only because you have a stake in the outcome of every moment, but because, after all, it's why we are here—to love and be loved.

Put all of those fundamentals in a pot, bring the soup to a boil, and it takes on a life of its own, evolving to a certain degree on its own accord and at its own pace. We, as individuals—and despite the intense protestations of our respective egos—are reduced to participants, and not directors, in our own story.

Then there is the final element—*surrender*—and whether the relationship is one with a "significant other" or a parental one, it's unavoidably a key ingredient in the soup. Releasing ownership and embracing relationship is, to be sure, a scary damn thing. But it is what makes having others in our life the most precious thing.

It might be getting pretty obvious at this point that my aim for you is to bring a new outlook to your relationship with your cat, by *seeing it as a relationship*. From this vantage point, everything that you might hope to gain from this book will be enhanced tenfold, in terms of getting positive outcomes from problem behavior. By observing your cat's actions with an empathetic eye, you'll have a very different reaction to the peeing on the furniture or any other form of "acting out." Instead of getting angry at your cat and berating him (or cursing yourself), your first thought will be, "Whoa! This isn't like him. What could be going on that would cause him to do something so uncharacteristic?" The *big why* and *big how* become integral to our responses, and that's exactly the mind-set we want to be in as we proceed with all of the upcoming tools in this section.

Further, empathy also grants us the gift of a certain degree of foresight. If we are able to react with emotional connection to the outburst, then it follows that we should be able to prevent it by seeing the lit fuse before the cat bomb goes off. The huge pee spot on the couch may have been prefaced by actions that would be imperceptible to an outsider: pacing, vocalizations that you may have never heard before, even behaviors that aren't connected to symptoms. Through the laws of relationship, you will be attuned to the "gut feelings," the nagging "something just isn't right" feelings that can oftentimes save a life . . . or at the very least, a couch.

AT THE TOP of this chapter, we said the most important thing was to understand that you are in a relationship with your cat. That relationship, like any you'll ever be engaged in, requires you to use tools to successfully navigate it, and in the coming pages we will give you plenty of those. That brings us to a final thought: all the tools in the world won't do you any good unless you have a place for them to live in and to operate from—and that place is the empathetic core inside you. In other words, *you are the toolbox*: Welcome to it.

Raw Cat 101
and the Three Rs

THE YELLOW BRICK road of Cat Mojo is paved with your cat's swagger, her sense of pride, her confident ownership of *her territory*, and her instinctive knowledge that she has a job to do in that territory. What moves her down the road is her daily routine of hunt, catch, kill, eat, followed by grooming and sleeping. If cats can engage this HCKEGS cycle with consistency, certainty, and confidence, they will experience *total* Cat Mojo, which is our Emerald City, always rising like the sun on the horizon.

For cats to reach the Emerald City, we need to provide an infrastructure through which all of these activities can unfold each day with predictability. And we do this with **the Three Rs: Routines, Rituals, and Rhythm**.

Every home has its natural rise-and-fall energy cycles, based largely around when you get up, go to work, come home, then go to bed. As you begin to establish rituals and routines with your cat, and base them on your home's energy spikes, you create a rhythm. This rhythm becomes the foundation for all of the primary, supportive interactions you have with your cat, such as when you play and when you feed.

But it's not just about getting your cat to conform to *your* rhythm. It's about folding their needs and yours into a *household* rhythm. Just as human rituals define our confidence and sense of stability, cats need their own.

So your day isn't just about taking your kids to school, dropping them off at soccer practice and piano lessons, then helping them with homework and preparing dinner; I'm saying that HCKE, cuddle time, and cleaning the litterbox are all locked into that rhythm as well.

THE ENERGETIC BALLOON

Cats sleep as much as they do in order to prepare for the hunt. As they sleep, they are collecting energy. They are, in essence, Energetic Balloons, starting as an empty vessel and, through sleep, filling up with energy. When they wake up, that energy needs a home—a target, if you will. Let's not forget that they are *programmed* by years of evolution, with a rhythm that demands satisfaction. The Raw Cat awakens and *needs* to hunt. Anything else that happens to cats (like being petted), or even *around* them (experiencing the lively rhythm of your and your family's day), becomes more air in the balloon—more energy that will seek release.

That's where our job comes in. We can almost guarantee a measure of mojo and proactively lessen the frustration of a quickly filling balloon by being the architects of this preexisting rhythm. When interacting with our cats, we are either putting energy in, filling the balloon, or taking energy out, opening the safety valve. It's that simple. Just as the rhythm of our day is determined by our various rituals and routines, the same is true for our cats. Each day in our home presents fairly predictable energetic spikes, and our cats spike along with the rest of us. When the family gets up in the morning, it's energy in. Our rituals range from alarm (and snooze) to shower, from shaving or makeup application to breakfast (both human and cat).

These rituals are the building blocks of our morning routine; everyone runs around the house, talking in loud volumes—*Did you pack your lunch? Are you ready to go? Did you feed the cats?* More energy in. Footsteps around the house, doors slamming, and all of those reverberations: still more energy in. We leave the house with a full balloon (our cat) left behind.

Imagine what happens now as the day passes. We've got birds outside the window, traffic noises, people in neighboring apartments making noise.

Now you and your family return home, and energy spikes. Dinnertime, everyone's home. *How was your day?* Feed humans and animals. Time to do the dishes! Get ready for the next day. In the meantime, the balloon is filling while you relax and unwind. Watch some TV before the last spike of the day when you get up again, get ready for bed, and prepare for the next day. At this point, all you have to do is breathe loudly and the balloon is going to pop.

What does a full balloon look like? Imagine if you had a balloon and that balloon had a mind and could feel it was ready to pop. That balloon would start to self-regulate—it would let some air out. Redirected aggression is an example of your cat letting air out, but there are more subtle ways. To me, the tail swish is that "balloon's" ability to let air out. Once the balloon is full, the tail becomes an air escape mechanism. Same thing with what I call "back lightning." The twitching that happens through the cat's back is, at least partially, a spasm, but also a way of getting that energy out. You may notice your cat walking across the room, suddenly stopping as if a fly just landed on him and then very deliberately grooming himself. This self-soother is also a self-regulator.

What is our role in filling up the balloon, in this overstimulation? For some cats, petting is air into the balloon in a way that is intolerable. It's energy in without an out. What might feel good for three or thirty seconds suddenly begins to feel like it's going to make their balloon pop. And then—bang! That hiss, that bite, their turning on you—running away or self-grooming are desperate attempts to let air out of the balloon.

The Raw Cat 101 tool focuses on the particulars of those key rituals and routines, so that you can enjoy a rhythm in your house that supports the Mojo-fied experience for your cat—every day.

PLAY = PREY

Now that you know about the Raw Cat Rhythm, do you still think that tossing a crinkle ball across the floor counts as play? Are you letting yourself off the hook because you have a bunch of plastic mice and a catnip cigar lying around the living room? Do you still, after all of this, have a vision of cat play being about them batting a ball of yarn around the carpet? If so, do not pass go, and definitely do not collect your two hundred dollars. Go back to the Raw Cat Rhythm (chapter 3), reread it, and meet me back here.

One of the most important things I can tell you about keeping your cat

Raw happy and Raw healthy is that play isn't a luxury, something that is a fun diversion if and when you have time. Look at it this way: If you have a dog, you have a collar and leash and you take the dog for daily walks. And likewise, if you have a cat, you have interactive toys and you use them for daily play sessions. These things should hold equal weight because for the respective species, they are a physical and behavioral necessity.

Having that interactive toy, however, is only the tip of the iceberg. Here's the thing: *play is a structured activity.* The difference between casually playing with your cat and truly engaging in the HCKE ritual is the routine nature of HCKE. Your cat likes things to happen in a predictable manner, and this is how you Mojo-fy playtime for them. You don't play Monopoly by sitting down and flicking around Monopoly game pieces with your finger. No, *this* is Monopoly: you roll the dice, you move, you pick up a card, you buy a house. A typical play session with your cat involves this level of engagement.

As you break out an interactive toy and replicate movements of prey, you're helping to reinforce the endgame—what the Hunt/Catch/Kill actually looks like—and you bolster the Mojo that goes along with the hunting process. You are essentially providing a structured outlet for your Raw Cat's behavioral yearnings. This is how you feed the Mojo.

"BUT MY CAT DOESN'T PLAY"

The reason so many people say to me, "Jackson, my cat doesn't play," is because they expect playtime to look like your cat is just running laps around the house for an hour. But remember, play (i.e., "the hunt") is not all about action; the preparation, or the "stalking," is just as big a part (if not a bigger one) of the process as the "pounce and kill" action part.

The exhaustion that comes from hunting happens even when the cat isn't continually moving; watching the moth on the ceiling exhausts, the stalk exhausts, those short bursts of energy exhaust. It's the mind-body focus that exhausts your cat. This is a directed action that your cat is 100 percent engrossed in. Expecting success to look like a track-and-field event will result in both you and your cat being frustrated. Don't set yourself up for failure: know what success looks like.

Every cat plays. You just need to know how *your* cat defines it. Your sixteen-year-old diabetic overweight Persian might just do "moth on the ceiling." For that cat, that is play. If all she does is moth on the ceiling, and when the moth lands, she just bats at the toy twice—that is still play. Expecting your sixteen-year-old diabetic Persian to run around the house leads you to say "my cat doesn't play," and then you never try again. Instead, get to know what that "alternate universe" of HCKE looks like for your cat.

. . . And you didn't think I was going to let *you* off the hook, did you? Creating ritual around play is only half the equation; your investment in that ritual is the other half.

The Cat Daddy Guide to Types of Cat Toys

Interactive toys: You're attached to one end; your cat is attached to the other end. You provide the Three Rs (**Routines, Rituals, Rhythm**) of what the hunt looks like. These are toys that stimulate the prey drive—like the wand with feathers, or small prey at the end of a cord. Without question, THE most crucial tool in the shed.

Remote toys: This is any toy that can be thrown and that you can play fetch with. It usually disappears under the couch or refrigerator and reappears during next year's spring cleaning. Examples are sparkle balls, crinkle balls, furry mice, and those odd, geometric rubber balls. These are fine, but not as an exclusive choice.

Self-activated toys: These are the lazy man's toys, usually of the battery-operated variety. You flick a switch and the toy does the rest. The problem is that if your "play partner" is a machine whose movements are entirely predictable, the thrill of the hunt becomes completely muted. To a degree, the HCKE ritual is like walking the tightrope between order and chaos. With no chance of anarchy, the ritual becomes somewhat meaningless to the cat. Am I telling you never to use toys like this? No. I get it—you might have had a crazy-long, crazy-busy day, and being able to flick that switch is a good alternative to doing nothing; so long as it's not the "spinal cord" of your interactive play arsenal, the self-activated toy still has a place in the Mojo-fied home.

A note on laser pointers: A laser pointer can help you start the engine for play. But I firmly believe that it is limited as a tool. It simply can't be the through line for ending the game. Why? Because it can't be "killed." It is a predatory tease—no biting, no all-four-paw wraparound—just an endless chase. Get that motor going with a laser, for sure; just make sure, at some point, that you switch to something physical that can be "caught and killed."

BE THE BIRD: ANATOMY OF THE KILL

 Play is a dedicated activity. The last thing I want is for you to text with one hand and wave a feather wand with the other, or talk to your spouse or watch TV while you're playing with your cat. If you want the benefits that come with a cat who has executed all of the elements of the Raw Cat Rhythm, then what is needed on your end is commitment. And I'm not just talking about time commitment, like committing to fifteen minutes of play. I'm talking about owning the role that you are playing in the "game." It's what I call "be the bird" or "be the mouse." What would it be like for you to actually be that prey? How would you move in the presence of a lightning-fast, fang-toothed mammal who is trying to kill you? With that in mind, let's take a look at how cats hunt and, accordingly, how you should strive to replicate prey movements during play.

First, I want you to pretend you're a bird.

If you're the bird, you're going to do that subtle, moth-on-the-ceiling movement for a minute, simply hovering, and then you do that thing that gets you caught: you swoop down and suddenly hit the ground. And now your cat is going to pounce. But what makes this a game? Just yanking the toy away and having the bird fly away again? No, you're going to play dead, and make it so your cat will then bat at the bird to test if you are really dead. Next, he will likely walk away to try to trick you into moving again.

From there, you might slowly begin to inch along, playing not-quite-dead, as you take faint little steps away and try to get to refuge around the side of the couch. You're heading in the right direction when you see wide-eyed, rapt attention, tensing muscles, and maybe a twitch at the end of the tail. And then the dilated pupils, the "head bob" as he sizes up the exact dimensions of the kill, and the famous "butt wiggle" right before he pounces tell you that your cat has stepped into that alternate universe. This is when your cat will run at you . . . but then you take off again!

Now it's time for you to decide: do you want him to catch you, or is it not time to be caught yet? And off you go again, repeating this sequence—moth-on-the-ceiling movement, wiggle butt, pounce . . . all the while thinking, What are your best methods to elicit that confidence, a.k.a. Mojo, from your cat?

Personally, one of the things that makes me really happy is when, toward the end of the HCKE sequence, a cat takes the feather from the toy in their mouth, starts to growl, and looks around the room for that perfect space to take his prey. Then he starts walking away, and I give him some slack in the line and follow him. To me, that is the Holy Grail. I have played so well that my cat has slipped into that other world—the world of the Raw Cat. Then I wait for him to drop the feather, and I fly away again. This is how you know you've hit Raw Cat pay dirt.

YOU HAVE ENTERED THE LAND
OF THE RAW CAT: POPULATION 2

This is a generalized list, so now the most important thing you can do is to find out who *your* cat is. Does she like ground prey or air prey? Is she a lizard hunter or a bird hunter? Can she go fluidly from one place to another? Some cats get fearful of bird motion—they may prefer ground prey.

HUNTING STYLES REMINDER

As discussed in chapter 3, cats will generally have a preferred style of hunting, innate to them. In general, they might prefer to *ambush* from an open clearing; *stalk-and-rush* from behind cover; or wait to *pounce on prey* that pops out of the ground. Incorporate these different strategies into your play and see what your cat responds to best.

TYPES OF CAT PLAYERS

Speaking of different styles, consider these two general types of players:

You've got your **sports car**, which is where you simply present a toy, and *varoom* . . . they're off! There is no gap. It's just turn the key, press the gas, and zero to sixty.

And then you've got your **Model Ts**. You have to crank that engine—sometimes for five minutes—before they actually respond to the toy. But when they do, they really do. And once their hunting mechanism has been cranked to the point of the key turning over, they're in the game. That's why we use toys like laser pointers. They're like those old-time engine cranks on the Model T.

Cat Daddy Dictionary: Boil and Simmer

The Raw Cat (and your cat) is a hunter built for speed, not distance. Trying to keep cats running around for fifteen minutes straight during playtime is not going to be practical (unless they are in the kitten-to-teenager age range). It will be not only an undesirable thing to many cats, but ultimately an exercise in frustration for the guardian (who will then exclaim, "My cat doesn't like to play!" or "I can play with my cat for an hour and he never gets tired!").

Instead, approach playtime on the Raw Cat's terms: shorter bursts of vigorous play, followed by a brief rest period. Think of a simple recipe that instructs you to bring the ingredients to a boil and then allow them to simmer. The only difference here is that in cat play, we will keep returning to a "boil."

So, start with bringing the activity to a boil: get them to chase a toy around, burn off some energy, and maybe even get them panting for a few seconds. (During this first boil—and just to get the engine running—would be a good time to break out the laser pointer if it's your cat's particular cup of tea.) Then let them come down to a simmer (rest) for a bit. You will likely notice that they recover quickly. They may act bored or indifferent (in other words, like a cat), but soon you'll easily be able to bring them back to that boil.

From there, repeat: let them get a little tired, rest briefly, then bring them back up again. Of course, at this point you want to move to a toy that is more truly interactive than a laser pointer—in other words, something they can "kill"! After a few rounds, you'll see diminishing returns and shorter bursts of energy during the boil. Once you get to the point of "one jump and done," or when the only way they will engage is if you bring the toy over to them, where it will receive a half-hearted swipe while they lie on their side . . . well, then—your cat is cooked . . . figuratively speaking, of course!

Cat Nerd Corner

Preventing Boredom While Playing

A 2002 study by Dr. John Bradshaw and colleagues tested cats' interest in playing with the same toy, as opposed to when the researchers presented them with a new toy. Unsurprisingly, offering the cats a new toy increased grabbing and biting behaviors. In other words, your cat might get tired of the toy before they get tired of playing.

While almost any preylike toy can get your cat moving, try rotating toys to hold his interest in a HCKE session.

CATNIP: IT'S A CAT THING—
YOU WOULDN'T UNDERSTAND

We all need a little recreation. For cats, it may come in the form of an herb. There are multiple plants that cats respond to, the most well-known ones being catnip, valerian, honeysuckle, and matatabi (also known as silver vine).

Catnip, also known as *Nepeta cataria*, is a member of the mint family. Nepetalactone is the active ingredient in catnip that cats respond to and, in fact, most species of cats—big or small—*will* respond to it. This response appears to be somewhere between hallucinogenic, aphrodisiac, stimulant, and relaxant. (Wow—where can I sign up?)

The most common behavior we see in response to catnip is rolling. This rolling behavior is similar to what female cats do when they are in heat, but in the case of catnip, both male and female cats will roll. We can't really say for sure whether the response to catnip is sexual, playful, or predatory, but it sometimes appears to be all three. Some cats prefer to lick and chew catnip, while others will just lie there, drooling with glazed-over eyes. Meanwhile, other cats get really amped up from it.

Approximately one-third of all cats, however, don't respond to catnip—it's a genetic thing. And kittens don't seem to respond to it at all, so the response may be related to sexual maturity (although being spayed or neutered doesn't diminish the response). The catnip reaction is relatively short: just five to fifteen minutes. After that, your cat will typically need a break of at least half an hour to show a response again.

Of course, *the* most important thing to know about catnip is how it affects *your* cat. By and large, catnip appears to reduce inhibitions, which, as with humans, can be a good or bad thing. Just ask yourself the question "Is my cat a happy drunk or a mean drunk?" It's the same question you would ask yourself about the friend you're about to spend New Year's Eve with—just so you're prepared. If your friend is a happy drunk, then at some point during the festivities, you can bank on him throwing his arms around you, saying, "I LOVE you, man!" and then finding a place to pass out. If that friend is a mean drunk? Then you'd better have bail money put aside because he will most assuredly be starting a fight with someone in the parking lot. This is to say that you need to be able to predict how your cat will act once her inhibitions are down. If a cat already has bully tendencies, then it might magnify her violent nature and send her over the top. Competition for toys might get a bit more fierce, and if she is prone to overstimulation behaviors, those might come much closer to the surface. For other cats, they either become more relaxed, or less fearful (which could then become a problem if they suddenly approach another cat in a more brazen way than normal).

This is to say that in a multicat home, catnip is at the very least worth trying, but I would always recommend a catnip test run with individual cats first, as opposed to with the whole group. If you have known tensions between cats, or are trying to introduce new cats to each other, it's a good idea to remove all catnip and catnip toys from the house. Why take the risk? And remember, since the catnip response during a single encounter is short-lived (and multiple exposures provide diminishing returns in terms of its effect), keep your catnip toys packed away, marinating them in loose catnip for even more potency, and bring them out for special occasions. This will enhance your cat's experience each time, and also provide a positive association when such a thing is needed. (For more info on this, see "The Jackpot! Effect" in chapter 9.)

FEEDING FOR MOJO

The HCKEGS life rhythm represents the direct line from the Raw Cat to our cat. That innate need to live one's life around the hunt doesn't begin and end as a series of rituals. The Raw Cat (and house cat's) psyche and body will only be satisfied with the product of that hunt. In other words, the Raw Cat, *and* your cat, are obligate carnivores.

My preferred and recommended food of choice for cats is a raw, meat-based diet, which includes all of the aspects of prey: bones, muscle, tissue, fat, organs, and even a small percentage of plant matter, the amount proportional to what would be found in the stomach of the prey they would hunt and eat. Since any commercially prepared diet is not an animal killed and consumed on the spot, there will be some nutrients lacking (for example, those found in the blood of the prey). That said, we live in a time where complete nutrition via raw feeding can be achieved through several commercially prepared choices.

I get that you might be grossed out by "going raw"; also, not all cats will vibe with the raw diet. Sometimes it's really hard to get cats into it. In that case, I recommend that you feed your cat a grain-free wet diet. Why is there rice, gluten, or other fillers in your cat's food? Because it's all cheaper than meat!

Nonetheless, *I would rather you feed your cat the worst wet food on the market than the best dry;* if you want to use dry, use it for treats. For older cats, however, sometimes anything goes. You just need to keep weight on them. At that point, philosophies about food go out the window, so if they insist on dry, let 'em have it. But my bottom line is: wet food is what is most natural for your cat.

I've got pretty strong feelings about dry food. Let's face it, most people like dry food because it's convenient. I guarantee that if you're feeding dry food, there's a high chance that you're also leaving food out 24/7, and that does not jibe with Raw Cat logic.

Why am I not a big fan of dry food? First of all, dry food is often full of carbohydrates. Research has associated high-carbohydrate diets for cats with urinary crystals, type 2 diabetes, and obesity. Sound like something you want to take a risk on?

Disease risks aside, let's go back to the Raw Cat diet: prey. Prey animals are high in protein and water. The process of making dry food, or extrusion, breaks down some nutrients in the food. By the time it's done being extruded, dry food has a moisture content of less than 10 percent. Wet food is about 60 percent moisture, which is much closer to that of a mouse (around 75 percent). You do the math. Cats fed dry food might drink more water to "compensate," but research shows they still don't make up that deficit.

And if you've heard that dry food can clean your cat's teeth, just throw that garbage advice out the window. Even if kibbles remove *some* plaque (which is questionable), feeding dry food is not an effective replacement for brushing your cat's teeth or having their teeth cleaned by a veterinarian.

The bottom line is, if you want to cater to Raw Cat, dry food isn't the way to do it.

DESTINATION: JACKPOT!

There is that moment when you will find yourself opening a lot of cans of food to find the right one. But remember, this is about a relationship. When you start going out with someone, do you have any idea what kind of food they like? No, so you ask them. You can't ask a cat, but you can present them with choices that fit both the criteria of what is good for them, and what they enjoy eating.

Which brings us to the importance of variety. The Raw Cat might love him some mouse, but that doesn't mean he will turn up his nose at the rest of the buffet the natural world has to offer him. Likewise, cats are not built to eat just one thing their entire life. And beyond that, it's important every now and again to put yourself in their shoes; if you ate the exact same thing every meal for your entire life, I bet after a certain point you'd become "finicky" as well.

The good news is that, if there's one thing we don't lack in today's burgeoning cat market, it's variety. For relatively little money, you can experiment with different proteins, textures, preparations, and variations that will inevitably lead you to your cat's gastronomical sweet spot. It comes down to due diligence. There are pâtés, shreds, chunks, and every stop in between. Maybe your cat prefers "roasted" or "grilled"—or you suddenly realize your cat loves spinach. There are hundreds of choices out there, and I can't stress enough the importance of finding what makes your cat yell, "*Jackpot!*"

Also, as a veteran of animal sheltering, I want to alert you to something that I hope never happens, but we need to be prepared for it: if your cat eats only one thing his entire life, and something happens to you, more often than not that spells trouble for him and those who need to care for him. If he ends up in a shelter or rescue situation, the combination of stress and his very limited palate provides an opening for a form of anorexia. In essence, consistently challenging your cat from a dietary perspective, and opening him up to new tastes and textures, is not only good for him but, in a way, helps to prepare your cat for different life challenges and changes.

Transitioning to the Raw Cat Diet

For some cats, the raw diet is like coming home. I recommend you try introducing it as a treat at first, and see if your cat goes for it.

If your cat is already on a wet food diet, you can also transition her to raw by mixing in a little bit of the new raw food with what she currently eats. In general, you don't want to switch her food too fast or you could have explosive diarrhea all over the house. (Fun for the entire family!)

Some cats do best if you start with browning the raw food for under a minute to strengthen the smell, which will increase your cat's interest (and bring the food up to its prey's average body temperature). Some cats like it if you add a small amount of water to their food to give it a little "gravy." You can even sprinkle some dehydrated meat on the top to get your cat started. Once she gets the hang of it, you may not need to incorporate these "tricks" to get her to go for it.

You can match the grind of the raw food to the style of food she already prefers, you can introduce different meats and cuts, chunks versus ground. Remember, feeding for challenge means presenting the palate with variety . . . even with raw meat!

MEAL FEEDING— A CAT DADDY NON-NEGOTIABLE!

We have to make the distinction between scavenging versus opportunistic hunting. One lifestyle suggests grazing; the other suggests HCKE.

Free feeding is leaving food out for your cat 24/7 and is basically analogous to scavenging. It's food for the taking, with no effort involved. It's unearned and, therefore, unrewarding. No Mojo. My experience is that free feeding undermines the work we try to do, not to mention the cat's own physiology.

Cats are built to eat several small meals a day, optimally around five to six hours apart. I advocate somewhere between two and four meals a day, matching the rhythm of your home. The difference between a wild cat who is hunting all the time and your cat is that your cat's circadian rhythm is hooked into yours. When your family wakes up in the morning, energy in the house skyrockets, and so does your cat's. So, ideally, that's when it's HCKE time. You come home from work, and the same thing happens: your cat's energy rises. And then once again before bed. Every time there's a ritualistic rising of energy in the home, you should be ritualizing play and food (HCKE) around that.

Controlling when your cat eats regulates your cat's energy. Regulating your cat's digestion gives you information about when he will eliminate. We tend to overcomplicate things. Keep it simple and connect the feeding schedule back to the Raw Cat!

How Much to Feed Your Cat

One-size-fits-all feeding guidelines are unrealistic. Don't take any one source's word as gospel on how much your cat should be eating. Do your research, but also get to know what your cat likes and dislikes and how much he likes to eat, and monitor his weight and activity level.

Cats require somewhere around twenty-five to thirty-five calories per pound a day for maintenance. One mouse is about thirty calories. Outdoor cats eat eight to ten mice a day, but that is after twenty or thirty hunting attempts. Cats who live outside have a different rhythm than our indoor cats and work a lot harder for their food.

Feeding Time for Multiple Cats

Of course, as much as I try to arm you with hard and fast rules for cat living, when it comes to multiple-cat homes, that's where rules go to die. In multiple-cat households, your cats might not all be on the same page when it comes to how fast or how much they eat. If you have an elderly or sick cat, he may need more access to food than your other cats. He might even need food out all the time. Also, cats don't share mice, and most cats don't want to share their food dish. So space your dishes out accordingly. Your house cat has a nice-sized personal space bubble that needs to be respected.

Some cats are part of what we call the "Snarf and Barf" crowd: they eat like there's no tomorrow. They might gulp their food down just to barf it back up. Usually it happens so quickly that you'll be cleaning up undigested food that looks almost identical to what you had just put in the bowl. The reasons for Snarf and Barf are varied. Sometimes there's an underlying physical problem like, for instance, hyperthyroidism. It's always smart to take repeated episodes as a symptom and have them checked out by a vet. Just as often, however, there are emotional reasons—the cat might have lived out on the street, competing with other cats for scant resources. It could be that before she came to your home she lived with a dog who liked her food as much as she did, and so she got used to speed eating before trouble came knocking.

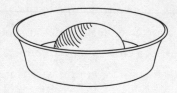

Whatever the cause, there is a simple solution. My favorite solution is a "slow down bowl." These have barriers or ridges that cats have to work around to get their food. You can make your own by feeding your cat from a plate with a few clean rocks she has to work around. Slow feeders not only put the brakes on Snarf and Barf, but can buy you precious time during pet introductions (see chapter 10).

Food for Challenge

You may have one cat who won't eat around everyone else because he is a Wallflower. However, you don't want to feed that cat in the other room just because he is scared. Instead, use mealtime as a means to slowly move him into the community.

Everything we provide for cats is an opportunity for challenge. Food is *it*. They are food and resource motivated, not human-praise motivated. It's not just routine and rhythm. You cannot get cats to do what you want if they're not a little bit hungry. When I first started filming *My Cat from Hell*, the network folks observed my "food challenge" methods and asked me, "Aren't you just bribing the cat?" Hell yes, I'm bribing the cat! And that's okay.

Preventing Pickiness

The first thing you need to do is take a look at your feeding situation. If your cat has dry food sitting out 24/7, do you think she is going to be that motivated to try something new? Is she being picky or is she just not hungry? This gets back to why cats need meals. They need to be a little hungry to try something new.

Whisker stress: Many cats do not like the feeling of their whiskers touching the side of the bowl. Feed cats from shallow bowls or small plates.

Texture: Some cats are particular about pâté, chunks, slices, and even the shape of dry food or treats.

Temperature: Food should be served at "mouse body temperature." There's no self-respecting Raw Cat out there that would choose to eat something out of a fridge.

Choice: Offer lots of choices, rotate foods, and note preferences.

Location: Make sure the food dish is in a safe location—that may mean away from other cats or with a view to see the comings and goings of other animals. And let us not forget: dogs love cat food. And young children love to play in it and with it. We all need and deserve a little peace and quiet when we eat.

> **Don't top off:** Some cats learn they can get attention by meowing at the bowl waiting for humans to "fluff up" their food.
>
> **Know the difference:** Cats that don't eat may not just be picky. Not eating, even just for a day or two, is a major red flag. Obese cats are particularly at risk of hepatic lipidosis (fatty liver disease), which can be deadly in no time at all.

GROOMING AND SLEEPING FOR MOJO

Unlike the other components of the Raw Cat Rhythm, the last two need very little help; they are products of the momentum created by the successful execution of the first four. In a way, they act as proof of full commitment on the part of the Raw Cat and his human shepherd. If your cat has hunted, caught, killed, and eaten in a way that signals completion—and a fully deflated Energetic Balloon—an infallible instinct to groom and sleep will be triggered to call an end to the HCKEGS cycle and get ready for the next one.

With that said, here are some general notes around grooming and sleeping:

To Groom or Not to Groom . . .

When was the last time you saw your cat grooming herself? If they're not grooming, something is wrong. Also, if your cat's fur is oily, or she's getting mats when she never did before, these are also warning signs. Either way, this is something you need to be vigilant about. If your cat is avoiding grooming, it can be a sign of illness or depression. It's also sometimes a sign of obesity; note whether your cat is grooming but avoiding her back or butt. The truth is, she may not be able to reach it, which should be a major wake-up call.

Does Your Cat Need Your Help Grooming?

All cats benefit from brushing, but for some breeds, it's not optional—you must brush them. Long-haired cats can get painful mats that may require professional help for removal.

Does Your Cat Need a Bath?

My question for people who bathe their cats all the time is this: why are you torturing your animal?

There is simply no reason to bathe your cat. In fact, unless your cat has been skunked or has soiled himself, he will *never* need a bath (with the exception of the hairless breeds, who, because of their unnatural state of hairlessness, need to have a bath once a week). Cats spend all that time grooming to cover themselves with their scent, a Raw Cat staple and a source of serious mojo, and then a human steps in and bathes them, erasing their ID. Some cats can be wiped down with a baby wipe if they are older and don't groom much, or are obese and can't clean themselves well. Otherwise, step away from the bathtub.

The Lion Cut: No, It's Not Cruel

I think people tend to look at cats with lion cuts and think, *Oh, my god, that's terrible! Why would you do that to your cat?*

A lion cut is not just something you do in the summer because your cat might get hot. Truth is, you don't see a lot of long-haired wildcats because it's not really a natural look. We have come to embrace the long-haired cat look because we have bred it into the gene pool. But cats with long hair are going to be even more sensitive to touch, and to the displacement of their hair during grooming or petting. This also explains why many long-haired cats don't like to be brushed, even though it's often a necessary evil in order to help them avoid matting.

Lion cuts are also recommended for senior or overweight cats who don't groom themselves well or often enough.

Just like anything else, ask yourself, *Is this for you or is this for them?* In this case, given that a lot of cats are a lot happier after a lion cut, we are actually doing it for them, even though the "cosmetic" nature of the cut might first suggest otherwise.

. . . Perchance to Dream

Sleep is a welfare issue, and cats under stress can be sleep deprived just like us. So make sure your cats have quiet, calm, and safe places to rest, especially in active households or homes with multiple pets. It's fine to let your cats share your bed, but they might want their own personal options as well. Offer different textures and styles of beds to see what gets your cat relaxed, and remember, some cats like to sleep up high, some like to sleep down low. (More on this in chapter 8.)

EVERY SINGLE STEP of the HCKEGS cycle seamlessly feeds confidence into the next. The beauty of applying the Raw Cat Rhythm to the rhythm of your home is that it can be done with relative ease, and the benefits are immense, immediate, and echo throughout every corner of a cat's life. But, as we'll see, while the Three Rs—Routines, Rituals, and Rhythm—provide the rhythm of Total Cat Mojo, confident ownership of the territory is the drum it's played on.

8

Catification and Territory

Mojo-fying the Home Terrain

BY NOW, I'M sure I'm sounding like a broken record, but . . . territory, the resources that it contains, and ownership of it—these are THE most important components of Cat Mojo. How important? Well, let's put it this way—I've already written two other books on the subject. In both *Catification* and *Catify to Satisfy*, the emphasis was on understanding Raw Cat territorial instincts, seeing how your cat expresses those instincts, and then building a world that satisfies those needs in a creative, not destructive, way.

Why would we need to build a world for our cats in the first place? As we continue our march together from a rural life to an urban one, the onus is on us guardians to do just that. Consider this: our own cats would naturally have a territory of about six or seven city blocks. By keeping them indoors and by living in higher densities, we are shrinking that territory down. The outward world is getting smaller while their inward Raw world remains the same. If that imbalance is not corrected, well, in my experience, bad things happen. Relationships become rivalries, competition for those valuable resources fester. And don't think I'm just talking about cat-to-cat relationships, either; the strain is felt by all species sharing the space between the four walls.

The good news is that we can beat the territorial squeeze. **Catification** is the art of creating an enriched environment that is acceptable to both you and your cat. Catification teaches us that every square inch of the home can be shared in a positive way. Allowing our cats to own spaces through scent distribution and finding confidence in the vertical world can be accomplished—all while respecting and adhering to our own personal aesthetics. In this new, significantly reduced world that we share with our cats, nobody loses as long as we embrace compromise. If we don't . . . well, like I said, it's a good bet that bad things will happen.

ALL CATS NEED a place where their Mojo can bloom. And that leads us to . . .

Base camp is a defined area of your home that is the heart of your cat's territory. It is often a place of introduction and acclimation (for cats moving to a new home) and it is also a place of safety.

Create a base camp for:

- Moving
- Remodeling/renovations
- Introducing a new animal
- Introducing new human family members
- Having guests over when you have a shy cat
- Preparing for emergencies

When cats have a base camp to return to, the stress of all of these transitions is minimized.

WHERE TO SET UP BASE CAMP

Base camp should be a room that you spend time in. It's a socially meaningful space where you can mingle your scent with your cat's. Offices, family rooms, and bedrooms are examples of a good base camp room. A laundry room, garage, or basement is not a great place to set up base camp, since these are not rooms you likely want to spend a lot of time in, and they probably don't smell strongly of you.

If you are introducing a new cat into a home with existing cats, you may not want your master bedroom to be the new cat's base camp. If your resident cats sleep with you, you don't want to kick them out of that "home within the home." No place smells more like you than your bed. You might be setting up your cats for a rocky start. (For more on introducing a new cat to your resident cats, see chapter 10.)

BASE CAMP EXPANSION

Base camp needs plenty of signposts. As your cat's territory expands, and he spends more time in the rest of the home, the signposts should also be expanded.

Base camp expansion happens when you move signposts out of base camp into other parts of the home as a way to introduce your cat to the rest of the territory.

The signposts and scent soakers you used in base camp will now expand your cat's territory in a Mojo-boosting way.

When your cat is ready to move out of base camp, take some of those signposts—a bed, a scratching post, or a litterbox, and place them in an adjacent area. When your cat explores the home, these familiar objects will help her feel like those new areas are already "home."

When are they ready, you ask? Cats are ready for base camp expansion when they are visibly at ease: tails up high, exploring the space, eating, drinking, and using those scent soakers. Use body language and behavior to inform your base camp expansion.

Base Camp Rotation: Replace objects that have been expanded out of base camp with new scent soakers and signposts. This means your cat always has areas of the home that smell familiar to her and give her a sense of ownership. Beyond these basic prerequisites of base camp, signposts, and scent soakers, we have to consider the entire house as territory.

Cat Daddy Dictionary

1. **Signposts** are objects that signify territorial ownership for your cat. By definition, a signpost is something your cat has left a visual sign or scent on, such as scratching posts, litterboxes, and cat beds. *We'll talk in great detail about litterboxes, the most important signpost, later in this chapter.*

2. **Scent soakers** are soft items that absorb a cat's scent and can also serve as a signpost. They say "I live here," and allow for rubbing, scratching, or lying in. Beds, blankets, carpets, cardboard scratchers, and scratching posts are all excellent scent soakers.

SCRATCHING POST
EQUALS SIGNPOST/SCENT SOAKER

What I often hear from clients is "My cat is wrecking my house." What they usually mean is "My cat is scratching the furniture, and I'd rather not have a beige carpeted cat condo in my living room." Fair enough.

In many cases, what humans experience as "nuisance" behavior is a necessity for their cats. Scratching on things like end tables and sofas is a good example. But for cats, scratching is not a luxury (or a pathology). Repeat after me: *scratching is not a luxury for cats.* It's how they stretch their back and chest muscles, how they exercise and de-stress, and how they shed loose nail sheaths.

But scratching serves two even more important and Mojo-rific functions for your cat:

1. Scratch marks are proof of ownership.
2. Scratching allows cats to mingle their scent with ours (and one another's).

To truly understand a cat's territorial impulse to scratch, consider this: we humans tend to decorate our living environment with stuff—material possessions, such as furniture, art, photos, books, and keepsakes. Cats tend to decorate their living environment with scent and visual signals, which they like to maintain and "keep fresh." Scratching is an excellent means to both ends.

When your cat has scratching options throughout the home, it leaves both a visual mark and scent in the fabric or wood. Just as you would update, rearrange, or tidy your photos, cats will "adjust" those scent marks as they pass by. Scratching gives them a sense of security and ownership—and turns those areas of your home into signposts and scent soakers.

And although cats want their own turf to scratch and mark, they might still want to scratch other areas . . . areas that smell like . . . you. Cats love to scratch couches and chairs that you use for a few reasons, the key one being: just like they create a "group scent" with other cats they live with, they probably want to do the same with the other mammals in the

home . . . especially the big, hairless ones who provide them with food and love. Your cat is trying to comingle her scent with yours to show the ultimate in cat sharing: co-ownership of territory.

Oh yeah: and your couch is usually nice and sturdy, covered in a very scratching-friendly material, and lives in a socially significant territorial destination. But we can provide all of these things for your cat in a scratching post. (See chapter 13 for more suggestions on keeping scratching where you want it.)

Cats usually have four key preferences that you need to know about:

1. Location

    Now that you know that scratching equals ownership, think about where your cat likes to scratch. Cats will mark things that are socially significant to them, whether that is a door frame, your couch, or a rug. This is where you need to be willing to compromise.

    When you hide a scratching post in the back office that no one ever spends time in, you are ensuring a lack of Mojo and a destroyed sofa. And because scratching equals ownership, you need multiple scratching posts, throughout the home.

2. Texture

    Cats want a scratching material they can dig into. Cats usually prefer textures like sisal rope, jute, wood, cork, carpet, or cardboard. Some cats have strong preferences, so it's good to offer some different choices and see what they like the best. When in doubt, match what they scratch!

3. Know your angles

    Watch your cats when they scratch; do they prefer horizontal surfaces like your rug, or do they go for the side of the couch in a fully vertical position? Or do they scratch the base of your bed frame? Some cats prefer an angle when scratching, and some cats love to scratch in all three positions.

4. Size matters

    Whatever you give your cat to scratch, it needs to be sturdy. Cats who are vertical scratchers need to be able to stand on their hind legs, extend their legs, and get a full stretch. Freestanding posts needs a wide base—if it wiggles or wobbles, "the couch wins."

URBAN PLANNING

Urban Planning is a process for setting up your home to accommodate the needs of everyone who lives there—humans and animals—in a way that promotes peaceful coexistence. The key is traffic flow: everyone must be able to move freely through the space without conflict.

This idea is especially useful for homes with kids and dogs, where we use, to our best advantage, the fact that cats are just as comfortable vertically as they are horizontally. Being able to plan the world completely on that axis makes for comfortable traffic in the house, allows us to find the Confident Where for our cats, push challenge lines (covered in chapter 9), and show them the world in a very positive way . . . all while they show us where in the world they are the most confident.

Here's a simple process for integrating some Urban Planning into your house:

Step One: Evaluate your current home "landscape"

In a city, traffic lights and street signs create an understanding among the inhabitants, give them rules to play by, and help facilitate optimal traffic flow. When looking at your present home layout, consider how efficiently the "traffic" flows and try to identify any of the following problem areas:

Hot Spots are the areas where any conflict or other behavior problems occur regularly. Fights, acts of aggression, or peeing outside the litterbox almost always point to a hot spot. Is it happening in the middle of the room? In a window? In a litterbox? To help solve the riddle of problem behavior in a graphic way, use painter's tape (it has bright colors but won't damage floor or carpet) to identify where the action is happening. Very simply, the more tape you are placing in a spot, the hotter it is (for more on how to interpret these patterns, see The Anti-Treasure Map on page 243). Hot spots demand alternatives so they don't become dead ends. Which leads us to . . .

No

Yes

Ambush Zones and Dead Ends are areas of conflict that are often created by aspects of the space, such as furniture placement, architectural elements, or even clutter. Ambush zones can occur near resources that only have one entrance/exit, such as a hooded litterbox, or a litterbox placed at the end of a hallway or behind the washing machine. Ambush zones allow one cat to block others from coming or going, causing "traffic jams." Be sure to identify and eliminate ambush zones and dead ends to promote traffic flow.

Cat Daddy Tip
Blocking off the Unders

If you have cats, there's no reason to have Unders. The Unders are those hard-to-reach spaces—under the sofa, chairs, and bed, in cabinets, or behind your stove—that a scared cat will be attracted to like metal to a magnet.

To prevent cats from caving, you'll want to completely block off the Unders. This might mean, for example, filling up the space under your bed tightly with storage bins, or sealing the bottom of your couch off with strips of Plexiglas, or using childproof locks to keep cabinets off limits. Blocking off the Unders encourages your cat to find his Mojo in other parts of the home, rather than hiding away 24/7. More important, it encourages YOU to provide cocoons for your cat—those safe but socially significant places where he can transform into his fully confident self (whatever that looks like for him). Of course, this process needs to be a carefully thought out series of attainable challenges. Learn more about the approach I call **the Challenge Line** in chapter 9.

Step Two: Optimize traffic flow

Adding a **Traffic Circle** to a hot spot can divert the flow of traffic and prevent conflict. Traffic circles can be a cat tree or other piece of furniture, and they function to diffuse potential conflict.

Once you have identified an ambush zone or a dead end, a **Revolving Door** can keep the traffic flowing. This usually involves a climbing structure—like a cat tree or some kind of shelving—that allows a cat to move safely up and out of a problem area.

Escape Routes prevent cats from being cornered. You can provide escape routes by offering an uncovered litterbox or by making sure all cubbies or shelves have multiple exit points.

Step Three: Utilize and optimize the full space potential of key rooms with the following ideas:

VERTICAL WORLD

We all know cats are natural climbers, so when we evaluate the Catification potential of any room, we must consider the vertical world that exists there. When possible, cats will inhabit all available space in a room, from floor to ceiling, particularly our Tree Dwellers. Remember, they like virtually any area off the floor—from chairs, to the tops of tables and bookcases, to the highest elevations of a room. Consider how the existing furnishings in a room might best be optimized as a vertical landscape.

Catification for Special Needs

What exactly qualifies a cat as "special needs"? One common denominator—whether cats are elderly, blind, deaf, have neurological disorders, missing limbs, or were born with other serious health issues—is that getting around their world is usually part of their challenge. Regardless of their disability, my goal for every one of those cats remains consistent: help them find or maximize their Mojo.

If you have a senior or special needs cat, you can modify your Catification pretty easily in order to accommodate him:

- Make sure he can walk right into his litterbox by cutting away the majority of the front of the box.
- Night lights along baseboards can make a huge difference for a cat who can't see his way around at night.
- Ramps at gentle angles, padding, nonskid mats, heated beds or pads, and comfy perches help your cat access those Mojo-fied areas and stay in touch with his vertical world and Cat TV.

Engaging your special needs cat with HCKE, and keeping him connected to the Three Rs, will also help him remain vital. Remember, self-consciousness and pity has little to do with the moment-to-moment life of a cat. We should meet him on his own terms. Through Catification and how we utilize it, we can keep these cats safe and simultaneously continue to explore the world of challenge.

THE CAT SUPERHIGHWAY

As one of the most compelling aspects of Catification, the Cat Superhighway enhances traffic flow and gives cats full access to the Vertical World, as it allows them to move through a room without setting a paw on the ground.

Some of the main features of a well-constructed Cat Superhighway include:

Multiple Lanes are imaginary lines that run along a vertical axis of the "highway," enabling ample room for multiple cats to traverse the area without crowding issues.

On/Off Ramps serve as both access lanes to, and escape routes from, the Superhighway. Multiple entry/exit points are essential, particularly in multicat households.

Destinations and Rest Stops make your Cat Superhighway more appealing and ensure that it will actually be well traveled. Destinations are the types of locations where a cat will undoubtedly go and spend some time—like a cat bed on top of a bookcase, for example. Rest stops are designed to be temporary stopping points along the way, where cats can pause and take in the scenery—like small perches or even a **Crow's Nest**, which is basically a lookout post where cats can see what's going on in their domain.

Here are a few things to avoid when designing your Cat Superhighway:

Narrow Lanes—When lanes on your highway are too narrow and cats can't easily pass each other, this can mean cat traffic "gridlock" . . . which can often mean trouble. Shoot for a minimum lane width of eight or nine inches (so two cats can easily pass), or arrange for a nearby exit ramp or alternative route.

Areas Where You Can't Reach Your Cat—Avoid constructing your Superhighway so "super" that you can't get to your cat in case of an emergency, or even a vet visit. You will need to be able to reach her at all times. This design feature will make cleaning day easier as well.

Hot Spots, Ambush Zones, and Dead Ends—Even without narrow lanes, conflicts can erupt for any number of reasons. Be on the lookout for any place along the highway where there might be a dead end or problem area. Extra lanes or on/off ramps can often remedy these issues quickly and get traffic flowing peacefully again.

THE ICING ON YOUR CATIFICATION CAKE

Okay, so we have established base camp. We have enhanced the home turf with our Urban Planning, creating free-flowing, room-to-room traffic and optimizing all available space on both horizontal and vertical planes. And then we have placed our scent soakers and signposts strategically throughout this Mojo-fied terrain. Now, let's talk about two more Catification staples that are true game changers.

The Cat Sundial

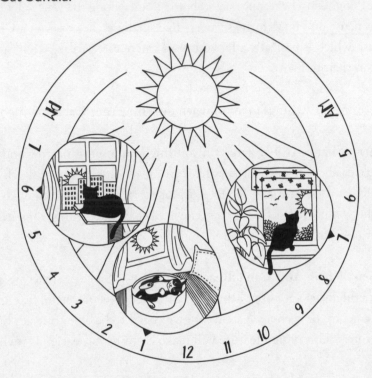

The Cat Sundial is the tendency for cats to follow the patterns of the sun throughout the home. The best thing you can do is know what windows let in the most sun at each time of the day. And then make sure you place scent soakers in those areas: beds, cat trees, perches, hammocks, or condos.

When you give your cats multiple resources in these highly desirable areas, you allow them to practice the fine feline art of time-sharing. Allow your cats to share, rather than fight over, territorial resources.

Cat TV

In our homes, the TV is a relaxation focal point. No matter how busy our day is, no matter how chaotic, we know that we can park ourselves in front of that ubiquitous appliance and, if provided with good entertainment, it will all disappear, if only for thirty minutes. Although we often talk about "vegging out," that's not the whole story; watching TV gives us that rare opportunity to relax and engage at the same time. We are not just watching but are using our imaginations, joining story lines, and investing in other lives. But we are doing so with a degree of detachment, so that the enjoyment outweighs the stress of actually living through those story lines.

With the exception of the pleasant heat that comes off the console, cats have very little use for our TVs. But that doesn't mean they can't reap the benefits of the concept. Cat TV takes the most important story line for cats—hunting—and puts it in a "box," so that they can experience the same relaxed sensation: an exercise I call "passive engagement."

The most common Cat TV watching involves sitting at a window to watch prey. The key to a stalk-and-rush hunter's strategy is the watching and assessing. The pounce is just a small part of the HCKE cycle, whereas sizing up prey and planning a possible attack is an activity that can engage your cat for most of his day. Think about it—we've all seen our cats obsessing over a moth that is circling a lightbulb. Cats can literally sit there for hours, waiting for that moth to make a move (or a mistake).

Just as you might design your living room with the TV as the focal point, look around your home for prime windows for creating Cat TV, and add things outside those windows to attract natural prey such as birds and insects. Think: a bird in a birdbath, bees visiting flowers, squirrels at a feeder. Make the window a destination location with a cat tree, perch, or cat bed that invites your cat to sit and binge-watch Cat TV to his heart's content.

Also, keep the **Cat Sundial** in mind when designing Cat TV. This way you can maximize the chance that your cat will actually use her TV perch based on the natural movement of sunlight throughout the day.

If you live in an apartment, it's a little tougher. Not only is window space itself at a premium, but the ability to hang things like bird feeders, birdhouses, etc., outside is usually sacrificed. In that case, there are other options. For example, although I'm not a big proponent of aquariums, they provide quality TV time without the benefit of an actual window (just take really good care of those fish!). There are also very cool "fake aquariums" out there that use plastic fish and jellyfish and are also pretty realistic. They are designed as decoration for humans but make for great Cat TV. Also, as long as you remember to make the existing windows available and inviting, then just watching the "ant people" down on the street can be an exercise filled with fascination and engagement.

Setting your home up with multiple Cat TV–watching stations will reap immediate benefits for your cat, and for you, as well. It prevents boredom, anxiety, and stress for cats who are left alone during the day. Just as important, it simultaneously complements your daily play rituals with your cat. Of course, there is no better way to drain air from the Energetic Balloon than to actually play with your cat, but allowing for stretches of passive engagement while you can't be there keeps the balloon from filling to bursting point the moment you walk in the door. As I've said before, every moment with your cat is an opportunity to either inject energy into the balloon or drain it out. Cat TV gives you the ability to make that choice remotely; the territory itself helps to keep her daily Mojo rhythm intact.

THE MOJO MAP

Up until now, I've been concentrating on the components of a properly Catified home. But in order to understand how those components come together to create an optimal *flow* within the territory, there's no better way than making a Mojo Map.

What goes in your Mojo Map?

Layer 1: The areas your cat uses

Layer 2: The things you have provided for your cat
- The elements of Catification in your home
- Cat TV areas
- How cat traffic flows in your house
- Where your cat pees, poops, eats, sleeps, and patrols
- Time-sharing of specific areas
- The territorial thrones of your home—for both cats and humans (the bed and couch)
- Areas where your cat spends a lot of time versus just sauntering through
- The Sundial
- Windows and doors

Start with a blueprint of your home. There are apps online that can actually help create that for you, or you can just go decidedly low-tech and sketch out the layout of your house with a pencil and paper. Put in the big pieces of human furniture, the windows, the doors, and what they lead to. That is the base of your Mojo Map.

The Mojo Map allows you to be proactive about **identifying socially significant areas (or SSAs)**—the "thrones" (the most coveted and oftentimes argued-over pieces of cat furniture), the heavily trafficked areas of the house, and, in multicat households, the points of contention. The Mojo Map will allow you to define patterns (and potential blockages) that inform Catification choices, such as *where you place your litterboxes and where you should add a cat tree.*

To help illuminate your cats' preferences and patterns and how you can complement them, I like using the old grade-school star stickers. Start by putting stars on high-value places: Where do your cats sleep more than a few hours each day? Where do they play? Where do they scratch (even if it's not where you want them to)? In the multicat household, give each cat his own star color so you can better acquaint yourself with each cat's core

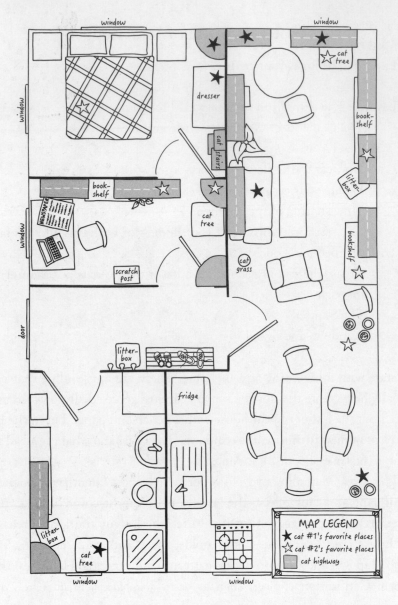

territory, how it overlaps with that of other cats as well as that of the humans, and what parts of your home don't hold much weight.

Speaking of humans, think about which rooms they tend to congregate in, and where the daily rituals are centered. Does your family spend most of its time in the kitchen? Or do you work from home all day in an office? Do you retire to a family room at night to watch TV? Or are the kids doing homework at the dining room table while you read in bed? This is a time to think about territorial co-ownership, one of the tent poles of Catification: these rooms, as important as they are to the human family, should be reflected in the map as being equally important to the cats.

The Mojo Map will help you identify the core of your cat's territory. And once you identify it, you've thrown that pebble in, and then you Catify the ripples. When you compare the human SSAs to what you are offering your cat, you will see, very clearly, what areas in your home need more Catification.

Now take a look at the various base camp–caliber items you have already provided your cats: Where are the feeding stations right now? Where are the litterboxes? The scratching posts? A cat tree? The cat beds? Do you already have a Superhighway? Put it all on the map. This process will reveal in what direction the Catification scales are tipping. If you find that all of your "cat stuff" is clustered in one corner of the map, well, now is the time to spread the love, according to who tends to favor what and where these pieces might be better placed to encourage optimal ownership and traffic flow. In our perfectly Catified world, signposts, scent soakers, Sundial pieces, and Cat TV would be evenly dispersed throughout the territory.

Remember, Catification is ALL about creating a space that works equally well for human and cat. But the key word in that definition is "equally." If we don't actively encourage a Mojo-fied relationship to the territory, we are tacitly encouraging the opposite. The choice is clear: *build with signposts, or prepare for graffiti.*

A LIVING THING

As you continue to build and refer back to your Mojo Map, you will find that it is a living thing; it is fluid, as are the relationships that it documents. Preferences will no doubt shift as the year progresses. As the sun hits different spots and your Sundial changes—or maybe if you crank up the furnace or fireplace—your cat's preferred spots will follow suit, since they tend to follow heat sources. This can affect how things are laid out as the year unfolds. And that's where your map comes in handy—to stay one step ahead of the territory. The more you keep that sense of urban planning up to the minute, the more confidence is built and maintained and the less territorial competition will rear its ugly head.

"SIGNPOSTS AND SCENT SOAKERS" should be one of your Catification mantras when looking at the inner architecture of your shared territory. The obvious foundational components are beds, scratchers of all shapes and sizes, towers, food bowls, water fountains, and, yes, your old sweatshirts. There remains, however, the king of all signposts and the mother of all scent soakers: the litterbox.

That's not exactly music to the human ear, I know. I *really* know. I think it's a safe bet that there aren't that many people who have seen firsthand the destruction that can come from a two-foot-square plastic box like I have. I'm not talking poop and pee, here; I've seen, time and again, how a litterbox can become a cause of conflict in the home, and all relationships—whether human-to-human, cat-to-human, and even human-to-house—can suffer for it. That's why I'm going to do my best to cover all my bases when it comes to litterboxes. The more you know, the less you'll blame yourself, your cat, your spouse, or that two-foot-square plastic box.

LITTERBOX 101 AND BEYOND

Do you believe in magic? If you've seen a cat use a litterbox—following her instinct to bury waste in soft, loose material, and doing so in a plastic box—then you should experience a moment of awe.

If your cat were outside, she would eliminate wherever she liked, and not necessarily in one predictable spot. When kitty litter was invented by Ed Lowe in 1947, it instantly revolutionized our relationship with cats in two ways: First, that relationship would deepen greatly because now our cats could spend infinitely more time in the house with us. Just as significant (and infinitely more complicated), that relationship became one based on expectations. In true human form, from that moment forward, we expected our cats to eliminate exclusively in . . . a box. After a long, *long* history of a laissez-faire arrangement, this sudden ultimatum happened in a blip in the timeline of our lives with cats. And again, in true human form, we weren't exactly patient about changing the course of evolution. If you consider how recently we brought cats into our homes, sternly pointed at that box, and said, "Now do it in there!" it's a damn miracle that they do it at all.

THE ELEPHANT IN THE ROOM

If you ask me, or anybody else who does my job, we wouldn't have jobs at all if it weren't for pee and poop in places other than litterboxes. Nothing will motivate a prospective client to either call me or to rehome their cat faster

than a serial "outside-the-box eliminator," whether it's on your couch, your carpet, your bed, or on you. So let's start with some time-tested prescriptions for preventing serial peeing and pooping through proper litterbox Catification.

First, however, I'm going to have to say it: the litterbox (along with its quantity and placement) is the proverbial elephant in the room that nobody wants to talk about. I know there are clients of mine who have thought long and hard about whether they would rather have pee on their carpet or another litterbox in their house. This, at the end of the day, is your call. The litterbox also represents that core compromise I've spoken so much about. Once you realize how important it is for your cat's overall sense of well-being, I hope it will push you toward the right side of that compromise. And there's one more factor to keep in the back of your mind while you ponder that litter-box–shaped elephant: if you follow these guidelines now, they will, in almost all cases, help to prevent litterbox problems further down the line.

I've already discussed scent soakers and how important they are to a cat's general sense of Mojo. These territorial signposts are like the things that define your life in your home. Keepsakes, souvenirs from the trips you've been on, photos that line the walls, the small design details you agonized over, and even the coatrack that is, at the moment, overflowing with coats, sweaters, hats, and purses—these are the things you walk by and you say, deep in your subconscious, "Yes, I belong here." You breathe easier, knowing that this is *your home.*

With this in mind, ask yourself: if you were going to take a long trip, and you know you get homesick, what would you bring with you to signify home?

As someone who spends roughly a third of his year on the road—and who also gets homesick—I think that one of the best pieces of advice I ever got was to travel with my bath towel. Sure, it's great to travel with pictures of your wife and your animals and put them next to your hotel bed. But a towel is one of the ultimate human signposts, because when you get out of the shower in a strange hotel, you're wrapping yourself in your scent, and the scent of your home. For you, your traveling signpost might be your slippers or a pillow. For cats, it would no doubt be their litterbox.

Think about it: for your cat, every room in your house could represent the strangeness of a hotel room or the intimacy of a bedroom. If you want to maximize Mojo, you will put litterboxes in socially significant areas. These are spaces that both the humans and the animals occupy equally. As humans, when we come home, we sit on the couch, and we go to bed, which makes those places major human scent soakers. This compels cats to spend time in these areas, complementing our scent with theirs, thus making your bedroom and living room the most socially significant spaces in the home. And yes—*those* are the rooms where you may need to place litterboxes.

I realize it might feel as if I just dropped a litterbox-shaped bomb on you. But this bomb could radically change the landscape of your home—in a mutually constructive way. This willingness to change the landscape of your home for your cat's well-being is the very definition of Catification. The win for you in putting litterboxes front and center in these living areas, and not thinking for a second about your general aesthetic values, is that it *will* reduce or help to eliminate peeing that results from territorial insecurity (which is behind the majority of all problem peeing).

Still, if a vision of a house full of litterboxes is freaking you out, think about it as a grand experiment. Along the way, certain litterboxes will be used and others will be ignored. This will show you what your cats consider to be socially significant areas, and at that point, you can reduce the total number of boxes.

Cat Daddy Dictionary: Litterbox Resentment

I just suggested that you put litterboxes all over your house. But what I don't want is for you to get to the point where the compromise is so painful that it starts to tear at the fabric of the relationship between you and your cat. This is something I call **Litterbox Resentment**: You are walking through your house when you look down and see a litterbox. Then you start to resent your cat, just as you would if, on a particularly bad day, you slip on your child's toys that are all over the floor and you find yourself starting to resent your child. Clearly, this calls for an intervention.

You have just come face-to-face with the fact that cats aren't the only territorial animals in your home. We want them to be happy, but the thought of them pooping in our living room is unbearable. However, just as your children's toys are integral to their development, the litterbox is critical for your cat's Mojo. Just remember, there's always a solution available. It's being solution-oriented that takes you one step away from the ledge that is Litterbox Resentment.

CAT DADDY'S TEN LITTERBOX COMMANDMENTS

While the following are more tips than actual commandments, they have helped to resolve most litterbox issues I've encountered with clients over the past twenty years. So take heart: the laws of litterbox maintenance have the power to deliver you from the days of ruined carpets to a glorious paradise of kitty compliance.

Thou Shalt Have One Box Per Cat + 1

This formula may as well have appeared on stone tablets, just like the original commandments. Though not a commandment, the "Plus One Formula" is a guideline that I strongly recommend you consider. It states that there should be one litterbox for every cat in the house—plus one extra. If you have one cat, you'll want two litterboxes; two cats, three litterboxes, and so forth. This formula is there to gently push you back into right-sized thinking. And speaking of that . . .

Thou Shalt Have Multiple, Well-Placed Stations

When I return to a client's home after having given them the above formula as homework, I often come back to a home that still seems curiously devoid of litterboxes, at least at first glance. That's when the client takes me to the garage, where four litterboxes are put side by side, creating not four litterboxes but one huge "litter station." Welcome to the hidden resort of Litter Beach, tucked privately away from the hustle and bustle of the home. Nice try, box hater! Litterboxes define territory, and every box should serve its purpose as a signpost by being placed in a different location in the home. Think of it as having multiple doormats. You wouldn't stack them all at your front door. You would have one for each door—front, back, and side—so they could serve their purpose as a sign of welcome to others, and a signpost for you.

Which brings us to: Location, location, location! You put the litterbox in the garage, the mudroom, or the laundry room because you don't want to watch your cat poop and pee, and you don't even want to be reminded that they do so in your house. Or you just don't want to have a litterbox or three destroying the appearance of a beautifully designed home. In the meantime, you might be asking your cat to walk down two flights of stairs, through a cat flap, and across the cold garage floor to a small, covered box on the outskirts of his territory. It's the equivalent of an outhouse—not convenient, not desirable, and if you had any choice, you'd find a way to avoid it. There are other significant drawbacks as well. In these types of locations, opening the garage door or starting the washing machine will startle your cat. The potential upshot of that scenario is that your cat might think that bad things happen when they go to the litterbox—so . . . he stops going to the litterbox.

So, I repeat: *location, location, location!*

There's just no way around this, in my experience: the box should be located where it works best for your cat, not you. Think of it as the lesser of two evils. It's either a litterbox where you don't want it, or pee where you definitely don't want it.

Thou Shalt Not Camouflage the King of Scent Soakers

 Your cat has 200 million scent receptors (versus only 56 million in humans), which tells you just how important (and sensitive) that particular sense is to them. That's why it's so important to cater to what your cat is attracted to, and, likewise, what they are repelled by. This is why I recommend only unscented litter, with no deodorizers in the litter and no air fresheners right next to the box. In my experience, those strong, artificial fragrances, including scented litter, can drive your cat away. Think about this: if you were trying to keep cats away from objects like, say, a Christmas tree, I would tell you to use an aversive scent. Cats don't really like citrus scents by and large, so I'd recommend zesting a lemon and putting it in something porous like a Ziploc bag with holes poked in it and tucking it right next to that Christmas tree. How, then, would an air freshener with similar properties placed right next to the litterbox *not* be aversive?

When it comes to scented litter or air fresheners, we are talking about the breakdown of the human/cat compromise. Same thing goes for other forms of camouflaging—that is, disguising your box as a potted plant, or using a robot litterbox, or toilet training your cat. These are things that are convenient for humans, but as you will see, rarely work for the cats. It's a cat's smell that makes the litterbox a scent soaker, and therefore incredibly important. From a human standpoint, as long as you're maintaining a well-defined scooping routine, there should be no discernable cat smell to mask. We'll get to that soon when I go over how to clean your cat's litterboxes.

Thou Shalt Observe the Law of Litter Common Sense

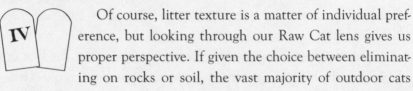 Of course, litter texture is a matter of individual preference, but looking through our Raw Cat lens gives us proper perspective. If given the choice between eliminating on rocks or soil, the vast majority of outdoor cats would pick the latter. Indoor cats avoiding the given substrate in their litterboxes will tend to choose softer items like bath mats, bedding, and clothes. Many cats (including declawed cats and seniors) can be very sensitive to the jagged nature of some crystal or pellet litters, or even to the roughness of many clay litters.

As with our previous commandment, when keeping Raw Cat preferences in mind, litter common sense calls for the simplest choice. The fancier the substrate, the more that can go wrong.

Thou Shalt Not Mindlessly Fill the Box

I think overfilling the box is a common problem simply because we think that more of a good thing will just make it a better thing. Every cat is different, of course, and we have to find out what works for the individual, which is a lesson we learn simply by observation.

One thing to consider is that for an arthritic, older cat, a full box of litter can cause discomfort—especially when pooping—because the cat must "grip on" to the litter to gain stability. Likewise, overweight cats can sink in large amounts of litter.

Long-haired cats dislike the feel of litter against the hair on their upper legs, butt, and belly. Remember, those sensitive hair follicles mean that when they squat, and the hair on the back of their legs touches the litter, it can create a tickling sensation. (For some long-haired cats, it may even be enough of a distraction that they will seek out a smoother surface to pee on.)

In most cases, try starting with just an inch or two of litter and adjust from there. But the lesson here is that everything about litterboxes, down to the amount of litter in the box, needs to be a conscious choice on your part.

Thou Shalt Honor the Right Box

VI Does your cat spend plenty of time digging in the box? Or does he gingerly enter as if potential dangers lie within? Are you asking your cat to use a top entry box even when your cat is elderly or in some other way physically compromised? Or is your cat overweight and the box is barely big enough for a kitten? Remember, the box should be attractive and convenient—in other words, a friendly place that your cat won't think twice about getting into.

Ideally, the length of the litterbox should be at least 1.5 times the body length of your cat. He should be able to turn around, do plenty of digging, and find a clean place to go without coming face-to-face with the wall of the box.

Also, gymnastics should not be required to get in and out of the box. Top-sided litterboxes might seem like a great idea, and for an agile cat, they might not be that hard to get into. But even the most acrobatic cat wouldn't choose the life of a jack-in-the-box when there's a much easier alternative: just pee on the rug!

Kittens, seniors, and obese or disabled cats might have challenges getting into (or out of) a high-sided or top-loading litterbox. Puppy litterboxes are great for seniors or cats dealing with mobility-based pain or discomfort. You can also cut down the entryway or sides of a regular box to make it easier for cats to walk in, rather than over, to enter the box.

Thou Shalt Not Cover

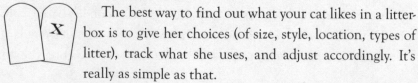

I'm not a huge fan of hoods on boxes. The idea that a cat needs privacy when peeing or pooping is classic human projection; it's what *we* want when we go to the bathroom, so you think it's what your cat wants. Wrong. Cats who go outside often go out in the open. In front of a bush. In a driveway. In your garden. On the side of your house.

Some cats might be fine with a lid, but lids can lead to ambush zones and dead ends, especially in a home with dogs, kids, or other cats. Covers can get pretty nasty after repeated use and are hard to clean. Also, long-haired or larger cats can get a static shock from touching the sides of the hood as they enter or exit. In other words, the risk-to-reward ratio here is heavily weighted toward risk—so at the end of the day, why bother taking it?

Thou Shalt Not Use a Liner

You might think that liners make your life a bit more convenient, but in reality, many cats don't like the texture of liners and can even get their claws stuck in them. Plus, liners get scratched and ripped and pool urine, resulting in a huge mess. That's not more convenient. Just say no.

Thou Shalt Keep the Litterbox Clean

When was the last time you scooped the box? Yeah, I get that you don't like facing a minefield of nasty clumps, but neither does your cat. A recent study demonstrated that when given a choice, cats unquestionably preferred a clean box to one that contained clumps of pee or poo logs. Yes, sometimes we do need science to tell us what we already know: scoop that litterbox every day.

Thou Shalt Allow Your Cat to Covet Another Box

The best way to find out what your cat likes in a litterbox is to give her choices (of size, style, location, types of litter), track what she uses, and adjust accordingly. It's really as simple as that.

Cat Daddy Rant: The Politics of Poop

When you walk your dog, you know what is coming out of him. You pick up your dog's steaming poop with nothing but a doggie bag separating your hand from the poop. This "firsthand" familiarity keeps you intimate with your companion's output and alerts you to any potential problems.

When it comes to cats, however, we seem to have taken more of a "see no evil, smell no evil" approach, in which we are constantly attempting to disinfect and sanitize away what are normal bodily functions. We will do anything to not have to deal with cat waste. Many have even resorted to having a "robot" handle this job in the form of an automatic litterbox. But if you let a robot do your job, you don't know what's going on with your cat; the robot makes the poop and pee go away, but as a consequence, you aren't as involved in the "inner workings" of your cat's life. (Besides, why pay a fortune for these automated litterboxes, which get all gummy and gross? They can also malfunction, and go off when your cat is in there, causing him to get scared and try to go somewhere else.)

It is part of your guardianship to know how well your cat feels based on the look of their pee and poop, and cleaning the box is an opportunity to get information about your cat's health. You should know what normal poop looks and smells like; how many times a day your cat urinates or defecates; how many clumps are normally in the litterbox; and whether there is ever any blood in there. And if your entire house is toxic after your cat poops, you might need to go to the vet.

Digging Deep—What Is Your Cat Doing in the Box?

A lot of people ask me about their cat's scratching and digging behavior in the box. First, they want to know why their cat scratches at the litter, scratches some more, and keeps on scratching. What is so interesting about this behavior is that cats can be so different. Some cats are "one and done," giving a quick, tidy toss of sand over their poop, while other cats will "dig to China," even scratching at the walls or floor near the litterbox.

On the other hand, many people have the opposite concern, and ask me if they can train their cats to cover their poop. You can't really "train" cats in this respect—they either do it or they don't. Sometimes cats don't cover because they don't like something about the litter. In that case, a cleaner box may help: no cat wants to scratch if it means getting her paws dirty or uncovering another cat's waste. For other cats, it could be a behavioral glitch related to early life experiences while learning to pee and poop on their own. What I'm saying is that if a cleaner box and softer litter don't do the trick, you can't necessarily change this habit (or lack thereof), and you might have to live with it.

"Covering" is often attributed to cats hiding their scent from predators. To your cat, this ancient ritual is so ingrained that it doesn't matter if there are no predators in your home. But the truth is that this behavior is probably way more complicated than just protection from predation. Outdoor cats will cover more when they are in the core of their territory—the areas where they rest and eat—than when they are peeing or pooping along the outer edge of their territory. Also, pee and poop are used to send messages between cats. This all just demonstrates how complex this poop-covering behavior really is, and the folly involved in trying to alter it. Chalk it all up to another Mojo mystery.

Trouble in (Cat Poop) Paradise

 Part of your litterbox detective work involves making sure you know what your cat does while he is in there. Believe it or not, this can tell you a little bit about how he is feeling. For example, do you know what it looks like when your cat doesn't like the litter?

Some telltale signs that cats don't love the litter or something else about the box:

- They don't put their feet in the box.
- They don't scratch at the litter before or after.
- They zoom out of the box as if someone is chasing them.

If you notice any of these behaviors, first run to the vet to rule out anything potentially serious. If all checks out, go through the commandments and see if there are some variations you can try with the litter or the box.

CLEANING THE BOX

This may not be the most popular stance, but I feel strongly that the more you sanitize the litterbox, the more you're doing a disservice to your cat. If you're scooping two or three times a day, scrubbing every week, disinfecting the box, then let's face it, you're doing that for you, not for your cat.

Think about it. Almost every source of cat behavior advice tells you that in order to prevent cats from returning to an area they have soiled, you must completely remove the urine odor. This is true. So why are we completely trying to obliterate the cat's smell in their litterbox?

Cats want and need to smell themselves. Pee and poop are heavy-duty territorial signifiers, ways of going around saying "I own this." Their pee and poop are symbols of territorial security, no different from cheek or body marking, or scratching on a post.

Ownership of the territory is of paramount importance to cats. If they can't smell themselves anywhere in the house, they will find ways to smell themselves. It might encourage them to pee in different places.

All you have to do is scoop the clumps every day—you don't have to go crazy. You can completely empty the box out once a month or so, and rinse it with hot water. This should suffice for most cats (and for you as well).

A WORD ON TOILET TRAINING

I was watching videos of cats who had been trained to use the toilet. Most people I knew who had seen these videos thought it was cute or at least very interesting that cats could be trained to do such things. Some began drifting into a fantasy about how convenient that would be, to not have to worry about litterboxes and the chores that go with them. At the time, I couldn't put my finger on what disturbed me about watching these clips. Over time, I realized it was because I could identify physical—and yes, emotional—stress in the cats. There was a look in their eyes that seemed to say "This is not natural to me, I don't like this, I feel vulnerable and uncomfortable."

Yes, there is the occasional cat who will actually use the toilet spontaneously. Opportunistic humans then took that and ran with it: if that cat can do it, why can't mine? Now there are multiple "training products" available to force your cat to use a toilet instead of a box. I've even seen cats trained to flush when they're done. If your cat wanted to use the toilet to pee and poop, he would have demonstrated that desire already. You might be able to train him to use a toilet, but it is a Mojo fail. Cats are meant to urinate all over the place to mark their turf, so the Raw Cat would never consider using a toilet; rather, it is something we instill purely for our gain.

WE'VE EXPLORED EVERY corner of the cat/human connection, from commandments and tools to gut-level empathetic observation. Now we can truly stake our claim on that piece of relational real estate where a Mojofied life is built, fostered, and maintained for a lifetime. This promised land is within our reach as long as we embrace our role as cat guardians, and its mantra: it's not what you own, but whom you parent.

The Art of Cat Parenting

I N CHAPTER 6, "Welcome to the Toolbox," we began to set the tone for this section by encouraging you to see yourself in more of a parental role with your cat, rather than as an "owner," or even a "trainer." Now it's time to take that relational springboard and do a double-gainer swan dive into the approaches you can take to encourage your cat's Mojo, while promoting harmony in your shared home.

While the case could be made that dogs find comfort and security in the guardian-companion training dynamic, cats do not. Not by a country mile. Think about it: did you ever wonder why we call people who work with dogs "trainers," and people who do similar work with cats "behaviorists?"

With dogs, training stabilizes their world and, when done well, provides the cement of our relationship. But with cats, we want to *maximize* our level of influence on their behavior, but then be willing to bring a spirit of *compromise* when it comes to the end result.

A "sit" on command from a dog or a cat looks the same on the outside. But while a "cat sit" approximates the shell of the human/dog relationship, we need to understand that there's still a cat inside that shell. Meaning that, on a relational level, while the dog is grounded by the "sit," the end result for the cat is a completed action and anticipation of a reward. That, however, is far from a hollow victory; we got our cat to look to us, follow our lead, and focus on completing a task that we asked of him. That's a win because it is a relationship builder, even though it doesn't *complete* the relationship like it might with a dog.

You could even argue that, compared to cats, many dogs *need* training for their well-being. It's not only in their DNA from our long-term relationship with them, but training also gives dogs coping skills in light of the expectations we place on them, in the many environments and situations we put them in.

Compromise is about us meeting cats in the middle, at the communicative and relational fence; the "training" process I've been talking about maximizes our ability to get the cat to willingly come to that fence—

something that doesn't come naturally. Don't expect to change cats in the way that training would change a dog. "Maximize and compromise" is the mantra that reminds us of what a "cat win" looks like. Which is to say that both parties will have an equal say in the outcome. It's a cat thing.

While the principles of positive reinforcement are universal, it would be naïve to assume that the effects of these principles are the same in every species. Cats' and dogs' brains are different; they have different motivations and solve problems differently. So our expectations need to be a little different.

Once again, I'd ask you to consider the parent-child dynamic as an analogy. We talk about "good parenting," as opposed to "good training," when it comes to teaching kids to be considerate of others in the home or to do their homework. But before you dismiss all of this as mere semantics, think about how your actual approach might differ in your quest to "parent" rather than "train." This subtle difference makes *all* the difference in what kind of luck you'll have persuading more desirable behaviors from your cat.

TO PUNISH OR TO
PRAISE—THAT IS THE QUESTION

The principles of behavior modification via operant conditioning apply to all animals—birds, chickens, gophers, dolphins, killer whales, and, yes, even cats and humans. Psychologist B. F. Skinner developed reinforcement theory to describe what motivates behavior. This theory is based on the principle that certain outcomes that coincide with a behavior increase the probability of that behavior happening again in the future. These reinforcers are usually things the animal likes. Punishers, on the other hand, are defined as things that decrease the future probability of a behavior.

Today, *scientists and animal trainers recognize that positive reinforcement is the most effective way to change behavior.* Although punishment might work temporarily, it doesn't change your cat's motivation, and it doesn't tell your cat what to do instead. Punishment also comes with a healthy dose of side effects like fear and aggression (not to mention a complete erosion of the trusting foundation of your relationship).

Still, in the wake of this reality, a common question that comes up is "Without using some form of punishment, how do I discipline my cat?" To which I respond: there is no such thing as disciplining your cat. They have no idea what you are doing when you scold them, shoo them away, or squirt them with a water bottle. Besides, for punishment to yield its desired result, it has to happen every single time the behavior occurs, and very shortly after it happens. There's no way you can police your cat 24/7—and would you even want to?

Our goal is to increase Mojo, to raise a cat's confidence. There is nothing in humiliation or punishment that will raise confidence. Even worse is a practice I've seen where humiliation is disguised as an attempt to "prove oneself alpha" over a cat. I'll say it again: any type of punishment, however clever the "concept" we cloak it in, is anti-Mojo. Anything that serves the purpose of enforcing your dominance over your cat is anti-Mojo.

It comes back to relationships. There is no successful relationship that comes down to establishing dominance. This book is about positioning yourself as a Mojo enabler, not a Mojo disabler. Invisible fencing, scat mats, shock collars, declawing, and, yes, even the ubiquitous spray bottle should all be thrown into the "things we used to do" pile.

Time-Out vs. Kitty Jail

When cats get aggressively overstimulated, remember that they are not making choices; the Raw Cat is in fight-or-flight mode. A time-out, as opposed to what it sounds like, is not punishment; it's a chance for the purely physical state I'm describing to subside. And then there's what we call Kitty Jail.

Kitty Jail is often mistakenly referred to as a time-out. But let's be clear; Kitty Jail is not a time-out. Time-out is a kind gesture at its core, a way to let your cat settle back into themselves after a Raw Cat explosion. Kitty Jail is punishment, and therefore lighting the fuse of a cat bomb.

Kitty Jail happens when guardians are at the height of their frustration and impatience with a problem—whether it's cats fighting, peeing in places other than the litterbox, or "nighttime annoyance" behavior. You just can't deal with it anymore, and now you're locking your cat in the bathroom and out of all the socially significant spots in the house. You're punishing him.

As we should know by now, punishment serves no function for cats. It may make *you* feel better in the short term, but it will definitely not solve the problem. Cats will not make that long chain association that, because they did something ten minutes ago, they're locked in the bathroom for an hour and a half. There is no such thing as "go learn your lesson." That falls under the category of taking your cat's head and rubbing his nose into his pee. They don't get it.

If you need to lock your cat out of the bedroom, let's say, because your bed is getting hit time after time with pee, I get that. It's a Band-Aid, but I get it. But Kitty Jail is not a Band-Aid. Kitty Jail is a bad news boomerang. It's going to come right back at you, and it's going to knock your teeth out.

When your cat goes into fight or flight, has redirected aggression episodes, or has freaked out on somebody or something, you can lead him to a small, confined environment, with lights down low, no sounds, no stimulation, no nothing. This decompression zone allows that cat to reenter his own body's orbit, to go from being absolutely glued to the ceiling energetically, to bringing it back in: to fuse the etheric body and the physical body and bring them back together in harmony. That's what purpose a time-out can serve. And a time-out can last five or ten minutes. It's just to get your cat out of DEF-CON 1 . . . out of fight or flight, and back into the real world. **NOTE:** If your cat is too wound up to be led into a time-out location, DO NOT attempt to pick him up and carry him there. In this case, bring the mountain to Muhammed, so to speak, by turning the room he's in into a quiet zone. Turn off the lights and leave the room. This should safely help accomplish the same time-out goal.

Remember, a time-out is there for your cat's benefit, not for yours. That's the distinction between a time-out and Kitty Jail. One is for your cat, to help him regain his equilibrium. And one is for you, so that you don't kill your cat.

GIVING UP THE BOTTLE

The spray bottle—it seems like everybody has one these days, and in some clients' homes, I've seen them in every room of the house. Somewhere along the line, this punishing tool has become as prevalent and acceptable as just saying a loud "No!" (which also isn't particularly useful).

You might be thinking "But, it works. I squirt, and the cat jumps off the counter. Now when I just show him the bottle, he runs away." But what is your cat actually learning? Is he learning that the counter is a bad place to be? No. He is learning that the counter is a bad place to be *if* you are present and holding the spray bottle. What's worse is that he is learning to be afraid of *you*. He only reacts when he sees you holding the spray bottle, which makes you the originator of the unpleasant feeling.

Remember our mantra "maximize and compromise"? Well, the spray bottle takes a blowtorch to that mantra. In other words, spray-bottle diplomacy is not diplomacy, not in any shape or form. Conversely, it is emblematic of our species' long-standing belief that we can bend our animals to our will. When your cat is cringing, it is because she expects you to do bad things, and that doesn't mean she's going to learn a lesson or understand what to you is a moral right or wrong.

There's always a positive alternative, but using the spray bottle means your cat will fear you. There is nothing positive about your cat (or dog or spouse or kids, for that matter) fearing you. There is no upside. If you have to resort to fear, you are doing something counterproductive.

Do Animals Know When They've Done Something Wrong?

People often describe their companion animals as "knowing they have done something wrong." So Dr. Alexandra Horowitz set out to determine if what humans perceived as a "guilty look" in dogs was actually related to *being* guilty, or if the "look" was just a response to the dog being scolded.

In the study, dog guardians were instructed to show their dogs a treat and then command them not to eat it with a stern "No." The guardian placed the treat on the floor out of their dogs' reach and left the room.

Then the experimenter either took the treat away or allowed the dogs to eat the treat. When the guardians returned to the room a few moments later, they were either misinformed or told the truth about whether their dogs ate the treat. If the guardians thought their dogs obeyed them, they greeted them in a friendly manner. If they thought the dogs disobeyed them, they scolded them.

Guardians attributed behaviors like avoiding eye contact, rolling over, dropping the tail, and moving away from them as signs of "guilt." But these behaviors were *only* dependent on whether the human scolded the dog, and not on whether the dog was actually "guilty" of eating the treat when the guardian told him not to.

The experiment showed that dogs weren't experiencing guilty feelings about eating that treat, but that they likely experienced fear and anxiety when scolded by their human. And if you see those "guilty-looking" behaviors in your cats, there's no reason to think they're experiencing anything different from those dogs.

TRAINING/TEACHING 101—CAT MOJO-STYLE

Think back for a second to when you were a student: Who was your all-time favorite teacher? What was it about that person that still sticks in your memory? Was it because he or she made learning fun? Because he or she invested in you and, at the same time, made you feel invested and passionate about the subject? Whatever the answer is, it probably isn't because the teacher simply presented facts that you memorized and regurgitated for a passing grade. Your favorite teacher gave the subject an emotional anchor, a reason to care about it.

As with any parental relationship, the one you have with your cats provides you with a constant opportunity for teaching. But what increases your student's ability to learn (and retain) is the mindfulness you bring to

each moment. As any good teacher will attest, you know you're doing it right when you are available enough to learn while you teach. As we move forward, I would urge you to pause often in the process and appreciate that teaching or training your cat can be a two-way street; this is an opportunity to learn something about yourself in each moment.

Early on in my work with cats, everything revolved around three things: hands-on experience, observation, and "book learning." The problem with the latter was that there was not a ton of information out there, and even less in the way of peers I could learn from in the cat world. So I turned to my friend and my shelter's head dog trainer Nana Will. Nana was not only great with dogs on an empathetic level, she was a walking encyclopedia when it came to the intricacies of animal behavior and the applications of operant conditioning.

I was in a rhythm of following Nana around and soaking it all up as she worked with both shelter animals and her at-home clients. I was adopting what I could from her techniques, short of trying to make cats act like dogs. But one of my most valuable lessons from Nana came about in an unexpected way.

We were going to the bank together to deposit our paychecks on the Tuesday after Memorial Day—which meant that the bank was absolutely bananas. Everybody there was in a bad mood because it was an unseasonably hot first day back to the grind after a long weekend, and the lines were out the door. The air was thick with collective postholiday bitchiness.

We were standing in line and Nana was telling me about positive reinforcement training as it applied to her dog training. It just so happened that, right in front of us, was a four- or five-year-old girl standing with her mom. All at once, she started pitching a hissy fit of epic proportions, screaming for ice cream. It was a demand that, within moments, we were all aware of because all that came out of that little girl's mouth, in every conceivable pitch, volume, and tempo, was, "I WANT ICE CREAM!!!" And when those four words didn't work, she became a live-action dictionary definition of a temper tantrum: first, she pulled violently at her mom's pant legs while continuing her ice cream demands; then, she dropped down on all fours, beating the floor and banging her head like a cartoon character; then she rolled over on her back, continuing to abuse the floor with the soles of her feet, and our ears with the escalating dog-whistle tone of her insistent screams. It was quite a spectacle, one that was exponentially increasing the level of the aforementioned collective postholiday grouchiness.

The cherry on top of this crap sundae, driving everyone to the brink, including me, was that the little hellion's mom was just ignoring her. I was getting really angry, and was about to say something. Nana grabbed my arm and said, "No, just watch." Finally, after the girl had exhausted her arsenal of vocal and physical acrobatics (and herself), she looked to her mom and wordlessly got up off the floor. There was a roughly five-second pause, and then the mom turned to her and said, "So, what are we going to have for lunch today?"

It couldn't have been more perfect. Nana felt my body relax and let go of my arm, knowing I got it. With a smile that was perfectly Zen in the face of the preceding chaos, she said, "See, that's how it works. We either reward the noise or we reward the silence. Everyone learns the same way."

Nana's first lesson was something I will never forget—it has remained at the heart of my teaching some twenty years later: Everyone from dogs and cats to chickens, possum, donkeys, turtles . . . and humans. All of us.

Whether rewarded for our noise, or rewarded for our silence, *we all learn the same way.*

THE TOTAL CAT MOJO TEACHING TOOLS

The basics of how I "train" are centered on a short list of techniques (for lack of a better word). There's Trust Gaining, Clicker Training, the No/Yes Technique, and the Challenge Line, all with an undercurrent of positive reinforcement. Trust Gaining, is, of course, what we've been talking about all along. Let's take a peek at the others:

Clicker Training

When I initially approached my dog-trainer friend Nana to pick her brain about her work with clicker training, she straight up told me that she had next to no experience applying these techniques to cats. I was absolutely fine with that; I never had any desire to get a cat to be a dog. I just wanted every tool I could find; afterward, we could figure out how to use that tool to build the house of Cat Mojo.

Clicker training is based on the ideas of operant conditioning put forth by B. F. Skinner. In the 1940s, two of his students, Marian and Keller Breland, took these ideas and ran with them, training animal actors in their "IQ Zoo."

What made their training methods so effective? Using a sound to inform animals that they had done a desired behavior. They happened to use a small "noisemaker" that emits . . . wait for it . . . a clicking sound for their training. The Brelands trained thousands of animals using these methods: chickens played baseball, pigs saved money in piggy banks, and pigeons were trained to guide missiles (I wish I was kidding).

The idea didn't really take off until the early 1990s, when Karen Pryor started offering classes to help people train their dogs using a clicker. Today, it is *the* method for training animals in a humane and effective way.

So how does clicker training work? Let's break it down.

1. You teach your cat that the sound of the clicker immediately leads to a delicious treat. They call this "charging" the clicker. Do this several times to help your cat learn this association. Click—treat. Click—treat.

2. Now you add the behavior. You activate the clicker whenever your cat does a behavior you like. This can be a behavior that you "capture" (catch them in the act of doing) or that you "shape" or "lure." When they do the behavior: click—treat.

It's that simple: behavior—click—treat. The clicker is not a command, and it's not a remote control. It is a bridge to the treat and a response to a behavior you like. Because those behaviors are reinforced, your cat will do them more in the future.

So what *do* I use clicker training for? I haven't really changed much since I first started learning about it—meaning, it's a tool, and wherever the tool fits, I use it. For instance, I use clicker training in a shelter setting where I often just teach simple tricks like sitting, waiting, and high fives. In the shelter, this work helps cats feel a little Mojo in a strange environment, and can even encourage them to come out to the front of the cage to greet potential adopters. It keeps their minds and bodies busy, and it provides a structured activity for staff and volunteers. This promotes a stronger bond, and the end result is also a much more adoptable cat.

Outside the shelter, I don't spend as much time on things like that. Don't get me wrong—training behaviors for fun has value for human and cat. For instance, I love setting up cat agility courses that help bring out the Mojito in every cat, and clicker training can be invaluable for this. Agility courses for cats differ from those for dogs because we get to use the vertical space as well. Seeing a cat who has never explored the "world of up" get to the point where they walk a Cat Superhighway as if they were on the ground? Man, that's good stuff—and instant Mojo!

On the other hand, teaching your cat to sit in a cat tree instead of on the kitchen table during dinnertime is useful and solves problems for both of you: the cat wants a vantage point, and you want the cat *not* to be on your table, pawing at your forkful of food. This can be an excellent application of clicker training.

Also, clicker training can help build much confidence when it comes to encouraging cats to accept things like: getting in and out of a carrier and accepting that carrier as a friendly place; having their nails trimmed; taking medication without struggling; even meeting new family members. These are the most common, and most helpful, applications when it comes to clicker training and your relationship with your cat. And that's the key word: helpful.

If you didn't know by now, I'm a huge fan of the Raw Cat. Logically, then, I'm not such a huge fan of using clicker training for tricks that I consider humiliating. The role assumed by the human and the role assigned to the cat in the process of clicker training is one that requires a great deal of trust on the part of the cat—and a great deal of empathetic diligence on the part of the human. So the question we need to ask when starting a course of training is whether this is helpful to my cat, to his Mojo, and to our relationship.

We need to realize that there is power we wield here, and it can be abused easily. Is clicker training ideal for teaching a cat who really wants to go outside that a harness is the way to go and shouldn't be a source of fear? Of course. But should we train our cats to better accept wearing a hot dog costume so we can blast it out on social media? Based on everything in this book about enabling and fostering Mojo, I sure hope we are in step when it comes to answering that question.

Of course, this is a pretty cursory breakdown when it comes to the ins and outs of clicker training. As simple as this method is, it still deserves a much deeper dive. If you want to learn to clicker train, there are plenty of great resources out there for you in the form of videos, websites, and books. I would recommend anything written by Karen Pryor as a good starting point.

The Jackpot! Effect

If I haven't made it clear by now, allow me to recap:

Cats, not being dogs, are not motivated by the thought of pleasing you. Cats, by and large, are most definitely motivated by food. The more they like a particular food, the more receptive they are to your influence and persuasion. Hence, whether you want to call it targeted food motivation or bribery, when it comes to working with your cat, food is not just any old tool; it's your best friend.

When it comes to "training" your cat, the single most crucial element, at least in my experience, is finding *that* food—the one that goes beyond simple motivation to the mystical world of your cat yelling "JACKPOT!"

Some behaviors or actions—like, say, a "sit" or a "high five"—can be accomplished by offering any ordinary treat. But when it comes to creating a positive association with something that your cat is challenged by? Then you better have your Jackpot! close at hand.

Knowing how monumental the Jackpot! is, we arrive at our first potential roadblock: the perceived finickiness of cats. Though it may feel like trying to find a needle in a haystack (or not—some cats are like four-legged vacuum cleaners!), the Jackpot! is there somewhere. Here are some recommendations for finding it:

- **The clean slate makes for a clean plate:** There's no reason to even attempt a Jackpot!-finding mission if your cat is full. Make sure she is hungry. This speaks even more eloquently to my desire that you feed your cat meals rather than leave out food to graze on 24/7. As long as you continue to free feed, Jackpot! is just not going to happen.
- **Flavor first:** If you were to present unprocessed meat and/or fish in their most natural form (meaning not in treat or cat food form), your cat will naturally gravitate toward at least one. So start there. Is it salmon, beef, or chicken? Just keep presenting until you get "that

look," the widened eyes and hyperactive nose that say, "Hey, what is *that?*"

- **Texture time:** Just as important to many cats is the feel of the food. For example, if you know, based on the flavor test, that salmon gets that initial Jackpot! interest, the next step is to figure out texture—and there are many to be had. Cat food comes in pâté, chunks, smaller chunks, strips, more gravy, less gravy . . . you get the drift. As for the "crunchy" texture that seems to motivate so many cats—I'm not a fan of feeding dry food . . . at least not for meals. If your cat sees her "crunchies" as Jackpot!, use it! Instead of a meal, you can now use individual pieces as Jackpot! treats.

- **The table scrap myth:** I don't know who came up with the idea that cats shouldn't eat "human food." Maybe it comes from the seasonings, such as added salt, onions, garlic, and other spices that are prevalent in human food and might be unsafe for your cat. That said, if your cat shows a proclivity to meat or fish marketed toward humans, we can't let that stand in the way of "JACKPOT!" So, as long as the aforementioned seasonings are not present, try cold cuts or other meats generally reserved for humans. Remember that you're not *feeding* these Jackpot! treats—they are offered in a restricted and measured rather than free-for-all kind of way.

- **Speak to the Raw Cat:** While there are many reasons to stay away from grains when feeding cats, it's just as important to avoid grains when trying to find small treat-sized portions, since those extra ingredients will quickly fill up your cat, and that means the end of motivation. This is why I like freeze-dried meat treats so much. They are everything a cat needs and nothing they don't; they approximate the crunchy texture for dry-food addicts, and as treats, they can be broken down into small pieces, which will keep the treat alluring for a longer period.

Once you find the Jackpot!, keep it Jackpot!. Your mindfulness and restraint when it comes to *how much* and *how often* you dole out treats is absolutely critical. Treats should be viewed as special, high-value delicacies that are only brought out at select times. Too often I see well-meaning folks impulsively shower their cats with treats because their cat is cute, or because they feel guilty for being gone all day, or just because. This behavior is problematic because treat time loses its magic, and you lose one of the only opportunities you have to influence your cat.

The No/Yes Technique

It feels like the vast majority of my introductory phone calls with my clients (and even conversations with strangers who stop me on the street) revolve around their desire to say "No!" to their cats. In other words, "Jackson, how do I get my cat to stop . . ." or "How do I tell my cat that [fill in the blank] is wrong?" If the question is being phrased that way, I already have a sense of exactly how behind the eight ball you are, and I can tell you, this is the beginning of that road to ruin. Rather than slapping a Band-Aid on a shark bite, getting an action to stop means stripping away the initial motivation of that action. This alone is ineffective because behind every action is the hope for payoff; so behind every "no," there must be a "yes."

One of the best ways to describe the No/Yes Technique is to once again reference the parent-child dynamic. Let's say you are regularly scrubbing your walls clean because you have a three-year-old who is constantly drawing on them. Now you can punish, yell, send her to her room, and take away her crayons . . . or you can buy her an easel. And if you buy her an easel, you're bringing out the best in this child and making sure her natural impulses aren't met with frustration. You can screw the cap down extra hard on the toothpaste tube, but if you apply pressure, the toothpaste will just come out the other way. You are not saying "no" to her impulse to draw. You are saying "no" to her initial choice of how and where she does it based on your needs and the rules you set in your home. You are providing her with another means of expressing this irresistible impulse. It's a "no" followed by a "yes," and the strength of both directives are critical to this equation.

Now let's return to one of the most common cat questions: "How do I keep my cat from getting on my kitchen counters?" Of course, there are very straightforward ways of saying "no" in that circumstance. The key is a consistent aversive. For instance, there are motion-activated air canisters that do the job well. If that canister is placed on the countertop, *every time* your cat jumps up, the sensor is tripped and a harmless but startling puff of air comes out in the direction of the cat. You could also use a few placemats with double-sided tape on them. Again, every time the cat jumps up, his game plan is thwarted because he lands squarely on a texture that is simply unpleasant. There it is, your "No!"

However, as in the case of our child artist/vandal, that "no" is simply a half measure. If you don't present that child an easel, he or she will just pick another surface to "paint," whether it's the front door or the dining room table. That drive to create art is irrepressible and will only transfer from one place to another.

In our kitchen counter–surfing example, our clear challenge is not finding the "No!" but determining where the "Yes!" lives—we have to find out what motivates your cat to go to that spot to begin with.

The first obvious motivation is to get to "that place"—the vertical world. Even if your cat is not a Tree Dweller in the traditional sense, he clearly finds mojo off the floor. So let's start by making verticality a part of our "Yes!" recipe.

The second part of the recipe is resources: what lives up on that counter that makes it so desirable? Well, it's the kitchen counter, which probably means food. Our "no" means keeping food put away so it's not a consistent temptation, and we aren't setting our cats up for failure. For our "yes," read on. . . .

That's the third part of the recipe—us. When our body clocks are in sync, the human and cat energy spikes are happening at the same time. Whether morning or evening, you can bank on the fact that when our family's energy is spiking, we are probably doing something in the kitchen. Getting up on the counter gives the cat front row access to that something.

Clearly, all "yes" signs point to giving your cat a place to go that is near enough to the action and the resources, just not on the counters themselves. My go-to solution is a cat tree that is near enough to accommodate these desires and far enough away that the cat doesn't use that tree as an off-ramp of the Cat Superhighway toward the counter. When introducing that piece of furniture, encourage him to go there during human energy-spike times. Use the "Jackpot! Effect" to your advantage, too, breaking out your cat's favorite treats only when introducing the new tree.

Now we have incorporated a "yes" that will greatly diminish the sting of the "no." This makes No/Yes a powerful win/win.

Extinction Burst

You have vowed to stop responding to your cat's pillow trotting, which has become a nightly ritual. It's been a rough few nights so far, but you've resolved not to cave in and pay attention to her. So you settle down into bed, and at 4:00 a.m., your cat begins her usual meowing. You grit your teeth and lie there, waiting for the meowing to stop. But it doesn't. Instead, it seems worse than usual. And then your cat walks across your head and starts knocking things off your dresser. Now it's 5:00 a.m., and you're freaking out, thinking "I can't take this. I'll get up and feed her so I can get back to sleep." You're ready to cave.

Wait! When you stop rewarding a behavior that you have previously paid attention to, your cat will initially escalate her attempts to get you to respond. This is called an **extinction burst**, a *temporary* increase in behavior when reinforcement is removed. In order to be successful at "extinguishing" annoying behaviors, you must make sure that meowing in the middle of the night serves no function for your cat, and is not in any way rewarded. And that means suffering through the extinction burst. Then, believe it or not, the peace and quiet of a solid night's sleep without pillow trotting will be all yours. (For more on Pillow Trotting, see chapter 16.)

Let's continue with one of the most foundational tools for effective "parenting."

The Challenge Line

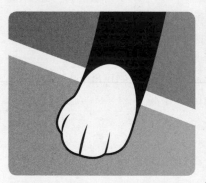

My work with cats began at the shelter that, for many years, I called home. I learned everything in that building, under the emotional and physical stresses that are unique to shelters. Most of my work back then was with cats who had completely shut down—Wallflowers to the highest degree. These were cats who already may have been Wallflowers in their previous homes, or, in many cases, cats who hadn't even been in a home in years. And worse yet, some of these cats were absolutely scarred, either physically or emotionally. Even if I could get these cats emotionally fit enough to qualify them for the adoption area, the next hurdle presented itself: how to make these guys feel vital, present themselves in their best light, and not go "kennel crazy" while they waited, sometimes for months on end, to find their forever home—all from the confines of a two-by-three-foot stainless steel cage.

Ironically, it was during this time working with cats inside a pressure cooker that I realized the job would never get done—and the cats would never find their Mojo—without crossing what came to be known as their Challenge Line.

Having faced way too many roadblocks with far too many cats, I began to dissect my process with them. I realized that I had a hard time asking cats to confront their Challenge Line, the precursor to transformation. The Challenge Line may as well have been called the Comfort Line because it represents the border of the individual's comfort zone. It's where one paw forward equals challenge, and one paw backward equals comfort. Comfort, however, is a misleading term. In the case of my shelter cats (as has been the case with tens of thousands I've met since that time), what passed for comfort was invisibility. They pressed themselves to the back of their cages and turned their heads from the door. We all know what it feels like to stay in a place of smallness because, well, it's just *easier*. Easy, as we know in our own personal journey, tends to keep us from moving forward.

Realizing I needed to challenge these cats was insanely challenging to me. I mean, after all they had been through, *how could I?*

But if I didn't, they would most likely never make it out of my shelter. And even if they did make it out, their uber-Wallflowerness would keep them from thriving in their new homes, almost guaranteeing that they would wind up being "cavers"—that is, under-the-bed or closet cats (or worse yet, get returned to the shelter). Helping them change became my motivation.

My goal for each one of these animals was to gauge where that very specific line was for them. And then I wanted to know how much I could acclimate them to that line and encourage them, one paw at a time, to cross it without feeling like a child jumping into the deep end of the swimming pool for the first time.

A child can be coaxed into the pool with their parents' assurance that they won't drown. These animals have no such assurance, but rather, a history in which the opposite was true: when they took chances, became "visible," and stepped out into the light, bad things would happen. So I started to increase their area of comfort, while decreasing their area of challenge.

By pushing the line, I define the line. And yes—sometimes the Challenge Line is a physical line that we can mark with tape on the floor. Here's a typical example of how the Challenge Line works.

CROSSING THE LINE

Recently I found myself working with a cat (we will call her Daisy) who was always shy around humans and other animals. The exception was her best cat friend Dexter. He was her older mentor who, since they first met, had been her "social bridge," the cat she could follow, and who would demonstrate Mojo that she could, to a degree, emulate.

When Dexter died, Daisy, like an emotional rubber band, snapped back into the life of a caver. Her guardians assumed that if they brought in some cat friends for Daisy, she would regain whatever sense of Mojo she had when Dexter was alive.

That didn't work. At. All.

The guardians adopted a bonded pair of boys, Alex and Possum, who promptly took over the territory and terrorized Daisy at every turn, chasing her back into her cave whenever she dared step out. Her guardians felt horrible—and their pity, sympathy, and guilt rolled together to create an anti-Mojo monster. They began to feed her in her "safe place," putting a litterbox under the bed as well. She literally had no reason to move into the light of day, and even when the boys left her alone, she remained where she was.

My challenge was to bring her back out. And once she un-caved, then the challenge was to get her to leave her safe room and come into the shared living space. And then go to the middle of the room, rather than hug the walls, army-crawling and making herself a target. A lot of challenges for me, but a lot of Challenge Lines for Daisy.

With Jackpot! treats, blocking off the Unders, and gradually moving her litterbox, sometimes inches a day, (and also working with her tormentors and their issue simultaneously), each line was crossed. Every step was calculated *not* to be easy. Proving to herself that she could be scared a little but still succeed was Mojo building and ultimately provided Daisy the wherewithal to not only take the middle of that living room, but eventually to give Alex just one slap upside his head while holding her ground. It was that Mojo-move that permanently changed the relationship dynamic and provided Daisy with a bigger place in the world.

Blocking off the Unders: The Reprise

As mentioned in chapter 8, the "Unders" are those hard-to-reach areas of the home where a scared cat might seek refuge—for example, under the bed, sofa, tables, chairs, etc. Blocking off the Unders is all about restricting your cat's access to these areas.

The "blocking off the Unders" tool is unique in that it integrates aspects of both the Challenge Line and the No/Yes Technique. By removing your Wallflower's option of always being able to hide somewhere, she is "forced" to confront her fears and engage her various Challenge Lines. At the same time, by saying "no" to "caving" (essentially hiding underneath furniture), we are saying "yes" to "cocooning," which will still provide her the cover she desires, but in a location that we control. In both cases, we are encouraging her not to feel invisible or insignificant and, instead, leading her toward more emotional and territorial freedom.

One caveat: going for broke in one fell swoop—i.e., removing every single hiding spot in one day—will almost assuredly backfire, resulting in not only a shy cat but one who is now completely panicked. Make the process of blocking off the Unders a gradual one so your cat can adjust to her new "Unders-less" environment.

The idea of pushing one's Challenge Line is a combination of desensitization and exposure therapy, which is to say that we are not just pushing a fearful child into the deep end of the pool. I'm not trying to forcibly numb cats to reality. Even saying I'm "pushing" their Challenge Line is a little misleading. I'm not pushing them over the line, but *encouraging* them over and expanding their safety bubble. With animals who have experienced trauma over and over again, this safety bubble is so close to them that it's almost a second skin. This process gives them the Mojo that comes from these small triumphs and proof that, over and over again, the results will always be positive.

You may cringe at the thought of the Challenge Line, but perhaps this is one of those moments when you may want to change your perspective to that of a parent. As a parent, you wouldn't avoid challenging your human children. On the first day of school, you have to be the bad guy and put your child on the school bus. Yes, there comes that difficult point when your kid is looking at you through the bus window, crying, and basically saying, "Why would you do this to me? I thought you *loved* me!" Yowch. And yet, you know that children *have* to go to school, because if they don't, the rest of their social existence, their intellectual development, and their ability to face challenges will be completely compromised.

But then what happens? They get to school, make friends, learn, and thrive. You have set them up to be the best version of themselves. And that's all we're doing when we push the Challenge Line with cats. Since we can't do talk therapy with them, we have to *show them*, over and over again, how it feels to cross a line that scared them five minutes ago. That's how they become card-carrying Mojito Cats.

THIS LINE IS YOUR LINE—ALSO

Our cat's Challenge Line is just as much our Challenge Line. Pushing those you love into a place where they're not comfortable, with the promise of a better life on the other side of that line, is a difficult proposition. And I urge every guardian to embrace it, because in all my experience with thousands of animals, I've never had a negative outcome.

When putting this Challenge Line philosophy into practice, it's absolutely crucial to act as if it is truly no big deal. In my experience, you will increase your cat's anxiety tenfold if you exude worry. Remember, cats are energetic sponges—and if you are projecting the knowledge of impending danger and an expectation of failure, they will absolutely absorb that energy, and they will respond accordingly.

If you want them to mirror confident behavior, then you have to present that confident behavior for them to mirror. Remember: it's a Challenge Line that we set up for them, with the knowledge that it's not a cliff, and we're not throwing them over that cliff and into an ice bath. We are asking for one paw—just one paw—over the line and offering abundant praise and reward with every step.

Within a certain amount of time, you're going to see a change in your cat. Tentative will give way to trust, and it usually happens in a flash. It could take a month for the line to move a few inches—like that "tick, tick, tick" of going up the first hill of a roller coaster—and then, suddenly, *whoosh*, they are just *moving* with the momentum of the ride. That's the payoff of your patience and your confident parental leadership, and your cat's accumulated experience of crossing the line with positive results (and more Mojo) moment after moment and day after day.

CHALLENGE IS DEFINITELY a continuing frontier in everyone's life, whether you have four legs or two. But one of the biggest challenges when it comes to your day-to-day home life is forging new relationships. For humans, it could involve adjusting to new roommates (and we've all had our nightmare experiences with that one), or taking a romantic relationship to the next level and going through the inevitable "period of adjustment." With cats, it's even harder; because they are so dependent on territorial ownership for their Mojo, learning to share territory can be daunting for cat and guardian alike. As we will find out in the next chapter, when it comes to the "Brady Bunching" Challenge Line, slow and steady wins the race—or, at least keeps that race from becoming a demolition derby.

10

Cat/Animal Relationship Mojo

Introductions, Additions, and Ongoing Negotiations

A	S THE RAW Cat integrates into our households, he will invariably find himself in a simmering stew of mixed company and varied relationships. Cat to cat; cat to dog; cat to kids—our modern human/animal families are often a colorful and diverse intermingling of personalities, and we guardians find ourselves traffic copping the wide-ranging and unpredictable dynamics of territorial change. Will these relationships be compatible or combustible? As with integrating human families, the key is respecting the individuals—their likes and dislikes, their habits and personalities. Hopefully you know my M.O. by now—cookie-cutter solutions don't work when navigating unique and challenging waters.

CAT-TO-CAT RELATIONSHIPS: COMPLICATED AFFAIRS

In section 4, we will address a number of common challenges (and opportunities) that can arise in cat-to-cat relations, once they are living together in a family unit. For now, let's start from the ground up, and examine the complexities of adding another cat, or more, to the present mix.

SHOULD I EVEN GET ANOTHER CAT?

When it comes to one-cat homes, the question I'm always asked is this: "I've got an only cat, I work twelve hours a day, and I know he's bored. I feel so guilty. . . . Does he need a friend?"

There are several components to that statement that we have to look at. I fully believe that cats should live with other cats. Unfortunately, what you see many times on my show are worst-case scenarios of cats who would definitely rather not. But in general, cats are communal animals who have been victimized by the stereotype of being asocial, aloof loners. The Raw Cat lives in colonies, as we've seen with feral cats. They problem solve as members of a whole community. The only thing they do solo is hunt. That being said, there are some cats who really don't mind being alone; it's about individuals.

In response to the question, you're right in one respect—a cat alone twelve hours a day needs more stimulation. But in order to find out if your cat is bored, you first need to do your boredom due diligence. Give your cat the proper enrichment so he won't be bored. Set up the home environment for exploration. Make sure there's always some form of Cat TV turned on for him.

Then comes time to put on the cat detective hat and take inventory when you get home: Is there destruction? Things used as toys that shouldn't be? Objects that have been ingested? Then yes, my friend, you have a bored cat.

And then there's your guilt, and a few really important points about it. First, regardless of the environmental solutions I detailed, none of them replace quality time with you. Making the space for just a little play in the morning before you leave and some cuddle time at night makes a big difference in a cat's day and goes a long way toward heading guilt off at the pass. The second point is that your guilt is the absolute worst reason to add a new family member. Break it down: Would you love to add another cat to your home? And, apart from your guilt, do you think it would be beneficial to your cat? If the answer is yes, then let's go, intrepid adopter, and find the right match!

MATCHMAKING MYTHS
AND LEGENDS: A CAT DADDY Q&A

Misconceptions abound at the prospect of expanding the family unit to include another cat or two. Let's address a few:

If I have a twelve-year-old female cat, should I get a kitten so she will mother him?

As always with questions like this, I have to err on the side of generalization. That said, if you've got a double-digit cat at home, please don't bring home a kitten. It's usually a bad match, energy-wise, given how superenergetic and hyper kittens tend to be. Then, as they enter the teenage phase (at around six months), they take what they learn and push buttons to see what kind of response they'll get. Older cats are usually not amused by this.

Also, a younger cat may pursue an older one in "play"—but it's not play to the older cat. As with the majority of humans, animals get to a certain age when they will want to take the path of least resistance. A kitten represents the most resistance to their day-to-day life this side of . . . well, a puppy. Or a baby. You get the idea.

I believe the maternal ideal is, for the most part, more about human projection than reality. That is to say, it's not something that your cat spends her days pining about. So, all of these factors lead to a fairly safe conclusion: a kitten will not bring out the "mothering" instinct in your older cat, and will more likely drive her crazy.

If you've already introduced a kitten to your senior cat and it's not going well—or if such a pairing is otherwise imminent—see chapter 14.

What about two kittens with an older cat?

That's a better scenario, as the kittens will at least entertain each other, and this gives them a great leg up in terms of their social development. Although this situation is less of a potential headache for the senior cat, it's still not the most optimal arrangement for him.

Should I bring home a female or male? An adult or a kitten?

I don't believe that it serves the matchmaking process to look for someone based on their being a six-year-old male, for instance. In my experience, I've found that these kinds of age/gender parameters are simply too broad, not to mention that they limit your ability to make a connection with a cat who falls outside of those parameters once you get to the shelter. Also, at least when it comes to gender, the fact is that most cats are neutered at an early age, so the effects of hormones and sex on cat relationships are nominal. Instead, I'm a big believer in considering more big-picture aspects of compatibility, which we'll be discussing in a moment.

I have an FIV+ cat. Can I adopt a cat who is not FIV+?

We are thankfully entering the age of enlightenment when it comes to FIV (Feline Immunodeficiency Virus). In the shelter world, we are, for the most part, abandoning the outdated idea that FIV cats should be kept segregated from noninfected cats both in the shelter and also when placed with a family.

FIV+ and FIV– cats can live together beautifully. There's not a problem, except if the FIV+ cat is very cat aggressive. That's when the line has to be drawn, because a deep bite wound is more likely than anything else to transmit the virus from cat to cat. Casual touching, and sharing food dishes and litterboxes are not an issue.

I have a declawed cat. Can I adopt a cat who is not declawed?

You don't need to feel too sorry in the defense department for your declawed cat. My experience teaches me that because his first line of defense is no longer available, his teeth are twice as fast as your clawed cat's, so whatever your clawed cat can do with her claws, your declawed cat *will* do with his teeth in the event of a conflict.

Also, the majority of declawed cats are not declawed on all four paws. In a fight, most damage will be inflicted not with the front claws, but with the back claws. That's where all the strength and the rabbit kicking comes from. That's what will eviscerate, and not just scratch.

All of this said, fighting should be at the bottom of your "top concerns" list once you do your due diligence in the matchmaking department. So, rather than thinking in terms of claws or no claws, the bottom line is—if you keep your clawed cat's nails trimmed, your declawed cat will take care of himself. And if you haven't yet declawed your cat . . . DON'T.

What role should selecting an alpha cat vs. a nonalpha cat play in adopting a new cat?

While we are still working to more fully understand the complexities in relationships between cats, I believe the ideas of alpha, dominance, and hierarchy actually damage our perceptions of cat relationships.

Many insist on throwing this pack mentality onto cats. However, taking what we know about cat relationships, we need to make empathetic, educated guesses, and then we run with it. As mentioned in chapter 5, this "alpha" status thing is not something I would advise trying to factor in to any criteria for whom you might adopt.

CHOOSING THAT NEW CAT

Okay, so you're in a position to pick out a new cat and you already have one at home. Now that we've gotten some of the more popular "myths and legends" out of the way, whom do I recommend you adopt?

In my opinion, the main criterion to factor in to matchmaking is to match cats by energy level. Even the cat's history should have less of an impact on your decision. I'd say that the first thing to do before even going to the shelter is to think about what personality type best complements your cat's.

For example, if your cat is five years old and a total Dennis the Menace, getting into trouble, wanting to play all the time, then you wouldn't want to bring home Mr. Wilson, who is more set in his ways and sedentary. A real Wallflower also wouldn't be the best match. Instead, it's a better bet to match his playful energy. So if you're looking at a colony-type room in the shelter, observe who the first cats are to come to the door. That's a good starting point, match-wise.

Now, I'm not saying that there's anything wrong with using this moment as an opportunity to expand your cat's comfort zone (and, thus, her horizons). But if you have a shy cat, you don't want that Dennis the Menace because he'll fray her nerves by trying to engage her constantly. However, finding a not-so-Dennis but still socially attentive cat can serve as a "social bridge" and help push your cat forward.

In general, you should try to complement rather than bring home a carbon copy. At the end of the day, the techniques of personality matching and introduction—which we'll cover in a moment—are key to the whole process.

KEEPING YOUR
PERSONAL PREFERENCES IN CHECK

In my experience, matching cat to cat in a vacuum seldom happens—the "human expectations factor" usually sneaks in. What often happens in this selection journey is that, instead of keeping an eye on being present in the process and staying focused on what's best for all, you decide "I want a long-haired black cat." Or perhaps you've recently lost a loved cat and are working through your grief, so you go in looking for someone who either looks or acts like him. Then you go to the shelter and that is who you zoom in on, even though he could be absolutely the wrong match for your other cat—who, in the end, should be the focus of your search.

There are also expectations to be managed. A lot of my past clients considered it a failure if their cats didn't snuggle together and act like best friends. Actually, at least at the outset, you're looking for them to simply tolerate each other. Right now, I don't have any cats in my home who snuggle, and that includes littermates. And that's okay. Everything is peaceful, and for someone who deals with cat conflicts all the time, that goes a long way. It's just about adjusting your expectations of what that relationship will look like.

SIGNS OF FELINE FRIENDSHIP

Spending time near each other

Grooming each other

Greeting each other with tails up

Nose touching

Playing together

Pillowing

WHEN A CAT
CHOOSES YOU: THE DESTINY FACTOR

Sometimes the best matchmaking happens when you're not trying to make a match.

You might be in a place where you're adamant about not adding another cat to the family, and a cat shows up on your front porch. The cat happens to be in the right place at the right time, the clouds part, and you realize that, as much as you would rather not deal with the responsibility, aggravation, and potential upheaval of adding to your current mix, this cat somehow seems destined to be in your life. So be it. There's something to be said for being open and available to the prospect of this happening. It's not always a smooth transition, but in the end, it's a beautiful thing.

Cat Daddy Rant: Single Kitten Adoptions

If you have the choice of bringing home two kittens or one, for the sake of the kittens, bring home two. Having a feline friend is better for them and better for you, and, as counterintuitive as it may seem, I guarantee they will be *less* work!

The cat's social world is based around family. Dr. Sharon Crowell-Davis's studies of feral cat colonies have demonstrated that their social lives are much more complex than anyone had given them credit for. The assumption that cats were asocial led scientists to completely neglect studying how cats interact with each other for years, and has led us to commonly segregate kittens from other cats as an adoption norm. People come to the shelter saying "I'm here to get a kitten," so there's never even a conversation about adopting two kittens together.

Dr. Crowell-Davis further suggests that when kittens are removed from their litter, it deprives them of the ability to learn to be socially competent adult cats. Cats are social learners! Kittens learn from their peers—how to hunt, how to play, and how to interact with other cats.

I'm not saying that if circumstances dropped a single kitten in your lap, then that cat is behaviorally doomed; there are plenty of "single-tons" I've met later in their life who turned out just fine. I am, how-ever, saying that if you are in a position of picking kittens from a litter, you *should* pick at least two . . . and that if it were my animal shelter—well, you just wouldn't have a choice.

COMING HOME:
THE STEP-BY-STEP
CAT-TO-CAT INTRODUCTION PROCESS

I think that the old common wisdom of introducing cats by "letting them work it out" is not only a recipe for disaster, but feeds the belief that cats are solitary creatures who are better left that way. Does it work sometimes? Sure, but it's cat Russian Roulette; when it *doesn't* work, you are triggering the territorial panic switch in your existing cat. Which means the Raw Cat senses a full-on invasion. Which means war.

You'll see in these steps that slow and steady wins the race. Not only are we trying to minimize risks, preventing a long-term lack of trust be-tween the cats, but we also go slow to make better friends!

Here is a time-tested recipe for successful integration that I've seen in action hundreds of times. Follow this step-by-step process to a T, and it will give you your best chance for a smooth integration.

Step One: Proactive Preparation

Before you bring your new cat home, there are some fundamental steps to accomplish that will give you a significant leg up on the process:

A. **No More Free Feeding:** As suggested in chapter 3, make sure you have switched your existing cat over to a routine of meal feeding, rather than free feeding her. As you know by now, this concept is foundational to my approach, and nowhere is it more important than during the introduction process, as we'll discuss in a moment.

B. **Proactive Catification:** Here is where we will customize and integrate some key Catification ideas from chapter 8.

- **"Childproofing":** Using this term can help you zoom right into what the term "proactive Catification" is all about. Before bringing home a new baby, you probably will have thought a few steps ahead to when he or she is more mobile and heading into the world of potential booby traps. Initially your new cat family member will be sequestered, but it's never too early to cat-proof. One difference, though: preventive measures for a solo cat might concentrate more heavily on child locks on cabinets, burner and knob covers on the stove, etc. Of course that should be done regardless, but for integration, things like blocking off the Unders is more of a priority. If you've ever tried to break up a cat fight under a bed, you'll know exactly why this is so important! Review some of the Catification ideas in chapter 8 so you can better childproof with your new addition in mind.

- **Territorial Diversity:** The way cats perceive territory is floor to ceiling, 360 degrees. If you have the choice, you want to bring a new cat to a home where the "top is popped." You've made it as territorially diverse as possible, so that when the cats do come into contact, it can be done at a safe distance, with each cat finding his or her Confident Where. Therefore, when you're Catifying for a new arrival, you want to make sure you're building the bare bones—a territorial skeleton, if you will—where you're giving equal emphasis to different spots on the vertical axis. This is because you don't know who this new cat's going to be, but you want to give her the ability to find her Confident Where *somewhere*, giving you the ability to build out her surroundings as you get to know her better.

- ❖ **Urban Planning in Action:** Speaking of the Confident Where (and the territorial skeleton), introduction time is prime time to make sure you maximize traffic flow, which will, in turn, decrease the conflict that can come with traffic jams. A Cat Superhighway around the most crucial social space—usually the living room or the bedroom—is a key element because multiple lanes of traffic, with various on- and off-ramps, provide vertical breathing room. Tunnels and cocoons on the floor, along with litterbox placement that prevents ambush and doesn't create dead ends, give you better traffic flow on the horizontal axis. Don't forget about cat trees placed strategically in the windows, with different levels on them! Urban planning maximizes the potential for discovery, time-sharing, and space-sharing required for cats to get to know each other, and makes the whole transitional period as noncompetitive as possible.

Cat Daddy Dictionary: Cat Chess

Cat Chess is a cat's strategic approach to the environment. Cats will look for vantage points from which they can gather information about the surroundings. For example, corners and dead ends are important for cats to know about, so they can trap their prey, or avoid being trapped.

Cats are always planning three steps ahead: *what will my opponent do and how will I react?* It is essentially based around the eternal question of how do they hunt and kill without being hunted and killed? It's fight or flight, as equally honed skills. It's a game with high stakes (maybe even life or death).

Cat Chess can play out in homes between cats. In an antagonistic, Napoleon/Wallflower relationship, it looks like a game of cat and mouse, of predator and prey. The aggressor cat surveys her field of vision within a certain part of the territory like a chessboard, looking to checkmate her victim at any opportunity. Great hunters plan ahead, predicting their opponents' moves, cutting off angles and escape routes. In the end, they leave the scene unscathed and move on in search of their next pawn.

Our job is to join the game, to become the chess master over the other players. The best way to do this is first to use your Mojo Map to ascertain the patterns and routes. Once this is done, then Catification is the tool that beats Cat Chess as obstacles are removed, multiple lanes created, and, ultimately, enough extra territory created that checkmate is virtually impossible.

Step Two: Base Camp and the *Mandatory* Isolation Phase

Although this part of the process might seem a bit lengthy and involved, remember: you have only one chance to make a first impression, right? That said . . .

A. **No Peeking:** One of the hallmarks of this integration method is that *the new cat and the resident will not initially lay eyes on each other.* This is a non-negotiable. Ignore this part of the introduction process at your own peril!

B. **Set Up Base Camp:** Decide where you're going to set up base camp for the new cat. This could be the master or a spare bedroom, an office, or even the bathroom when there is no other option. As long as the human scent is strong, it will help the cat establish a sense of home by comingling scents. See chapter 8 for a refresher on base camp.

Now comes that wonderful, exciting moment. . . . It's time to bring your new cat home! Make sure your resident cat is temporarily tucked away in a back bedroom or someplace where he will not see you bringing your new cat into the house, then proceed directly to the new base camp. Get your new cat settled in as best as you can, keeping in mind that anything you can bring along from the shelter or his foster home that has his scent on it—bedding, blanket, toys, etc.—is a high-value bonus for his comfort and acclimation process.

THE NITTY GRITTY

Now that we have everything set up and ready to roll, let's get down to the business of getting your cats to meet each other. Steps 3 through 7 can be performed at whatever pace is necessary for your situation. Let's go!

Step Three: The "Other Side of the Door" Feeding Ritual

In the feline world of highly attuned senses, introducing the cats one sense at a time is the most nonthreatening way to do it, starting with their infamous sense of smell. This feeding ritual, which is all about creating a positive association between the newcomer and the resident cat, has evolved over the years, but by and large has always worked for me. What's involved? Very simply, mealtime will consist of bowls set up on either side of a closed door. These bowls should start out far enough apart so the cats will walk up, eat, and walk away without incident, but close enough that they sense there's another cat on the other side of the door. From there, we gradually move the bowls closer. Here's how it works:

A. **Segregated Mealtime**: Set up dinner plates—one for the newcomer, one for the resident—at an equal and respectful distance from your "feeding door."

- When choosing a door on either side of which they'll feed, you always want to make sure that you have ample distance available on both sides of that door—realizing that, at first, your cats might not be comfortable with any less than a six-foot distance from the door. In other words, if you're doing it at a doorway that leads down to your basement, and one of the cats has to eat on the stairs, that is probably not the best space. (Using the base camp door as your main feeding door is usually the best way to do it.)
- As for the "respectful distance," that's basically defined as the minimal distance each of the cats need to be from the door in order to walk up to the dish, eat, and walk away without feeling the need to look around, run up to and bat the door, or swat, hiss, or engage in any other shenanigans that occur when cats are stressed out. This distance, at least initially, becomes the sweet spot at which each cat is aware of, but not threatened or distracted by, the other one.

When your cats are introduced to each other via this "remote handshake," they smell food every time they meet. And the only time they smell food, they're engaged in that handshake. This is what building positive associations is all about: other cat = food = good.

Look at it this way: if twenty bucks fell from the sky every time you met a stranger and were trying to size him or her up, you'd probably take it as a sign that the universe wanted you to like this person. In the same way, you are using a cat's hunger as your main source of leverage.

B. **Work the Challenge Line**: Once you've identified that "safe" distance, it essentially becomes your cat's Challenge Line. From there, every meal becomes a step of one paw over the line—by getting each plate incrementally closer to the door, and thus closing the distance between both diners, the cats get increasingly comfortable with one another . . . all while they are enjoying their food.

- If you've moved the bowls closer and you see that one or both cats stare at the door, start to flick or wag their tail, and show irritability, you are likely on the wrong side of the Challenge Line, and your cat will just decide that dinner is more trouble than it's worth. If this happens, move the food back and find that sweet spot again. (I recommend using painter's tape to mark that spot on both sides of the door. Defining that Challenge Line visually is actually a great way of marking your cat's progress, and yours.)

- The goal is to get as close to that closed door as possible, with the same predictable result each time. Don't move that Challenge Line until you get total compliance; there must be no shenanigans whatsoever. Once you've had two or three meals where there's no response at all, it's time to move the line closer. But don't get overzealous and move your line so much that someone freaks and sends you back to square one. Slow and steady definitely wins the race on this one.

- Once you get to the point where the cats are eating every meal about a foot away from either side of the door and walking away without issue, then it's time for the next phase: allowing visual access.

CONCURRENT TO YOUR "Other Side of the Door" feeding ritual, these scent-driven, Mojo-building protocols should also be followed:

Step Four: Scent Swapping

This is another way of getting one cat's scent in front of the other in the most nonthreatening way possible. It's as simple as it sounds.

A. **"Gift" for the Resident**: You will take a "scent soaker" from the newcomer's base camp—a blanket, soft fabric toy (that most easily retains her scent), or even something like a doughnut bed—and temporarily place it near the resident cat for his inspection. (You can also gently rub a clean sock or washcloth around the face of the new cat to pick up scent that way, then use it as a "scent soaker," *provided that she doesn't mind you doing that.*)

B. **"Gift" for the Newcomer**: You will take a scent soaker from the resident cat and place it near the newcomer. In both cases, the key is not to force her to smell the item, but to let her explore it at her own pace. And don't worry, she will get to it, and it will accelerate the initiation process. Think of scent swapping as another type of remote handshake.

C. **Signposts**: Here is yet another Catification concept that can be utilized to help with the introduction process. In this case, you would take a more significant item from the new cat's base camp (like a cat tree) and place it out in the living room, in a major window. This allows your resident to mark the base camp piece with his own scent, establishing a peaceful co-signpost in the home.

Hint: You can up the ante by providing a scent-soaking double whammy—place one of your "gifts" on one of the signposts!

Step Five: Site Swapping

Once your new cat demonstrates mastery of (and Mojo in) base camp, it's time for the next step: Site Swapping. How will you know she's mastered base camp? She will appear to be 100 percent comfortable, sitting at the window watching birds and not army-crawling, hiding under things, or jumping every time the door's opened. And then there are the most obvious signs: when she's sitting right by the door, trying to dash past you every time you open it, or when you hear her scratching/vocalizing on the other side of the door.

Site Swapping allows each cat to explore the other's territory without ever laying eyes on each other. This is also an opportunity for key signposts—like cat trees, litterboxes, etc.—to take on a shared scent.

You Site Swap on alternating days so no one owns too much land. But you also site swap because if a cat is locked up all day, his energy can build up into a potential "cat bomb." Here's how it would unfold:

1. Carry the newcomer out of her base camp, put her in the bathroom, and shut the door.
2. Allow the resident cat to walk into the newcomer's base camp, then shut that door.

3. Allow the newcomer to explore the rest of the home.

4. Rinse and repeat.

From there, it's just a matter of them having quality time in each other's environments. I wouldn't put a timer on it.

Make sure that you're swapping back at predictable times during the day, so you're not asking your existing cat to be in a closed space for extended periods or asking the newcomer to sleep around the rest of the house all night long, right off the bat.

Hopefully, this process allows cats to get to know one another really well before they ever see each other, which happens next.

Cat Daddy Tip

When it comes to site swapping, there are no hard and fast rules about when and how often, as long as you are consistent. You don't want to swap randomly, and you don't want to allow anyone to get too comfortable in one space. You can swap once a day, every other day, or even two or three times a day if the cats are happy. Just don't let yourself fall into a rut.

Step Six: Visual Access

With both cats now acutely aware of the other's scent, it's time to let the cats actually see other. The work that you've done up to this point has resulted in predictable behavior between the two cats and a cordial (or, at least tolerant) "scent handshake" at every meal. It's a mistake, though, to assume that they will be just as cordial once the visual element is introduced. Instead, begin at the beginning and reset the Challenge Line; take the feeding line back all the way to where they can see one another and eat with little or no disruption. And now, do the process all over again.

But first, you have a choice to make. Do you simply crack the base camp door, or set up a pet gate or screen door?

Option One: It's often fine to just crack the door. You can grab a couple of those triangular rubber door stoppers from any hardware store and place one either side of the door (to guarantee that no one's going to swing that door open). Or a hook-and-eye door latch also works just fine to keep the door slightly ajar. There should be only enough space that if some kind of swatting or swiping breaks out, it can happen with no damage done.

Option Two: In my experience, the better option is to introduce the cats by either using a pet gate or a screen door. A pet gate works better than a baby gate because pet gates are high and have a walk-through door in them, so that the human doesn't have to disassemble the base camp door every time he wants to cross that threshold.

Raising the Curtain

Once you've decided on whether to use a pet gate or screen door, drape a blanket over that gate or use clothespins to hang it from the screen. This gives you a much greater sense of control over the degree of visual access because you can "raise the curtain" gradually over a period of time. The curtain allows you to start with the absolute bare minimum of visual access. For many cats, this added layer of security makes all the difference in giving them the confidence they need to take that next paw over their Challenge Line.

The "Screening" Process

As you've seen on my show, I prefer to install a screen door at the base camp door. That sounds like a very big undertaking, but in reality, it's not. The costs of a screen door with sturdy pet screening, and the elbow grease to install it by taking your door off the hinges and putting this door in, are fairly minimal. And you can even do it in a rental apartment. I highly recommend going with a screen door because it allows for control of access in a way that nothing else can. There are no gates to jump over, no doorstops to budge out of the way, and no worry about how high the crack might be under the door.

Cat Daddy Tips

Whichever method you use to introduce visual access, the following tips will help:

- With some cats, you might have to start with no visual access, and then move them into each other's sight line slowly. (The blanket technique works well for this.) This then becomes the first Challenge Line to cross—moving from "I know you're there but can't see you," to actually eating while in the sight line of the other.
- Oftentimes a glitch occurs when one cat eats like a vacuum cleaner while the other picks, pecks, and walks away. You can use a slow down bowl or other food puzzle to buy you more time on the vacuum cleaner's side, while making sure not to provide too many treats between meals and choosing "Jackpot!" food for dinner for the finicky diner.

- When you just crack that base camp door, even if you maximize the angle so the cats are almost looking at each other, it still has a hunting game vibe to it, because each cat gets only glimpses of the other cat. With the screen door, there is no question about the message: all body language is obvious.

- I've seen this process take weeks. But I've also seen this process take just a few days. Your cats will tell you when they're comfortable. Knowing what your cat's body looks like on the side of comfort and on the side of challenge really tells you everything you need to know moving forward.

Once you get to the point where you've raised the curtain completely, allowing total visual access while the cats are eating fairly closely to each other (remember, it's not reasonable to expect two stranger cats to comfortably eat within six inches of each other, even if there's a door separating them, but you get as close as you can), then you're ready for our next step.

Step Seven: Eat Play Love

I'm a huge hockey fan. The game has changed tremendously since I was a kid back in the '70s. To put it mildly, hockey was a superdangerous sport back then—and not just because you were playing at very high speeds on a sheet of ice with 1/8" wide metal blades, holding a wooden stick and dodging a solid rubber projectile traveling sometimes in excess of 100 mph. No, back then, the real danger was that the players would not hesitate to beat the crap out of each other once they were engaged in the game. Sure, fighting is still a fairly common part of the game today. But back then, in a way, it *was* the game.

With inevitable violence looming once the whistle sounded, I always thought the most fascinating thing was the pregame ritual, when both teams would skate out onto the ice for their warm-up period. Each team would occupy an opposite side of the rink, with the red line dividing the ice right down the middle. The players would skate in circles, warming up their legs and taking shots at their goalie. And they would occasionally glance over at their opponents at the other side of the rink, who were also skating in circles and warming up. Sworn enemies, engaged in the same activity, separated by a painted line. What kept these continual circles moving while this unspoken frenetic energy, boiling beneath the surface, dictated that, at any moment, a staredown would lead to a full-scale throwdown? The fragile peace was kept by virtue of the ritual itself; the players knew that "this is the way it always happens—and it never has or will result in a brawl."

This is the vision I had in mind when designing the next step of introduction, which I call **Eat Play Love** (EPL). Philosophically, this is an extension of the "other side of the door" exercise. Before, you were just creating a positive association based on food. Now you are going for the whole enchilada. These three things—eat, play, and love—represent the highest of high-value experiences we humans bring to our cats in the course of a day. When this exercise is in play (no pun intended!), all of these experiences are withheld until they can be broken out as one big feel-good extravaganza. (To the best of our abilities, of course. You can't just go on a snuggle strike—that would be ridiculous!) I'm serious—this ritual has the potential to be Christmas morning every day, and the one caveat is that it happens with a strange cat in the room.

The gist of EPL is pretty simple: You're bringing one cat into a room where there's another cat at the other end of the "rink," so to speak, who is already engaged in a high-value, fully engrossing activity. And your challenge is to keep them "skating" in their own circle for as long as possible through treats, positive reinforcement, play, and . . . well . . . *love*—without that staredown/throwdown happening.

Fire Drill

The earliest I remember the "Fire Drill" was 1973. I was six years old, which would make my brother two or three. We lived in an apartment in New York City, something that made my dad ultraparanoid when it came to emergencies, since you were, to a degree, held hostage by the building itself. So, with getting out of the building being the thing that would keep us alive, he made sure we knew the exact steps that would get us out, and also the exact and graphic consequences if we didn't follow those steps. Believe me, he had us motivated.

Of course, he had to take it a step further. That's where the fire drill came in. In the middle of the night, dad would suddenly come running into our bedroom, turn on the lights, and, while banging on a pan with a wooden spoon, yell, "Fire! Fire! Fire!"

My brother and I, after first soiling our pj's, would go into full-on fire drill mode. The first couple of times, you're half hysterical and fully dazed, struggling to recall the protocol. But after three or four times, the banging, the lights flicking on and off, and his booming voice became an association: *get on the floor.* Both of us lying flat, my brother would get on my back. I would turn into a turtle and crawl to our bedroom door and put my hand on the doorknob to see if it was hot. If not, we kept turtle crawling, staying low. We did that with every closed door in the apartment until we got to the front door and felt it. If it wasn't hot, we would head outside, being sure to use only the stairs—never the elevator. We would then head out into the lobby of the building, steps from emerging onto freaking Broadway at three in the morning. And there's your fire drill.

That was nearly forty-five years ago at the time of this writing, and I remember that fire drill in my bones. It's muscle memory. To this day, if someone came running into my bedroom banging a wooden spoon on a pot in the middle of the night yelling "fire," I would get out of that house in a very safe way. Then I might come to my senses and have the crazy person who got into my house arrested, but that's not the point. The point is that staying prepared so that anxiety is put on the back burner while a job gets done . . . that's the fire drill.

This is a great concept to apply to many "cat parenting" functions like giving your cat a pill or helping him into a carrier (which we'll get into in chapter 12). For now, though, how does this concept apply to our present circumstances? "Fire drill" in terms of your cats in a multi-cat household is having walked though every eventuality in such a complete way that you will metaphorically get your ass onto Broadway.

The bridge that is crossed when moving from introduction (or reintroduction) techniques to one where we balance technique with a degree of trust is a crucial part of the journey. That said, the bridge doesn't have to feel like it's going to give way at any moment. The following checklist helps keep the cats safe during the process, but, just as important, keeps you feeling in control—which is just as important as the steps themselves. Our cats are so energetically sensitive, and are already feeling the raised temperature in the room. Your sense of unease, the pervading "What if . . . ?" thinking from moment to moment, can very well be the spark that sets the bridge on fire.

Therefore, it's important for you to break down and anticipate the possibility of conflict. That way, when you're finally at *that* point—with the cats in the same room together, barrier-free—you will know what to do if conflict begins to unfold and the fire alarm sounds.

The Eat Play Love Checklist

1. **The Unders and the Outs**—When we lose control of exercises like EPL, many times we lose it to the environment itself. One thing I can tell you from experience—fights start with chasing. Chasing very often ends in a room, in a closet, or under a bed or a piece of furniture you never in your wildest nightmares thought was big enough for one cat, let alone two. You can control the chaos by controlling the space—and that means blocking off the Unders and sealing off the Outs. If your EPL session takes place in the living room, then

it's up to you to seal off the Outs—meaning doors are closed, gates are up, and you are now working in a playing field that you alone have defined. Further define that space and block off the Unders. The only way to make sure you're not going to put your hand into a "trash disposal" of fangs and claws is to make sure there's not going to be a fight under a bed or couch!

2. **Have Your Sight Blockers Ready**—A **Sight Blocker** is something that: (a) the cats can't see through, (b) is solid enough that you can place it between them and they can't bust through it, and (c) is high enough that you don't have to bend down to place it between the two cats and your hands are out of the "danger zone" should a fight break out. Flattened and taped-up cardboard boxes of the appropriate height have always worked best for me, or you could try a thick piece of foam core. Don't use a blanket or something flimsy. They'll just run through it.

When you see that first sign of doom—usually it's the moment at which movement stops and the staredown starts—it's *game over*: sight blocker down. If you can't control them with toys and treats, lead them away. Use the sight blocker to guide someone out of the room. Again, your goal is to end everything on a high note, or at least not a low note.

3. **Last Resort Removal Option**—In the event of a serious lockdown, when you can't get the cats to budge even with sight blockers down, or if, despite your best efforts, a fight breaks out, a blanket can be a good friend. Just toss it over one of them, scoop him up, and remove him from the room. Another tool to have on hand is an empty soda can with pennies in it and tape across the opening. As opposed to using your voice, which will just add bad associations on top of an already bad situation, shaking that can will help shock the cats out of the moment they are locked into. The thing that unites these tools? They help to keep your panicked initial response from happening, which is just to scream and stick your hands into the cat blender. That will never end well for you.

4. **Be "Fire Drill" Ready**—Sight blockers, penny cans, and blankets should be placed so that no matter where you are in the room, you

can quickly access them while you are also allowing the organic process of the two cats comingling to happen. In other words, the last thing you want is to hover—you've got to have the confidence to step back, be cool, and remove panic from a stressful situation. That's why we think of all eventualities, and proactively incorporate our tools. Ask yourself: if they begin to fight, where will it be most likely to break out and where will it end? Mark those areas with sight blockers, cans, and blankets. At the same time, you need to be able to spring into action should the proceedings go south. The key is, though, that springing into action contains steps that you've thought through enough times—which means your response will be measured, appropriate to the situation itself, and not driven by emotions.

 **Another note:** It definitely takes two to tango when it comes to the Fire Drill process for cat introductions. Your partner in the Fire Drill is not only on the same page, but the same paragraph, the same sentence.

YOUR ENDGAME HERE is to create an even fuller immersion into the positive association experience we've been working on throughout this entire section. In this case, there is no barrier between the two cats, hence the pre-hockey game metaphor, and you will ultimately shoot for both cats eating a meal in the same room. Success here is the final frontier before full integration.

Here is the step-by-step process for pulling this off:

A. **Know Your Players:** Get to know who you're dealing with.
- What type of players are your resident and newcomer? Model T? Sports car? (See chapter 7 for more info on types of Cat Players.)
- Do they tend to be more food motivated or love/attention motivated?
- What is the highest order of pleasure on their cat "Jackpot!"

meter? What would go beyond *really liking* something and guarantee engrossment? Would it involve a favorite food/Jackpot! Treat, a special toy, or something like brushing or petting? Keep in mind that these treats/activities need to be something that keeps his motor humming and motivation high even when another cat is in his space.

B. **Prime the Jackpot! Pump:** You may be absolutely sure of what your cat's favorite treat or toy is, but it will only become "Jackpot!" after a period of absence. This is to say that, before getting into the EPL festivities, you must withhold her favorite things. I know, it's going to be hard not to dispense treats or favorite tastes whenever she gives you those big baleful eyes or that mournful "Why do you hate me?" meow, but don't give in! Delayed gratification will turn all of these things into a Jackpot! party!

C. **Ritualize an Optimal Play Session with Each Cat:** Once you know your player's preferences, it's important to have a successful session with one cat in the absence of the other cat, so you know what it looks like when each cat is engaged vs. when each is distracted. This will help you evaluate and monitor the Eat Play Love session when they are both in the same room, and, just as important, it will help end the session on a high note. Just like with food, we need a Jackpot! when it comes to the type of toy that starts your cat's engine. Once you find one, find others. Rotating toys plays into the Raw Cat Rhythm because it mimics variety in types of prey and, of course, keeps the game fresh day after day. Ritualizing is essential because you will know both what they like for play, and also when they are about to be turned off. Instead of giving them the opportunity to dash for the other cat, you are ending the session while they are still distracted by the play. You'll stay one step ahead of the game.

D. **The Eat Play Love Session:** Ready to go? To prepare, choose the common-area room in which to have the joint session. This should be the largest room with the most amount of empty space; a crowded, smaller room gives the cats too many things to focus on and too many opportunities to get away from you and to get at each other. Next, enlist the help of a friend, significant other, family member, etc. As I said, I'm always a proponent of having human partners to aid in these introduction steps, but this exercise, specifically, is one you just can't do solo.

Important: Remember the hockey analogy—we want both cats moving in those big, opposing circles. Momentum is on equal par with engagement during this exercise, and, likewise, stasis is our greatest enemy.

1. **Start with One Cat:** Begin by playing with only one cat in the room at first. Make sure he is engaged, and keep him moving. If you are dispensing treats, get that bread-crumb trail going; as he is chewing one, you put the next one down where he can see it, so that he is moving toward his next goal as he's finishing the previous one. The same goes for toys; you need to be in control of your cat's head—the rest will follow. In times of potential staredowns, nothing is more your friend than your ability to move your cat's eyes where *you want them to look.*

2. **Bring in the Other Cat:** Casually have your partner bring the other cat into the room with her already engaged. In a perfect world, you would lead the cat into the space with whatever is her Jackpot!, whether that is food, a toy, etc. This way you are not creating that extra static energy on your cat's part by being carried into the space. You should aim for giving her that extra dose of Mojo that comes from thinking that she is making all of her own decisions.

3. **Keep the "Rhythm" Going:** The *most* important component when you bring the cats together is establishing and maintaining a rhythm of play once they hit the room. This is where your partner's help is invaluable, because he or she can work to focus the other cat on the session while you do the same with yours.

4. **End the Session:** The session will end in one of two ways: either the cats will end it, or the humans will. It goes without saying that you would prefer the latter every time. Knowing your cats' physical language tells you when boredom is setting in, which leads to being easily distracted. That said, you can't possibly retain all control all the time. Here are some extra tips to prevent a throwdown:

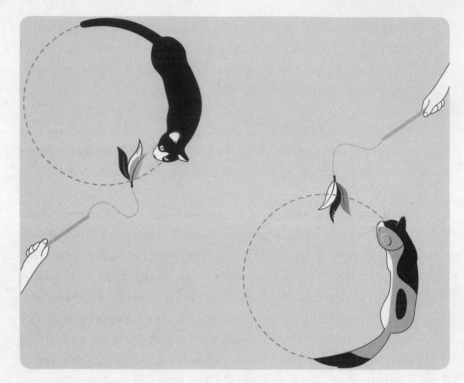

- The moment one cat stops moving, stares at the other cat, and will not be redirected, you might as well call it a day.
- A perfect-world end to a session would be to lead them out of the room with a toy. As I said, I always prefer, for the sake of Cat Mojo, for cats to feel like they are making the decisions. If that decision, however, is looking like it's going to be a messy one, and if you need to pick up one of the cats and bring him into another room before the cats take action on that decision, then that's what you do.
- Always choose to end the exercise on a high note. Remember, you are trying to create positive associations, which is a check we can cash only with consistent, positive endings. Listen to your gut—are you adding one final challenge to the day's proceedings or one too many brushstrokes?
- Cap off the EPL sequence—no matter if it ends good, bad, or ugly—with dinner. Chances are that your cats will probably be on the full side if the day went well, so you may need to hold off on mealtime for a bit, but keep the consistency going. At this point,

the cats expect to eat dinner on either side of the door/gate, and it's one last chance to end the day on a positively reinforced note.

5. **Final Goal for Eat Play Love:** Once you are secure in Eat Play Love—when you can accomplish EPL without having to end it prematurely, and it's a ritual that has become a part of the everyday cycle—then you can break down the door/gate barrier for mealtime and end the session by feeding the cats on the side of the room that they occupy. Just remember that imaginary "red line" in the center of the room. Start with a more respectful distance on either side of the red line, just as you did initially with the door feeding ritual. In the end, eating tends to be the easiest path to détente that I know of.

Cat Daddy Eat Play Love Tips

Switch It Up: Use the principles of site swapping when doing Eat Play Love. If you do it the same way every single day, with one cat entering the perceived territory of another cat, then you're inadvertently setting up a dynamic for overownership or lack thereof. Switch off: one day, bring the newcomer into the room where the resident is playing, then the next day, bring the resident into the room where the newcomer is playing.

Subdue the Staredown: As you go forward with this exercise and do it multiple times, you'll know how to best redirect your cats if they start to stare. Distraction left unchecked can lead to the dreaded staredown. Knowing *when* distraction is about to happen means that you have an opportunity to retain control, redirect their attention, or choose to just call it a day. Essentially, really knowing their body language keeps you a step ahead of the game . . . and the cats. Remember: it's on you to conduct these exercises without a fight breaking out.

Baby Steps to Success: At the beginning of this process, look for success in very small increments. If the going has already been a little tough during the introduction, having the two cats in the same territory and occupied for just one minute is a win. Although it might seem silly at first, write down the exact amount of time that this brief session lasted. Tomorrow, when you up it by five, ten, or even fifteen seconds, you've won that day, too. Sometimes the biggest successes come in the form of just a few seconds.

Don't Sweat the Setbacks—Just Step Back

 There's always a possibility that, despite our best-laid plans, a fight breaks out. That shouldn't be the end of your work; that should just be the end of the day. But it doesn't mean that you're doing everything wrong. Sometimes, you're just working against what these cats have conditioned themselves to act like around each other. Sometimes, the cats are just having a bad day, or something stressful occurs in the home to throw off the predictable rhythms. Again, it's important to remember that in the course of any relationship, there are fights. We just use words—they use claws. For your well-being, remember that an argument doesn't define a relationship; it's what happens afterward that does.

So what do you do if this happens? Back it up a step. For instance, if your first attempt at Eat Play Love ended before it ever began, with chaos erupting as soon as the exercise commenced, take it back to the last spot of repeated and predictable success. In this case, let's say that the last time you fed three meals in a row without even a sideways glance from either participant was: opposite sides of the door, full visual access, three feet of separation. Then that's where you go back to. If that's asking too much (meaning either or both cats avoid eating, engage in too much growling, etc.), retrace the process back **one step** from there. You will find, very quickly, an acceptable Challenge Line where you can restart the process.

FIFTEEN SECONDS OF PEACE

Even in the hardest cases, if you have fifteen seconds of peace and you keep building, you will have success. Just like I spoke about regarding the Challenge Line, introducing cats is like the beginning stages of a roller coaster. Have faith, there will come that moment when, all of a sudden, boom—the tracks take over, it just breaks free, you have a group rhythm in the house, and all is well.

Commonly Asked Questions

What If You Have More Than Two Cats?

If you have more than two cats, I recommend that you build relationships one pair at a time. Start with the "easier" cats if possible, so they can create a social bridge for the other relationships. Do all of the exercises with different combinations of cats, being sure not to overwhelm the newcomer with too many cats at once.

Do Cats Need Their Own Litterboxes?

Is it a sign of impending territorial strife when one cat is using the other cat's box to pee or poop? There is no such thing as one cat's box. You want to have n+1 litterboxes, but each litterbox is a communal signpost and should have every cat's scent in it. In the cat's social world, there is no sense of the proprietary. One cat does not (or should not) put his name on any object to the exclusion of any other cat. Every cat is going to use those signposts, at some point, if they so desire.

I've had many clients over the years who, for one reason or another, clung to the notion that each cat should have his own litterbox, and that the cats perceive it to be a great social transgression for one cat to use another's box.

Not only is this a case of human projection, but keeping this perceived social order intact will, more often than not, backfire. There's no way to tell a cat, "Don't use this box, but use that box." Anytime you try to stop a cat from going into *any* litterbox, you are simply sending mixed messages that will often end with that cat rejecting *every* litterbox. Very simply, let the cats decide which boxes they want to use.

What If We Have Two Cats Who Simply Will Not Get Along, Despite Our Best Efforts in Implementing All of This "Introduction" Advice?

This is tricky. How long do you continue to try and make it work when the cats are letting you know that they don't want it to? Knowing when it's just not a good fit is a very personal decision, so it's tough for me to weigh in on it in such a general way.

One thing I can say is that throughout this process, your expectations have to be realistic. Ultimately, you can't *make* cats get along. There is always the chance for human misinterpretation of the relationship. I've seen this countless times—the cats *are* getting along, but the relationship just doesn't look the way you want it to look. Maybe you want your cats to groom each other on the bed or act like littermates, but in many cases, cats getting along means they simply tolerate one another. As far as I'm concerned, as long as there is a cease-fire, and as long as they have a truce in which they declare, "We can share space," all is good. That means the groundwork is set for dialogue, and for the building of a lifelong relationship that will, like all relationships, grow. That said, check out chapter 14 for a number of Super-deluxe remedies to common cat aggression problems.

MOJO MAINTENANCE

Now that the introduction period is in the rear view, here are a couple of helpful hints to keep things harmonious between your cats in the years ahead:

Stay Resource Rich: One of the common denominators I see in the long-term success of feline relations is that there remains an abundance of resources available for all resident cats. Do you have enough resources to go around? How is the Sundial situation? Is there plenty of vertical space for everyone? Are you maintaining separate food dishes and plus-one litterboxes?

Keep Everyone Tired and Happy: Cats who play together, stay together . . . in relative harmony. However, we can't always presume that "playing together" will mean that your cats will be playing with each other like a couple of kittens every day. That's where your commitment to HCKE factors in. By keeping up with your "Play = Prey" strategies (as discussed in chapter 7), we help to burn away that excess energy buildup that can lead to problems between cats.

Expecting to Expand the Family with a New Dog or Child?: In the same way that there are optimal procedures to introduce cats to cats, there are optimal procedures to introduce cats to dogs, as well as kids. Stay tuned.

CATS AND DOGS

If you are anything like me, you got most of your childhood animal education from Saturday morning cartoons. I'll admit it—by the time I turned seven or eight years old, I just *knew* that cats and dogs were born to hate one another. I was also positive that dogs hated smart-aleck rabbits, cats hated tweety birds, and coyotes hated roadrunners. Well, coyotes pretty much hated everyone, but that's because of their superiority complex. . . . Anyhow, I digress.

The point is, regardless of where we were taught that the old saying "fighting like cats and dogs" was the norm, any of us who proudly identify as "bipetual" will tell you that real life is not a cliché. Cats and dogs *can* get along just fine. There's not always a cat waiting around the corner to hit a dog with a frying pan, or a dog looking to chase after a cat until he runs out of chain and chokes himself. Life is not like cartoons—at least not most of the time (although it is true that coyotes can be pretty smug).

If you bring a new dog into your home, and your cat has never even seen a dog before, you're asking a lot of your cat to withstand the stress of coming into contact with a new being. All new beings are potential predators in the mind of the Raw Cat, so it's part of his wiring to be cautious. In this section, we will be concentrating on getting past that suspicion in much the same way I've described meeting other cats—through positive associations. However, no matter what we do to tell your cat that the new being is friend, not foe, there's work to be done on both sides of the leash; we still have to be able to cash that dog-shaped check.

DOGGIE DUE DILIGENCE

Here are a few things to consider if you're thinking about adopting a new dog into a cat's home.

Do Your Research: It should go without saying that it's important to do your research if you're adopting a dog into a home with a cat. Socialization with other animals at a young age is good for cats and dogs, so you might look for a dog who has lived successfully with a cat in the past. Certainly you'd want to avoid adopting any dog who has had bad experiences with cats. Also, most shelters do their dog due diligence when evaluating dogs for adoption. The aforementioned prey drive is a big factor. Similarly, if the shelter received information about a tendency toward resource guarding in the dog's previous home, that, too, is a red flag. A fearful dog might actually present a problem since panic might lead to redirected aggression.

Individuals, Not Breeds: In the animal adoption world, there has always been persistent discussion/argument about avoiding certain dog breeds when it comes to matching them in a home with a cat. While it's true that certain breeds might be more prone to having a heightened prey drive, for instance, I believe it does a disservice to the potential match to judge a book by its cover, or a dog by her breed. As always, it comes down to the individual dog.

Personality Match: You want to match compatible personality types, just as you would when picking a new cat. Age, breed, and energy level should be at least part of your adoption criteria, and many if not most shelters have even tested how dogs respond to cats at the shelter. At the end of the day however, the most important information you need will be available once you have the dog in your home environment. That is going to tell you how things are going to go and what you might need to work on as far as the dog's side of the relationship is concerned.

Training: In a perfect world, whether the dog in the equation is the existing resident or the newcomer, he or she would be well trained, and predictably under voice command. When it comes to implementing the exercises I'm about to take you through, that training is a security blanket like no other that we can wrap around the proceedings.

Of course, we don't live in a perfect world. Although it's becoming more and more the norm to have training classes for dogs while they are still in the shelter, they are still a four-legged question mark when they cross the threshold of your home for the first time. Likewise, a dog that has lived with you for years still probably gets away with more than a little, but that little becomes a lot when a cat comes into his life.

Being undertrained, however, is not a crime; it just illuminates a need. By no means am I telling you *not* to adopt a dog that you're falling in love with just because of this need—it just means you need to get down to work.

A Little Help from My Friends . . .

Introducing a cat to your dog is a surefire way to uncover some gaps in your dog's training work. This is no time to go it alone. If your dog cannot accomplish a down-stay or similar calm behaviors as a cat walks across his path, then (1) you're introducing them too soon and (2) it's time to call in the cavalry and find a good dog trainer with a solid background in positive reinforcement–based methods. The good news is that most likely there's a qualified trainer in your area who can help. And with all of the stress you're dealing with in bringing a new family member home and creating new relationships, you should ask for that help!

If possible, I would recommend bringing in a qualified dog trainer for a few in-home sessions. Having the trainer come to your home provides a vantage point to the dog's behavior that the trainer just can't otherwise get, and that means you will then have tools that are customized for your dog in this new, very specific situation.

Whether you opt for private or class-style training, hiring a dog trainer also prevents a lot of frustration on your part as you make your way through the first few weeks of introduction. With training, solid Catification, management, supervision—and a little help from your friends—there's no reason most cats and dogs can't live in harmony.

"LIKE PEANUT BUTTER AND JELLY": THE STEP-BY-STEP CAT-TO-DOG INTRODUCTION PROCESS

A cat-to-dog introduction can happen one of two ways: you either bring a dog home to where a cat lives or you bring a cat home to where a dog lives. Each introduction scenario will unfold in a way similar to our cat-to-cat process; you'll even utilize the same seven steps. When reviewing the cat-to-cat section, just remember that when introducing two cats, you are following the letter of the law. When you are introducing cats and dogs, it's more about the spirit of the thing and not necessarily about following every step religiously. Any subtle distinctions in approach will be noted with each step.

Let's begin with a few more dog-influenced particulars in the first step:

Step One: Proactive Preparation—Cat-to-Dog Style

A. **Scheduled Meals Only**

If you currently leave out food 24/7 for your resident dog or cat, remember: *scheduled meals are your friends.* And it's important to note that we're not just trying to convince the cat that the dog is a good thing, but we're also making sure that the dog has a positive association with your cat. No more free feeding.

The Catification aspects of cat-to-dog cohabitation are very specific and, for various reasons, a little different than cat-to-cat:

B. **Catify the Living Areas**

Remember, the essence of Cat Mojo is confident ownership of territory. So, before you bring home a new dog, make sure that your space is fully Catified for life with a dog. *The most important consideration is proper use of the vertical world.* Your cat, if threatened, needs a home above the floor. This space should be above the reach of a dog.

There is no better occasion to introduce the concept of the Cat Superhighway than now. The Cat Superhighway is another way of saying that we want to Catify so that a cat can circumvent the major living spaces, such as the living room, without touching the floor, if they so choose. Review chapter 8 for more on this concept.

Our Cat-to-Dog Mantra:

The Sky Is Owned by Cats in the World of Cats and Dogs.

That means that cats may be either sharing or relinquishing control of the floor, to a certain degree, but that's a decent trade-off. Don't forget, in a cat's-eye view, their world is floor to ceiling. The volume they perceive in terms of vertical territory, if it is accessible to them, is the whole megillah. Dogs, on the other hand, are terrestrial for the most part. And this is where cats get an advantage, in terms of overall space utilization.

The best way for a cat to meet any new family member—whether human, cat, or dog—is to be able to get some distance between them, in order to get comfortable and make sense of a completely foreign body, so to speak. This is especially true where dogs are concerned: How does a dog move? What are those sounds they make? Where's that smell coming from? Why are they interested in X, Y, and Z? Cats want to be able to survey what's going on around them, and Catifying the space allows them to do that safely.

Cat trees are not only a great way for cats to get that vantage point, but cat trees can also act as on-ramps and off-ramps to and from the Cat Superhighway. Cat trees are a great way to prevent dead ends—that is to say, if things go south and the dog chases the cat and the cat runs out of floor, she has the vertical world to rely on. And again, there's nothing like having a cat tree that looks out a window. While your cat is watching the new creature in the house, she can also take a break and watch some Cat TV.

C. Catify the Litterbox Areas

This is a big deal because most dogs are attracted to litterboxes as if they were a buffet. Cat waste is protein heavy and a great snack, as far as dogs are concerned. As disgusting as that may sound to a human, it's even worse for the cat, and here's the big reason: the litterbox has to be a safe place—make that a *sacred* place—for a cat. If a cat is in a litterbox and this huge snout comes along, waiting not-so-patiently for what is coming out of the cat, that litterbox has lost its sanctity. And what that means is that your cat is going to start looking for a safer place to pee and poop.

So what can you do?

1. **Make sure that any litterbox is uncovered**, so that your cat has escape routes. They get in, they have a 360-degree view, and they can get out.
2. **Avoid dead ends.** Those who really hate my first suggestion might compensate for taking the lid off by putting the box in a place where nobody can see it. This might very well create a new problem: Let's say that you put the box in the corner of the bathroom, behind the toilet. From a Catification perspective, you've created a dead end—which is an ambush zone. If the dog follows your cat into the bathroom, blocking off exit routes for the cat, then the cat will just stop

going to that box in favor of an area where she has a safe, 360-degree view of the terrain. The takeaway here, as always, is that you're best served putting your aesthetic desires behind the built-in needs of our Raw Cat, who is not going to go anywhere unless he is assured multiple escape routes.

3. **Keep litterboxes in rooms that dogs can't access.** Ordinarily, I'm all about litterboxes being available in socially significant spaces. But in the world of dog and cat, you might have to make some concessions. One of my go-to moves is putting up a baby gate in a room where the litterbox is. Then you can raise up that baby gate around eight inches off the ground—maybe a little less, if you have a small dog. That way, the cat has the ability to go either under the gate or over the gate, and we can rest assured that the litterbox is safe from prying snouts (or toddlers, who think that *any* sandbox is an invitation).

We can't blame the dog for seeking out a protein-rich snack (any more than we can blame the toddler for creating a poop-festooned sand castle). What we can do is try to head off that problem at the pass because nobody wants to get dog kisses from one who just left a litterbox. Take my word for it.

Step Two: Base Camp and First Time Through the Threshold

It's always crucial to know what your first moves will be when you enter your home with your new family member, be it dog or cat. Having a concrete game plan gives you a measure of immediate control, not to mention peace of mind. This step has two main components:

A. **Base Camp:** Although setting up base camp is less critical when bringing a dog into a cat's territory (since the cat has already established herself there), this process is still important; base camp becomes the "safe zone," a panic room of sorts, for the cat to retreat to whenever she's feeling a bit uneasy about her new roommate. It's also a front-row seat to the territory where she can be surrounded by familiar scents and owned objects that provide reassurance. Obviously, you will want to set up base camp in an area that's naturally off-limits or inaccessible to the dog.

That said, since we are not relegating the cat to base camp, she should be able to explore the world that the new dog is occupying at her own pace, not ours, especially by this part of the process. Again, as long as the dog is on leash, the cat should feel free to explore, since making her feel like a guest in her own territory would be a punch in the gut of Cat Mojo.

When you bring a cat to a dog's home, it will be business as usual, just like we described in the cat-to-cat section; the cat will start off exclusively in base camp.

B1. First Time Through the Threshold—Dog into a Cat's Home: It's all about the leash.

When you first bring a dog into a home with cats . . . repeat after me:

The leash. Stays. On.

The fact is, you don't really know your new family member very well, and despite all of your due diligence before the adoption (and, likely, on the part of the shelter or rescue organization), you just have no idea what triggers may be pulled the first time your dog sees a cat, or the first time a cat sniffs the dog's toys, food, or even water. So once your cat and dog are in the same physical space, I would still keep your dog on-leash for a little while, until you feel safe, and while that trust bridge is still under construction.

The leash gives you a reliable and consistent degree of control over your new family member. At least in my home, it's not until the dog earns our complete trust that he goes leash-free. We don't even necessarily have to be holding onto it, especially as the days go by and the introduction process is well underway. If the leash is still on, and the dog makes a sudden move, we can "foot" (quickly pin the leash to the ground with a foot) that leash and regain control. Getting your dog under complete voice command is a process; the right to wander the house freely is definitely one that is earned.

B2: First Time Through the Threshold—Cat into a Dog's Home: Go directly to base camp.

When you first bring a cat to *any* new home for the first time—it doesn't matter if you are bringing that cat into a home with a dog or no dog, other cats or no other cats, or six other cats, four dogs, a box turtle, and a partridge in a pear tree—*base camp should be set up, and your new cat should be delivered directly there.* No matter how tempted you are to do otherwise, don't just let the cat out of her carrier in the middle of the living room floor. The universal truths of Catification and building Mojo by gradually building a territory that cats can feel complete autonomy over are just that—universal.

THE NITTY GRITTY

Once you make it to this point in the process, review steps three through seven in the cat-to-cat section (pages 168–77). Although the techniques and intent remain the same, there is a major difference. We proceed at a very measured pace when it comes to cats meeting cats because it is all about convincing two animals who depend on the sanctity of their territory that the new being in the space presents no threat, and can actually be a positive thing. In the case of cat meets dog, the two species have very different needs, and the name of the game really is getting the dog to be less frantically curious (or less fearful) and the cat more trusting (or less fearful). Among other things, this means that the steps are a bit more fluid, and can be performed at whatever pace you observe is necessary for your individual situation. The following are some notes for each step that are cat-to-dog specific. Onward!

Step Three: The "Other Side of the Door" Feeding Ritual

As described in the cat-to-cat section, you will still follow our ritual of feeding dog and cat on opposite sides of a closed door, and work toward bringing those food dishes closer together over time. Once again, the idea is slow desensitization: if every time food is served, the cat smells the dog—and, in fact, the *only* time she smells the dog is when there's food present—chances are she's going to think the dog has good things to offer.

Of course, there are a few things to bear in mind that make this step different when considering cat-to-dog vs. cat-to-cat: when excited, fearful, agitated, etc., dogs *bark*. Sudden barking will scare the cat-pants off of most cats and put a good dent in the positive association business. When in the initial feeling-out process of this step, err on the side of caution and move that Challenge Line back far enough so that we can move past the initial stages of dog excitement. Also, there's by and large a lot less hesitation on the part of dogs to get up close and personal with something (or someone) they are curious about. Cats, again generally, will be much more deliberate about how they approach. Another good reason to have a leash on your dog, even when doing this initial ritual: a dog rushing the door is also a good way of telling the cat that the door isn't exactly safe.

Step Four: Scent Swapping

This remains a handy protocol for both parties. One thing that unites cats and dogs is their superior sense of smell—they glean a lot of information from this sense when sussing out new situations. As you would when introducing a new cat, you should let the resident cat have at the dog's bedding and toys and vice versa before any face-to-face introductions happen.

Step Five: Site Swapping

When introducing cat-to-cat, site swapping assures the participants every step of the way that territorially they are safe and not in danger of losing ownership. With cat-to-dog site swapping, on the dog's part it's more about satisfying curiosity and allowing for full exploration than making sure the coast is clear, so to speak.

Hint: A great time to allow the cat a bit of impromptu site swapping is when you take your dog for a walk.

Step Six: Visual Access

With this step, you add to the scent stimulation you've already established by setting up a baby gate or screen door during our feeding ritual. Many of the same visual access strategies discussed in our cat-to-cat introduction process will work here: a cracked door, pet gate, or screen door, along with the idea of the gradual reveal via a blanket.

Only you will know when the time is right to try this.

If you attempt a little visual exposure and the dog tries to sniff too hard, or gives excitement/anxiety cues like stiffening or whining—or the cat gets freaked out (and you should know what that looks like by now!)—simply take it back one step and then try again over the next few sessions. Repetition with predictable outcomes is what convinces everyone that the new "other" can be trusted. And you'll know you're making progress when the dog barks and the cat doesn't have every hair standing on end; or if the cat smells or sees the dog and she doesn't start to hiss, with ears flattened, because she feels completely threatened.

Step Seven: Eat Play Love (EPL)—Cat-to-Dog Style

I think that EPL is just as valuable when introducing cat-to-dog as cat-to-cat, but, as you've seen with these other steps, for different reasons. The main goal of this step when dealing exclusively with cats is *successfully sharing territory* and having the experience of pure Jackpot! only in the presence of the other cat, repeated over and over again, until that positive association is cemented. Again, it's about planting the seeds of communal Cat Mojo. In the case of cat-meets-dog, the endgame is a little different because the species are different. Here, the goal remains much the same for the cat, but there is the extra bonus of getting a crash course in Dog 101. By watching a dog play, solicit love, respond to that love, get excited, and eat and pursue food, the cat can learn a foreign language at a physically safe distance.

You might be asking "Can't this education be done while life is just happening?" Meaning, while the family is just hanging out with dog safely on a leash and the cat is free to explore and learn dog language at her own pace? Yes, the education can and will also happen that way over time. But if your cat is already a Wallflower, leaving her to explore this new and potentially scary other at her own pace may just mean that it's not going to happen anytime this year. With EPL, you turn this education and exposure into an enforced ritual, helping the cat to get over that initial Challenge Line faster than if we left her to her own devices.

Because each animal's energy level will naturally be heightened during this ritual, you also get valuable information that can prevent some pretty negative outcomes down the line. For instance, if the dog is watching your cat play and suddenly his predatory instinct is triggered, that's information that you need, and a pretty strong indication that it's time to bring in a dog trainer to prevent what could be a pretty dangerous problem.

Also, let's not forget that cats can be dangerous to dogs, too. One of the great things about EPL is that you are dictating the distance, excitement level, and tempo of this part of the introduction/education. Let's say that the dog, playing with maximum excitement, triggers your cat's fight-or-flight response or at least heightens her anxiety level to a point where a redirected aggression or overstimulation incident could unfold. The ensuing fight would not be just physically damaging, but damaging to the trust you are trying to instill. The dog now feels unsafe around the cat. Remember: although cats are defensive rather than offensive animals by nature, if cats feel threatened, they are accomplished fighters who know how to stay alive. There's a reason why, in the equation of fight-or-flight, fight comes first.

"DOGS ARE GOOD"

As I've said before, the world of building positive associations is not complete until promises that were made are fulfilled (especially when a cat's instinctive fight-or-flight alarm bells tell her not to do that something you want her to do). Let's imagine the situation as if your cat were your human child who will not sleep without the lights on in his room because he is convinced that there is a monster under his bed. You can reassure him by checking under the bed every night while he watches, telling him with confidence that the coast is clear, and saying good night. The chances of being able to turn the light out still remain iffy. If you can get him to look under the bed with you, praising him mightily as he crosses his Challenge Line nightly, you've helped build his mojo so that he can participate in the decision to go lights out. That said, whether cat or child, all of that mojo building still depends on one singular outcome: a monster can never appear.

Coming back to our cat: the day that alien dog-being enters her life, it's like you hand the cat a little note that says: "Dear Cat. Dog is a good thing. Love, Human." My point is that, from that moment on, and through the course of the introduction techniques, the monster can never appear from under the bed. All our positive associations go straight out the window if the dog chases the cat, cornering her under a bed or on top of the fridge. Of course, it's not an insurmountable setback, but the process is about building trust—and you'd rather not be in the position of rebuilding.

MANY TIMES WHEN I'm approached by those who identify as "cat people," they will express surprise (and sometimes disapproval) that the "Cat Guy" posts so many pictures of his dogs on social media. At which point I will bring up my surprise that the "cat person" vs. "dog person" division still exists. I use the word "bipetual" as a lighthearted way of declaring my devotion to both, and I hold that sign up proudly every day because I want *everyone* to experience it.

Yes, dogs and cats are Yin and Yang—they bring very different, but at the same time very complementary, energy to one's home and life. Hopefully, this section has given you not only the tools but insights into a bipetual life that, once implemented, can lead to lifelong friendships . . . and not a world dominated by cartoon frying pans.

11

Cat/Human Relationship Mojo

*Introductions, Communications,
and Your Role in the Mojo*

B Y THIS POINT, one thing that I hope I've impressed on you, especially as we dove into chapter 6 and the Mojo Toolbox, is that your life with your cat or cats is not an arrangement of ownership but a primary relationship. This very basic tenet is also the primary plank in the Cat Mojo platform. Now we're going to dive into what it means to own the relationship at different stages of the human experience, and how the status of that relationship drives your desire to make the best life possible for both of you.

CATS AND KIDS:
RAISING THE NEXT GENERATION OF CAT LOVERS

In my close to decade-long tenure at an animal shelter, I worked almost every position imaginable—which, many years later, I realize was an incredible blessing. I've had the horrible responsibilities associated with the pet overpopulation crisis, but at the same time, I've been given a periscope that allows me to scour the landscape and help chart a new course toward a more humane future.

One of my jobs along the way was director of community outreach. Although I was admittedly in the dark when it came to children, I relished the idea of being able to help instill in them a love for, and empathy toward, animals while they were at such a crucial developmental phase of their lives.

One of the more challenging aspects of life in the trenches of any movement is that . . . well, that you're in the trench; you can't, for the most part, *know* that the work you're doing is of any value. But you know it feels good, and it feeds your soul.

Today, there's nothing that gets me more emotional than to see children who are growing up with animals—children I meet at fund-raisers or work with in my practice. More and more, those children "get it." They truly love their animal companions, and at the same time, they demand that others around them do the same. That radical empathy from such a young mind often brings me to tears—really! I know, beyond a shadow of a doubt, that child is going to be one more body in a growing army of compassion.

That's one of the reasons this section is so important to me. All children should grow up with animals in their lives and learn empathy and compassion (not to mention that it's amazing and fun and cool!). Kids should be part of raising a cat, not just as witnesses but as guardians. These kids are the next generation of cat lovers, and the reason we won't be killing cats in shelters in the future. If you want to help ensure that your child grows up aware of the world around him, instilled with the desire to be of service, add an animal to his life.

The other reason this section hit home for me is this: far too often, I've noticed that when a couple is expecting a new baby—especially a first baby—their cat ends up in the shelter. The guardians are often saying good-bye before the baby is even born, and, sadly, this decision is often born out of tired old myths, the likes of which we'll be addressing in this section.

We'll also talk about establishing real-life preparedness for bringing home a baby to your cat, or a cat to your kids; what you can do in terms of Catification to ensure a better life for your children and your cat; and, of course, how to set the stage for your child to become a member of Team Cat Mojo twenty years from now.

CATS AND BABIES: MYTH BUSTING

If you're expecting a baby and have a cat, you may have gotten hints from friends, family, or even your doctor that you should brace yourself for the possibility that you'll need to "get rid of" the cat. These suggestions are largely based on myths we cling to about safety when it comes to cats and kids. Let's start with busting some of those myths.

Myth 1: The Cat Will Suffocate the Baby

People still believe the myth that cats will somehow "steal a baby's breath," either because they are jealous of the baby, or because they are attracted to a baby's "milk breath."

Backstory: This myth most likely originated from an incident in the 1790s, where an infant's death was attributed to a cat. The report stated, "It appeared, on the coroner's inquest, that the child died in consequence of a cat sucking its breath, thereby occasioning a strangulation."

Truth: Sadly, the infant may have suffered from something more common, such as Sudden Infant Death Syndrome, or an asthma attack—not from a cat stealing his breath.

Did you know? As mentioned in section 1, these irrational allegations were not uncommon for those times. Since cats were associated with witches back then, they were unjustly blamed for a lot of bad that happened.

Myth 2: The Cat Will Give the Baby Allergies

Expecting parents wonder, Is my child going to be allergic to cats because of exposure to them when they are infants?

Truth: While some newborns could turn out to be allergic, research suggests that growing up with pets may actually *help* children avoid allergies. But for those children who wind up with a legitimate cat allergy, there are a number of ways to manage the issue, from air filtration to allergy shots and many stops in between. Since this landscape is quickly changing (for the better), due diligence is your best friend.

Did you know? One study showed that exposure to multiple pets (cats or dogs) during the first year of a child's life could reduce the risk of responses to multiple allergens at the age of six or seven. A study of children who lived in urban areas (where they are at higher risk of respiratory disease) found that exposure to cat dander before one year of age was associated with fewer allergies when the children were reassessed at three years of age.

 ## Myth 3: My Cat Will Give Me or the Baby Toxoplasmosis

Due to the connection between toxoplasmosis and cats—and the misinformation about how the disease may be transmitted—many concerned parents feel it's too risky to have a cat in the home with a pregnant mother or an infant.

Backstory: Toxoplasmosis, and the danger it presents to fetuses, has always seemed to cause waves of panic in expectant couples. A few years ago, this panic hit a fever pitch when a scientist claimed he had evidence of links between toxoplasmosis and various mental disorders. Since then, two large-scale studies that followed people from birth to adulthood found no effect of toxoplasmosis or growing up with a cat on mental health.

Truth: What's the connection with cats? Typically, a cat eats an infected mouse or rat and the *Toxoplasmosis gondii* parasite lays eggs in his digestive tract, which spread to other animals via contact with the cat's poop.

T. gondii is a common parasite. Over 60 million humans in the United States alone are believed to be infected, but for most of those who have healthy immune systems, you'd never know it. For pregnant women (or those with compromised immune systems), toxoplasmosis *can* be a serious health threat, and since toxoplasmosis can cross the placenta from Mom to her in utero baby, prevention *is* paramount.

Did you know: Toxoplasmosis is so easy to prevent that *the Centers for Disease Control does not even consider being a cat guardian a risk factor for contracting it.* The biggest risks? Eating undercooked meat or unwashed vegetables.

What to do: Even with this minimal risk factor, here are a few more facts and precautionary tips:

- It takes one to five days for the eggs to become infectious after being shed in the cat's poop. If you scoop the litterbox every day, you don't have to worry about exposure.
- Cats shed toxoplasmosis eggs for only a few days in their entire life; it's one and done, further reducing your risks.
- To be extra safe, pregnant women should either not scoop the litterbox, or scoop daily while wearing disposable gloves.
- Indoor-only cats are rarely exposed to toxoplasmosis because they aren't likely to eat those infected rodents. This is yet another good reason to keep your cats indoors!

Myth 4: My Cat Will Be Jealous and Pee on the Baby's Stuff

When a cat pees in the nursery or on the baby's things, we humans often presume it's because the cat is jealous of the new addition and all of the attention that is being directed her way. Worse yet, many anticipate this behavior as part of a cat's "jealous nature," which then leads to unfortunate decisions being made to avoid such behavior.

Backstory: This is classic human projection, based on how human siblings sometimes respond to a newborn's arrival into the home. So when humans observe this kind of behavior from a cat, they presume it's because "the cat must be jealous of the newborn."

Truth: In almost every case I've worked on in which a cat peed on an infant's things, it was a territorial issue. Typically, when expectant parents prepare for their baby's homecoming, they set up a nursery (or special "nursery area"), and bring in new objects and furnishings. These adjustments are too often deemed "off limits" to the cat, a move that backfires completely. First, it constricts the cat's territory on two levels: by total volume, and by causing the cat's scent to disappear from the room she's been banished from. And then the anti–cherry on top is when the baby comes home and everything in the cat's daily routine changes, so that everything revolves around the room she's been banished from. A cat's ensuing reaction is a classic Napoleonic example of "overowning"—marking key places in the nursery as a highly insecure way of claiming ownership of an area that was taken from her.

What to do: There are plenty of proactive strategies you can employ before the baby comes home to minimize or prevent this kind of thing from happening. Most revolve around having a more cat-inclusive attitude regarding the nursery areas, and acclimating your cats in advance to some of the new sights, sounds, and smells that will be turning up in their territory. We will be discussing specifics later in this chapter, in "Prepare Your Cat for the New Baby."

Myth 5: My Cat Will Hurt the Baby

A lot of new parents are concerned that their cat will randomly attack their baby or younger child.

Truth: Cats don't "randomly" attack for no reason and, by and large, they don't attack offensively; they aren't going to make the first move, for example, and run at a target from across the room that they think at some point *might* be a threat. Remember—one of the things that has helped cats successfully endure as a species for this many thousands of years is that, as equal parts predator and prey, they are keenly aware of how *not* to pick a fight.

That said:

- Cats can attack in a *defensive* manner when they are cornered, if they feel their safety is threatened, or in a knee-jerk reaction to rough handling (tail pulling, etc.).
- Cats can also "respond" in a predatory or playful manner when their need for ample, energy-burning playtime (HCKE) has not been fulfilled, and there is something beckoning their hunter drive. In this case, wiggling toes under a blanket could be gleefully treated as a play target, just as much as your ankles would be as you stride across the living room floor.

What to Do: There are a few things that will help prevent these kinds of mishaps between cat and child. We'll cover these suggestions in more detail in this section, but for now, here are the essential CliffsNotes:

1. One of the first things your child should learn is empathy, respect, and proper "handling" of his feline family member. We cover this

in Do's and Don'ts a bit later in this section. Until he is old enough to learn these lessons, *proper supervision is an absolute must whenever the cat is in the proximity of the baby.*

2. Make sure your cat has a proper outlet for the draining of her energy. The last thing you want is for your Raw Cat to be amped up to ten, with her Energetic Balloon ready to pop, while hanging out with your child who, at that moment, is moving like prey. In this case, there is a more appropriate play victim—an interactive toy!

3. Try to plan cat/baby interactions when both parties are on the sleepy or mellow side. This is all about the Three Rs of your household and knowing when the energy levels are most favorable so the outcome can be positive for all parties.

THE BLUEPRINT FOR BEST FRIENDS

Our chance to build positive associations between children and cats starts before they ever meet—meaning, before your baby is even born. With every intertwining stage of human and animal parenting comes not only opportunities for enrichment and appreciation, but also significant potential roadblocks that need to be navigated. In this section, we'll map a course through the world of cats and kids; it begins with safe boundaries, continues with planting the seeds of cornerstone values—love, compassion, and empathy—and culminates with a thriving and mutually respectful day-to-day relationship.

BEFORE THE FIRST STEP:
BRINGING A BABY INTO A CAT'S HOME

Introducing a cat to a baby is in some ways similar to how we introduce cats to other furry family members. There are advance steps that can be taken along the way to get your cat acclimated to the new reality of a human sibling joining the family before it actually happens. And don't worry—I know you'll have a lot on your plate. Just know that whatever you can manage to do in advance will pay dividends in the transition process.

Step One: Make the Nursery a Junior Base Camp

I know it's probably the last thing you're thinking about as you set up a nursery while counting down the months to your new arrival, but I can't tell you how many problems you'll prevent by considering the needs of your cat as well as your baby. One of the best ways to initiate Cat Mojo here is to start thinking of the nursery (or designated "nursery area") as a junior base camp.

> A. **Scent Soakers:** Gather up any scent soakers you can find to put in the nursery so the cat and child can start mingling scents (along with yours). This doesn't have to mean a cat bed in the crib. However, putting a cat bed or cat tree on the same side of the room as the crib is a great big hunk of Mojo.

B. **Mealtime in the Nursery:** Stop free feeding (if you haven't already) and start feeding your cat meals in the nursery—their cozy new junior base camp!

C. **Cat Superhighway:** Consider providing a complete Cat Superhighway in the nursery. Once the baby has arrived, the cat is then able to get up in the vertical world, look down at the crib and changing station, and say, "Huh . . . is that what all the fuss is about? Is that what that strange sound is? So that's where that smell was coming from . . . interesting. . . ." All of the observations, as well as the learning of an alien language, are done at a safe distance.

Should I Keep the Cat Out of the Crib?

Some might think that there's a fine line between trying to keep the cat out of the crib and sending a tacit message that cat and baby shouldn't mingle. Not so! I encourage mingling (even in the crib). Mingling is a good thing that provides indelible moments of foundational relationship building. If you consider the big picture, these mingle moments are all profit and no loss as long as these visits are supervised.

That said, if you build a Cat Superhighway and have some other elevated space for your cat to traverse, the crib becomes *not* the most interesting place in the nursery for the cat to be, and *that's* a good thing. Of course, I'm not saying we will ever be able to eliminate the crib as a destination—it's soft, it's somewhat of a cocoon, and between the baby and the bedding, it's a nice warm spot—but with Catification on board, it won't be the *only* one. Conversely, if you have no cat furniture or vertical space to claim ownership of in the nursery, your cat will rightfully think that the crib is the new bed you got for *them*.

At the end of the day, though, it's about your comfort level, and it's your call on how you want to raise your baby and your cat. If you decide to say "no" to the cat being in the crib, bear in mind all I've said about the territorial importance of the nursery—and make sure to give the cat a "yes" somewhere else!

Step Two: Desensitize Your Cat to the Sounds and Scents of a Baby

Now that you've welcomed your cat into the nursery, it's time to introduce him to sounds and scents that are part of the baby package deal. We're going to use a well-known process known as *desensitization*—which is commonly used in human therapy to help people with fears and phobias. It works with our companion animals, too.

Desensitization is helping an animal become less sensitive to something that is potentially unpleasant (such as the sound of crying babies) through repeated exposure at a "safe level" that you gradually increase in intensity. The bonus technique is called *counterconditioning*, and that is when you change your cat's emotional response from potentially negative to positive by pairing that unpleasant something with things he likes, such as treats or play. Let's put it into action.

Sounds: Strange as it may seem, there are plenty of recordings of babies screaming, crying, gurgling, and laughing available online. It's a great idea to get your cat used to some of these sounds before the baby arrives. And here's an interesting little fact: regardless of species, most mammalian distress calls happen to be similar in pitch, which means that those baby cries might trigger an alarm response in your cat. In other words, desensitizing to these sounds is a classic "better safe than sorry" scenario!

- First, use a version of Eat Play Love to find your cat's Challenge Line, by playing the recording softly as you feed a meal or Jackpot! Treats. Or, if the cat is more play motivated, engage him with his favorite toy. Make sure your cat is absorbed in this activity, enough so that the sound is not a distraction.
- With each EPL session, creep the volume up, taking note as to when the primary activity starts to get clouded by distraction, anxiety, or fear. At what point do the cat's ears start to move, does the fur on his back begin to twitch, or does he begin to demonstrate any kind of tension, including looking around the room? Does he completely abandon ship from the activity, deciding that the risk he is exposing himself to is just too great?
- That fine line between comfort and challenge—in this case, the vol-

ume that begins to make your cat uncomfortable—is your cat's Challenge Line. Once you identify the Challenge Line, you can desensitize your cat to it, by turning the volume down, then slowly trying to inch it up again until your cat is desensitized to the sound. Then you can start again at a higher volume.

Scents: Expectant moms often know other moms. If you can bring home blankets or clothing that smell like a baby, even if they don't smell exactly like your baby will, you can introduce that very distinctive scent to your cat early on. Let your cat explore the blankets at his own pace. You can place treats nearby, but never force a cat to get close to the baby blankets. There is a school of thought that would have you actually rub the blankets on the cat as a way of introduction. Make no mistake—whatever school that is, it's not mine!

There's no way to guarantee that when you bring your cat and newborn together, your cat is going to be all unicorns and rainbows about it, but if he's allowed to *survey* the weird before attempting to interact with the weird, it will be, well, less weird.

Step Three: Three Rs—Before and After

We want to start co-constructing the Three Rs (Routines, Rituals, and Rhythm) around cat and baby, even before the baby shows up. In this case, you will go through an HCKE session (chapter 7) with your cat as you normally would. But the twist is this: *conclude the session by leading the cat into the nursery for mealtime.* This will reinforce positive associations with this "new" space, and also help to develop a seamless flow from the familiar territory of the house to the new or revamped territory of the nursery. This will also help to define the new routine, ritual, and rhythm of mealtime in the household once the baby shows up.

Why is this important to establish before the baby arrives? Sleep will be at a premium, and the pressures of caring for a newborn are momentous. If you don't actually build these concrete Three Rs in advance, you'll find yourself facing a slippery slope that unfortunately I've seen some of the most well-intentioned new parents slide down. It begins with exhaustion, then leads to less *integration* and more *separation*. Your cat, of course, responds to the separation negatively. If you restrict cats from that territory, they get insecure about it; if you let them in without the right preparation, they may pee on things or hiss at the child. So you might end up locking them out more, but now they're peeing everywhere else more. You have inadvertently broken down the bond between you and your cat. You can avoid this.

Building the Three Rs has a key focal point, just like the ones we build when introducing a new animal into the home: mealtime! Therefore, I recommend feeding the cat in the nursery when you're feeding your child. This gives you the invaluable opportunity to be as inclusive as possible; *as you build rituals around your baby, build your cat into those rituals.* While you're sitting in your rocking chair nursing your child, what better time to feed meals to your cat?

Bringing a Cat into a Child's Home

If you already have kids and you're thinking of adopting a cat (or two), there are a few things you can do to help ensure a successful relationship. You'll notice this process tends to be a bit simpler than bringing a new baby into a home where a cat is already established, since you're not having to "shake up" your cat's territorial certainty.

Choosing Your Cat

The Energy Match: When you're at the shelter, foster home, or rescue agency, try to match energy to energy, just like you would if you were bringing home a new cat for a resident cat. If your kids are younger and/or rambunctious and active—and you have lots of other kids visiting—look for a Mojito cat: perhaps a teen or adolescent who is ready for nonstop fun. They can be a great match for an active household.

History with Kids: A cat who has a positive history with kids would also be ideal, because then you'll know she isn't going to be overwhelmed by the hustle and bustle of a home with several kids running through it.

Older vs. Younger: An older cat may be better suited for a more mellow home, or or one with teenagers who are a bit more chill. While we are often drawn to kittens because they are so damn cute, just keep in mind that they are fragile, and need much more supervision, both for their own sake and for that of any small children.

Preparing for Your New Cat

Set Up Base Camp for Your New Arrival: As a family, you can plan out setting up that room, and what kinds of scent soakers you'd like to arrange for, etc.

Basic Catification: As mentioned earlier, your new cat will immediately see and evaluate her new home vertically. Make sure she has some "higher up" places to traverse, especially if there are some enthusiastic, high-energy children in the house from whom the cat might need to take a break!

Initial Introductions: Once you bring the new cat home and get her set up in base camp, let her settle in for a bit before meeting *anyone*. Then later, when introducing the cat to your family members, do it supervised and one at a time. If there are multiple children all seeking the cat's attention and getting excited about their new animal brother or sister, it will most definitely scare the newcomer, at the very least. It's never too early to exert control and help dictate the tone and tempo of their relationship.

THE NEXT STEP AFTER THE FIRST STEP: CATS AND TODDLERS (A.K.A. KIDZILLA)

One fascinating element of cat communication is the language expressed through spatial recognition and respect. This is why I spend so much time on the traffic flow element of Catification (chapter 8). Especially in the shared horizontal world (the floor), we see the dynamics of territorial co-ownership—one cat who hugs the wall yields power to another who gets the center lane of traffic, or they may time-share prized scent soakers and signposts and resources like beds that mark the movement of the sun throughout the house. It reminds us that every position is a potential move in Cat Chess; a lot of these moves are subtle, and not completely understood by us, but as cats pass each other in the most delicate of ballets, we know without a doubt that this language is written in the Raw Cat's DNA.

And then . . . Kidzilla enters the living room like it is downtown Tokyo, and turns the ballet into a mosh pit.

On average, babies take their first steps at between nine and eleven months, and by fifteen months they are fully cruising/toddling/walking/ wreaking havoc. In the carefully choreographed landscape of cat urban planning, there may be no disruptive force quite like Kidzilla. Why? Not just because of the unpredictable movements, nor the fact that he or she ignores all traffic signals, moving with gleeful abandon through the center of the room, cornering unsuspecting Wallflowers and thumbing a nose at overowning Napoleons. No, the true threat resides in the total lack of self-consciousness. Kidzillas don't know where they want to go. Really. They don't have the developmental skills to navigate left or right in a quasi-straight line or the communicative skills to back off if they terrify the four-legged family members. There is no adherence to the rules of Cat Chess. You know that look on your cat's face—the "Oh god . . . what is that?"

look—as she realizes there are no escape routes. Kidzilla is closing in, and the fight-or-flight alarm bells sound.

If you have not already invested in Catification, this is that moment. You should be measuring just how far up your child can reach, and then build your Cat Superhighway up from there. Your cats have to know that they have somewhere in the vertical territory that is safe.

As mentioned in the Myth Busting section of this chapter, cats are not naturally offensive; however, they may become *defensive* when their exit routes are cut off . . . which is to say that the only reason they'll "go after" the Kidzilla is because they perceive that Kidzilla is coming after them! Don't wait for this potentially explosive situation to happen; if you subscribe to proactive Catification before your baby is born—or just prior to bringing a new cat into a home with youngsters—you'll be in a much better place . . . and so will the cats.

Your ultimate goal at this age range is to have territory within the territory that belongs to the cat and gives the cat a childproof vantage point while giving the child a cat-proof vantage point.

Putting the Super in Supervised Visits

Good Catification will keep any inadvertent child/cat encounters to a minimum and, as discussed, provide your cat with a necessary escape route if need be. But what about some planned time for your child to interact with the cat, or vice versa? Three things:

1. When your child is in this toddler age range, it is imperative that all "official" interactions between child and cat be supervised. No exceptions, please!
2. It is best to plan for these supervised interactions at "lower-energy" times in the household, when both cat and child are at their mellowest. This might be after a play session with your cat, when his energy has been expended, and/or near bedtime or naptime for the child.

3. Touching, for children this age, is what they are all about. Remember, however, that their motor skills are not fully developed, nor is their sense of what may or may not hurt an animal. Supervision also means allowing them to pet with your hand guiding, so you can stop the hands from grabbing and pulling, and, in general, avoid a hiss and scratch response.

LITTERBOX ENLIGHTENMENT

 The second your child can toddle and you can lose track of him, you should be worried about him going into the litterbox. The box represents ground zero for the best- or worst-case scenario of cat/kid introductions simply because it is a primary destination for both partners in the dance. Of course, for cats, it is the epicenter of activity and identity; for Kidzilla, it's a playground. Watch out for the classic anti-Mojo move here, which is to reflexively think, "I definitely do not want my kid getting in the litterbox . . ." and off all the boxes go into territorial exile—the garage, the mudroom, the laundry room, or the unfinished basement where the child won't get to them. This, of course, violates one of my most sacred tenets when it comes to litterboxes and Catification; you wind up subtracting Mojo from the equation in the name of what *might* happen.

Another example of this Mojo subtraction is taking existing litterboxes, disguising them as something else, putting lids on them, and facing the opening of that box toward the wall in an attempt to dissuade your child from getting into them.

Hint: A decorative shoji screen can create a barrier to the box, or you can use a high-sided box with a small entryway cut in it. If you find yourself leaning toward the avoidance side of the coin, making baby-related "what if?" changes based on your aesthetic instead of on what will work best for cat and kid, remember: *payback is a bitch.*

On the toddler side of the coin: if your child is dying to play in the litterbox, give her other things to play with. Whether animal or human, the

No/Yes works for everyone. You don't want to remove the most important component of a cat's territory in the name of what might happen.

Cat Daddy Tip

You can use a baby gate, raised up eight or so inches off the floor, so at least you're not hiding the litterbox. That way, the cat can get underneath or over the gate, and your baby can't get through either way. There are also pet gates with cat doors in them, which get the job done with minimal guardian hurdles to jump.

One concession to be made on the feline side of this Catification conundrum: if the baby tends to play in the living room, maybe the litterbox should be in the bathroom or bedroom—rooms to which the baby won't make her way unsupervised. However, conundrums provide great opportunities to put your imagination to the test; for instance, although ordinarily you might think this an absurd idea, raising the litterbox off the ground is absolutely fine by most cats (if they are agile). If you can live with it, remember, it succeeds in keeping your cat Mojo-fied and your child out of the box.

The upshot of all this is that I don't have a hard and fast rule for this potential roadblock—because we are in the world of cat/kid compromise. Anything goes as long as you try to adhere to the rules of Catification, and keep your kids from seeing a litterbox as an engraved invitation.

For the cats' sake, all I'm asking you to do is not give up and make the litterboxes completely unappealing for the cats, or put them all in the garage . . . or the garbage.

THE THREE RS REMINDER

By now, your family will have fallen into a certain rise-and-fall pattern of energy cycles, based solely on the particulars of your household activities. As discussed in chapter 7, you will want to establish key rituals and routines with your kids and cat, and base them all on your home's natural energy spikes. This creates your unique home rhythm.

Earlier in this chapter, we described the routine and ritual of feeding the cat while feeding your baby in the nursery, to create a particular household rhythm. But as your child grows older, your Three Rs will evolve, and you'll find other ways of *intertwining* the various routines and rituals, so that your evolving family rhythm stays in sync. This will make all of your various "times"—mealtime, playtime, bedtime—rise, fall, and flow like a Beethoven symphony.

The last word on this topic: the making of all beautiful music requires the willingness to make hard choices. Whether it comes to the temptation to close off the nursery or access to litterboxes from your cat, I would encourage you to make the opposite choice; figure out what makes the choice risky, examine your hesitation or even fear . . . and run straight at it!

MATURING MOJO: EARLY CHILDHOOD AND THE CLOSING OF THE CAT GAP

Much of what the parental role is in the early years of cat/child relations falls somewhere between a diplomat and a referee. We are attempting to protect one from the inadvertent actions or reactions of the other, all while fostering a common respect and reverence between them. Once the child gets beyond the toddler years and is better able to take direction, we can begin to instill those key foundational, Mojo-building do's and don'ts that will set the two on a lifelong course as the best of friends.

ANIMALS ALSO FEEL EMOTIONS

Empathy and respect are two of the most prized Cat Mojo virtues that children could ever learn when it comes to their relationship with cats. At around the age of three or four, children are starting to put words to their own emotions. They can answer questions like "What does it feel like when you're scared or happy?" This is also the age when kids start to understand other people's emotions, too. They are beginning to understand that other individuals have their own thoughts and feelings (an ability known as theory of mind).

The more similar to herself your child can perceive your cat to be, the more accurately she can identify your cat's emotions. She won't be able to take it much further yet, but you can still help her draw parallels. For instance, you can ask, "When scary things happen sometimes, how do you feel?" and whatever the answer is, you can say, "And do you think that when scary things happen, Fluffy feels the same way?" Of course, discussing positive feelings works wonderfully, too. For instance, "How do you feel when we go ride the merry-go-round?" and, whatever the answer is, "Do you think Fluffy feels that way when we play with *her?*"

From there, you can use the same kind of dialogue to talk about comfort, love, and physical pain. These questions, and the way you guide your child's answers, are the roots of empathy and the cornerstones for deep relationships with animals down the road.

CAT DADDY DO'S

Model Compassionate Interaction

- First, use a stuffed animal to demonstrate how to handle a cat: explain that we don't pull the tail or ears, and that we pet *gently*. If your child is rough with the stuffed animal, ask him to pretend he is your cat, and to tell you how he thinks he would feel if someone treated him in such a rough manner.
- Next, teach your child how to let the cat "pet" him, and where most cats like being petted the most, which is usually around the cheeks (for more on this read about the Michelangelo technique on page 232).
- You should already know what kind of petting your cat appreciates, but with most young children, one-finger petting or petting with an open hand are safest. This is also a great time for kids to learn that most cats are not wild about repeated head-to-tail pets (which is not necessarily true for all cats, but avoiding this type of petting helps to avoid petting-induced overstimulation. May as well stay one step ahead of the game!)

Remember: You can't blame a young child for wanting to grab, and you can't blame a cat for wanting to get away. But a lot of cats get only one strike before they are out, so you can supervise, give direction, and model good behavior to help your child be more gentle with the cat.

Teach kids to always talk softly and gently to the kitty: No yelling or loud, excitable talking at, or around, the cat.

Teach proper language—your cat isn't an IT. I feel that this "do" is one of the most important because it addresses the big picture, and helps to cement what we hope to be the most compassionate generation in history. Hyperbole? No way! Internalizing the concept that an "IT" is a suitcase or a baseball, not an animal with a beating heart and emotions, will help tip the no-kill scales in our favor (and, of course, in favor of millions of cats). Plus, when it comes to the smaller picture, i.e., your cat, it will help her get treated in the way I've been discussing here. So, always refer to your cat by name or at least gender, and encourage your child to do the same.

CAT DADDY DON'TS

Never be rough—ever: No hitting, spanking, "patting," or backwards petting (against the direction of the cat's fur).

Respect the "personal space bubble": Don't disturb the cats when they are eating, sleeping, using the litterbox, cocooning, or in their vertical space.

Hands are not toys: It's never too early to teach this. We can't count how many cats wind up in shelters thinking hands are toys, and that ends up being a huge strike against them for getting adopted. Be consistent and use toys for play. Hands should be for holding the other end of an interactive toy—which is tons more fun than having your hand scratched up anyway, right?

Teaching Kids the Basics of Cat Body Language and Vocalizations

As I've been highlighting throughout, teaching kids to develop their own sense of empathy (just as you've done in becoming the Cat Mojo Toolbox) is a more organic process than just giving them a list of do's and don'ts. By tapping into their sense of how they would feel about and respond to certain situations, the talk about how to approach cats, and when *not* to approach them, becomes easier. For example, if the cat's tail is swishing, her eyes are big, or her ears are flat, these are all indications that she is not feeling especially sociable at the moment. A low growl, a moaning vocalization, and of course a hiss or a spit (whether it signals fear or agitation is inconsequential) are fair warning!

For more information, humaneeducation.org is a great resource.

MORE MOJO-BOOSTING IDEAS FOR KIDS

If you're wanting to get the kids more proactively involved with your cat's life, that's great! Here are a few ideas:

Things young kids can do with or for cats:

- Have your child help with feeding so that your cat associates him with great things.
- Your child can tend a cat garden; he can grow herbs such as parsley, sage, or catnip. Nowadays, there are plenty of easy-to-use kits available.
- Young children can play with the cat using an interactive toy once they have some motor control—but no earlier than that, because they can all too easily move a toy too fast and scare the cat (not to mention that a simple fishing pole toy can resemble a medieval weapon). That said, with parental supervision and guidance, interactive play can be a great way to engage both cat and kid, and can be an amazing educational tool about the nature of the Raw Cat.

CAN KIDS HELP TO TAKE CARE OF THE CAT?

A lot of parents want to teach their children responsibility by giving them chores related to taking care of a companion animal. It's great for children to understand the idea of being responsible for another's life, and the concept of guardianship and being a pet parent. We just have to keep in mind what is reasonable and what is setting them up for failure.

A child's level of responsibility for a cat's care depends on the parents. You should communicate with your children about what needs your cat has. Help them see that their needs and their cat's needs are not that different. Being a good friend to their animal means providing their cat with a clean bed and litterbox. Cats need food, water, a warm and dry place to stay, and an animal doctor to go to when they are sick.

Should a six-year-old be scooping a litterbox? It depends on the child. But generally you can at least have your child *assist you* with the food, water, and litterbox duties.

Again, day-to-day life provides plentiful and wonderful opportunities to reinforce empathy. Keep reminding your child that this is not simply a chore, but a way to show your cat how much you love him. After all, this is what a parent does; we demonstrate how much we love our family members by taking care of them, feeding them, keeping their rooms clean, etc.

BEST OF FRIENDS FOR A LIFETIME: YOUR ROLE IN THE MOJO

One of the reasons I loved telling you all about your Cat Mojo Toolbox in chapter 6 is that once the concept becomes more than a concept, once it is a part of you that you can call upon, it becomes a gift for others, and I don't just mean the animals in your life; the toolbox is a gift to be passed down to your kids.

Cultivating their own toolbox also makes it much simpler to reiterate one of the foundational points of Total Cat Mojo to your kids: *you are in a relationship with your cat.* So you are not providing them an education just on animals, but on the concept and nature of relationships. They learn how to listen with compassion and how to act toward another as if it matters to their own life. They will also be better grounded in the notion that the quality of relationships (with other humans or animals) will hinge largely on two things: how well you communicate with them, and how accurately you can interpret and better respond to what they're communicating to you.

In the case of our relationship with cats, this process can be uniquely complex, as it will involve both spoken and unspoken communication—*and*, let's not forget that the language being received is a completely foreign one. Spoken communication is (obviously) all about the words you use to communicate to your cat, and also about the words you use to *internally* define the various communications your cat is transmitting back to you. You might be tempted to think, "How could any of this matter? My cat doesn't know what I'm saying, let alone thinking." Aahhh, but *know*, they do.

Unspoken communication is more about the overall "vibe" you're projecting—body language, emotion, gestures—and what we often perceive to be the "harmless intangibles" we carry around in the presence of our beloved cat, not thinking they would even notice. Aahhh, but *notice*, they do.

In the case of both spoken and unspoken communication, there is an ongoing dialogue that you are having with your cat, around the clock, that she not only is aware of, but is often responding to. Therefore, the Total Cat Mojo factor in our relationship with our cat is largely on us.

In this next section, I will reveal a handful of the most important ideas that I've learned over the years that we can embrace, and actions we can take, to help ensure a thriving, long-term relationship with our feline family members.

HUMAN EMOTION AND BODY LANGUAGE

Cats feed off of human emotion, and this is largely displayed, subconsciously or otherwise, by body language. Cats will mirror your energy, and if that energy is frenetic, it takes just a single spark to set them off. For example, if you are fearful, tentative, hovering or hunching over them, cats will sense that you don't trust them. Or if you are supernervous when you are petting a cat and jerk your hands away, he might perceive this as prey running away, causing this simple, unconfident gesture to lead to a misunderstanding, and maybe even a bite or a swat.

So, how should you approach a cat you're either just getting to know or who is a bit skittish? First, put your fear aside; when guardians are confident, that positive energy feeds off of itself. It's all about energetics, and you need to come from a place of stillness and calm. Be a nonthreatening ambassador, and carry a friendly message, entering feline territory with quiet confidence. This is especially true in the face of Wallflowers or Napoleons, who are just looking for an excuse to either run away or make a power play.

Another way of saying this is that for the most part, the best way to approach a cat is just to ignore them. This is especially true with fearful cats. Back off, get low (meaning off your feet, not hovering over the top of them), and let them come to you. Have you ever thought about the fact that in a room full of people that cats have never met, it's not the ones who identify themselves as "cat people" that the cats are attracted to? It's the ones who are either allergic or who identify as "cat haters" or "dog people." Because, in not wanting anything to do with the cats, those humans have opened themselves up to being scoped out and explored by the cats, who, at the same time, are avoiding and dodging the hands and forward-leaning bodies of those who are busy trying to convince you that "ALL cats LOVE me!"

CAT GREETINGS

Let's take a closer look at the subtle art of the cat greeting, starting with one of my all-time favorites. This one will work anytime you meet a new cat, and also as a reliable way to communicate good Mojo to your own cat.

The Slow Blink (a.k.a. the "Cat I Love You")

Cat behaviorist and author of *The Natural Cat* Anitra Frazier learned, perfected, and wrote about a technique she called the "Cat I Love You," just by looking at cats in windows on the streets of New York. She observed that, when approaching, if she softened her face and gazed at the cats, the cats would slowly blink at her. She took this as a cue and began initiating this when approaching—and the cats, or at least the vast majority of them, would blink back. Using this discovery with her cat clients, many of whom were traumatized, anxious, aggressive, or flat-out untrusting and scared, she found that the blink was a Rosetta Stone, an "in" to the hieroglyphic nature of cat language.

So why is it called the "I Love You"? In my opinion, it's because this moment is rooted in demonstrating trust through vulnerability. Remember, cats are also prey animals, and slowly closing their eyes to you is not something they would naturally do. In the wild, it's in their wiring to "sleep with one eye open," 24/7. So to close their eyes to an "unknown entity," a potential aggressor, is the ultimate show of vulnerability, trust, and, therefore—in the language of the predatory world—love.

We humans can return that vulnerability by offering this reciprocal display of trust. When I do the Slow Blink to a cat client, especially a hyperaggressive one, I'm essentially saying, "You could scratch my eyes out right now, but I trust that you won't." I generally start with the Slow Blink as an initial greeting to a cat because I need to demonstrate, right off the bat, that I am truly vulnerable (which cats know; you just can't lie through your body language to a cat, any more than you can verbally lie to a polygraph machine). This demonstration of trust is key. (Conversely, staring into the eyes of a prey animal like a cat can elicit a fight-or-flight response—the last thing you want when you're trying to build trust and make friends.)

When practicing the Slow Blink, make sure you keep your eyes "soft" and simply *gaze*, as opposed to *stare*. There's a very subtle but very important distinction to make between gazing and staring. Go look in a mirror right now and try both. You'll notice that a gaze is light, relaxed, nonconfrontational, and will set up the trusting Slow Blink; a stare is uneasy, obtrusive, confrontational, and will possibly set up a claw to your face if it's a strange cat who is already feeling threatened. Focus on your cheek muscles, your jaw, even your neck and brow. Before meeting, if you are the least bit unconfident, try a progressive relaxation exercise in which, for instance, you raise your eyebrows to the ceiling, hold them there for a ten count, then release. Do that for all of the muscle groups from the shoulders up, and you should soon be in a place of physical neutrality.

Now try it with your cat: Gaze at her, soften your eyes, blink, and think, "I love you." "I" with eyes open, "Love," eyes closed, "You," eyes open. Wait for an eye blink back, or at least for her whiskers to go neutral. Even a partial return of the Slow Blink is a good sign. If you don't get a blink in return, look away or down, and try again.

Of course, some cats just don't return the blink, and for others, it's about proximity, and you may need to step back a few and try again. The point is, it's about learning a new language (for the human), so don't take it personally if you aren't getting the response you desire; at the very least, you both learn something very valuable about the other, and that "in," that Rosetta Stone, still exists between you.

Three-Step Handshake

Many years ago, I was thrown into a situation in which I had to kind of intuit what I call the Three-Step Handshake. I was working at an animal shelter, and a woman had just dropped off a young cat who had been hit by a car. She couldn't afford his treatment, and, honestly, it didn't seem like she wanted him anymore. When she handed his carrier off to me, I knew he was in pain and needed to be rushed to the vet clinic.

In case you can't see where this story is going, I ended up adopting this cat and, as I chronicled in my memoir, *Cat Daddy*, he basically saved my life. But my first face-to-face with Benny required me to think on my feet about how I was going to let this injured and terrified cat know that I was there to help him.

I think of this as being an ambassador to a foreign country that has been isolated from negotiations and trade. The citizens are suspicious and wary, and have every reason to be. The same was true for Benny. He had no reason to trust me, so I had to give him one.

As he was sizing up his situation (*"I'm in pain, strange human, I'm stuck in a box, trapped in a moving vehicle . . ."*), I was thinking about what I could bring to the table—a peace offering that would be more than just a truce between two countries to not bomb the crap out of each other. It had to say, "I carry a friendly message." I started with that Slow Blink, but I wanted to strengthen that message.

Knowing that scent is so important to cats getting to know each other,

I also tried offering Benny the earpiece of my glasses—something that smelled strongly and distinctly of me, and that I could present at a less-threatening distance. When he responded positively and rubbed into the earpiece, complementing my scent with his, I next offered my finger to that space above the bridge of his nose: the feline "third eye."

Bingo! He pushed his cheeks into my finger and just *relaxed* right into that touch. And that was the moment I knew that these three different techniques could be combined into the equivalent of a handshake that thaws a chilled relationship between two countries. This was my diplomatic gesture that made us allies.

So, to review, the Three-Step Handshake breaks down like this:

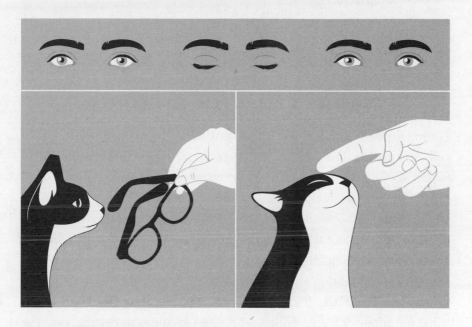

Step 1—The Slow Blink: Present yourself in a completely nonthreatening way to the cat.

Step 2—The Scent Offering: Offer the cat something that smells like you. I like to use the earpiece of my glasses or a pen.

Step 3—The One-Finger "Handshake": Offer your hand to the cat in a relaxed way. Take one finger and let the cat sniff it like he did the glasses or pen, and bring that finger toward the spot between and just above the eyes. Allow him to push into your finger; he will press in so you can gently rub his nose and up to the forehead (a more in-depth exploration of this technique in a moment).

Let Your Cat Call the Shots

One study looked at over 6,000 interactions between humans and their cats in 158 households. The interactions were categorized by whether the human approached the cat or the cat approached the human. When humans initiated contact with their cat, interactions were shorter. When cats were allowed to initiate the contact with their human, interactions lasted longer and were more positive.

TEACHER'S PET: A FEW GUIDELINES

Petting is one of those things I feel conflicted about when offering up a full-on tutorial. The act of petting is, to a degree, a very individual experience—an expression of the relationship you have with an individual cat. Still, approaching that experience with "Toolbox Thinking" will allow you to figure out soon enough how, where, and for how long your cat likes to be petted. I can't tell you how many times I've offered up universal "rules of engagement" like "Don't pet the belly!" only to be told in return that the cat in question absolutely *loves* it.

Just like the **Three-Step Handshake** and the **Slow Blink**, there are some techniques I always fall back on when it comes to petting a cat I've just met. I never want to make assumptions about where (or if) a cat wants to be touched. Here are my go-to guidelines:

1. The best introductions are made by asking, not telling. When a cat walks up to you, greeting him with a full head-to-tail stroke is just rude, and expecting entirely too much. Instead, I rely on the **Michelangelo (a.k.a. the Finger-Nose technique)**. I'll use this technique if I'm seated on a chair and a cat comes to explore me, or if I

encounter a cat while standing and he is in a vertical place (i.e., not on the ground). As the cat approaches, I will allow my hand to relax and, palm down, extend my pointer finger—not extended rigid, but relaxed, so that it almost seems to be coming off my hand like an upside-down "U." This presents the tip of my finger in a way that's similar to the way one cat might present his nose to another's. Touching noses is a universally friendly gesture between cats, so I'm just trying to let that greeting happen.

2. Whether I get the green light from the Michelangelo technique, or just initiate petting with a cat that I already know, the beginning of that session always begins with **Letting the Cat Pet You:** As soon as that "nose-to-nose touch" is accomplished, I straighten out my finger to provide just a little pressure to the touch. If the cat is feeling affectionate at this point, he will push the bridge of his nose into my finger. From there, he will give you direction—up toward the forehead, side toward the cheek. Just go where he tells you and you can't go wrong. It's all about listening!

3. The universal places I usually assume I can pet are: the cheeks, chin, and forehead. I see these as **Gateway Touches.** Gaining trust and eliciting a pleasurable response from these areas allow me to know if petting below the shoulder will also be a good thing for both of us.

4. The next technique is one I call the **Assisted Groom**. This is one I use once I've moved past some of the other more introductory moves, and there's a bit of trust inherent in my touch. Knowing that grooming is not only a built-in *need* but also a self-soother for a cat—something that, if she is feeling stressed or anxious, helps her calm down—I use my finger to simulate the action. Beyond just being plea-

surable, it really helps cement the bond between us. I'll start with al-most an extension move from Finger-Nose: the finger goes from nose to side of mouth/cheek. I will inevitably get some of the cat's saliva on my finger from that move from nose to tracing the mouth, so I will continue by taking that finger and tracing the bridge of the nose between the eyes and up to forehead to nape of neck. Many times when I present my finger initially doing the Michelangelo, the cat will lick my finger. Again, I will use that finger to spread her own scent around the areas that are already scent gland–heavy (cheek, forehead, etc.). Sure, it might sound a little . . . out of the ordinary? But try it and you'll see why I do it.

5. Another "advanced Mojo" move is **Hypno-Ear:** I call this advanced because, like the Assisted Groom, there's a measure of trust that needs to be gained before attempting it. I call this "hypno" because if done right, it absolutely gets the cat into a bit of a zombie-fied state. All it involves is a circular massage with the thumb on the in-side and finger on the outside of the ear. The top two-thirds of the ear is definitely the most sensitive part. In terms of the exact spot and speed of the circles, as always, it comes down to the individual. I can say, though, that the pressure is not tickle-light, but rather a medium pressure.

We would be doing cats a disservice if we said that *all* cats like to be petted in certain areas, or hate certain types of petting, so get to know *your* cat's preferences. Once you do, the main thing you'll need to concern yourself with is whether or not your cat is prone to overstimulation.

Overstimulation is a form of aggression that occurs when your cat passes a threshold for interaction. Petting-induced overstimulation is the most common form, although sounds and pain, and just general energetic chaos, can also take your cat over the edge.

RECOGNIZING, PREVENTING, AND MANAGING OVERSTIMULATION

I know I'm about to date myself here, but do you remember the commercials with the Tootsie Pop owl? He conducts a highly scientific test to find out how many licks it takes to get to the center of a Tootsie Pop? (One . . . two . . . three . . . CRUNCH!) Similarly, you'll want to take a sort of petting inventory to see if your cat is an "overstimulator." Of course, it would be a whole lot better if you could determine your cat's threshold before the "CRUNCH"—which, in this case, would probably be a swipe or bite to your hand. Here are a few suggestions for navigating overstimulation:

Recognizing Symptoms

Since cats who get overstimulated tend to have their own unique recipe for what causes it, your astute observation will be key here. Here are a few "tell-tail" signs (sorry, couldn't help myself). Much of the time, these types of behavior are somewhat out of character for your cat.

- Dilated pupils
- Piloerection (hairs on end)
- Ears back
- Quick head turns
- Licking, rubbing, or other affection that becomes too exuberant
- Tail swishing—usually means that the Energetic Balloon is ready to pop. As the tail goes from an intermittent twitch to a swish, things are increasing in intensity. Unchecked, this behavior will finally graduate to wagging like a happy dog . . . except they are not dogs, and they are definitely not happy! At this point—right before the pop—it's like your cat is screaming at you.
- Back Lightning is a type of twitching that happens through their back that is, at least partially, a spasm, but also a way of getting that energy out. You may notice your cat walking across the room, then suddenly stopping as if a fly just landed on him, and then very deliberately grooming himself. This self-soother is also a self-regulator.

It's also a reliable indicator to you that your cat's energy tank is just about topped off.

Preventing the "Blowup"

Be aware of energy in—For some cats, petting is air into the Energetic Balloon in a way that is intolerable. Energy in without any means of release fills them with a sort of static . . . and then finally . . . bang! What might feel good for three to thirty seconds suddenly feels like it's going to make their balloon pop. That hiss, that bite, their turning on you, running away, or self-grooming are all desperate attempts to let air out of the balloon. Think of these behaviors as engaging a sort of safety valve in the balloon. Be aware! For other cats, extreme enjoyment may actually trigger overstimulation—especially if you're petting in an energetic way, with heavier than normal pressure or faster than normal tempo. You might notice the cat bringing her tail up to meet your hand in an equally excited way.

Take an inventory—Note what happens when you touch certain areas of your cat's body. Try stroking the tail alone, then a full-body, head-to-tail stroke. Now a belly touch, handling paws, head, cheeks, and shoulders. Note the difference between petting once, twice, three times. How many full-body strokes can you give your cat before you tend to incite overstimulation? And most important, if your cat gets overstimulated, what was the obvious thing that caused it, the straw that broke the camel's back?

It's sometimes hard to think of ending your petting session because it's obvious that the cat is enjoying herself, but you are tempting the Tootsie Pop CRUNCH! If you are mindful of these changes and notice these signs and stop, the aggression—which we tend to call an "attack"—simply won't happen.

Managing Energy

Try to regulate your cat's daily energy intake/output. By your practicing HCKE, he should be more relaxed when he is finally on your lap. If the Energetic Balloon has been active all day (meaning in a state of inflation-deflation that you or the environment controls), then the stimulation-o-meter will average about a four out of ten. It stands to reason that getting him to be at a six instead of a nine on that meter during a petting session will save you an unpleasant encounter. Not to take the cat's side (well, actually, yeah, that's what I'm doing), the popping of the balloon is on you. Energy buildup–related outbursts are nothing you can really justify being mad about because you can learn to anticipate and prevent them.

Cat Nerd Corner

Why Do Cats Overstimulate?

One theme that we've discussed at length is how nature has not missed a trick when it comes to the gifts of survival bestowed upon the Raw Cat. One such feature is the incredibly sensitive touch receptors all over the cat's body. These receptors detect direct pressure, air movement, temperature, and pain, and they transmit information about the environment to the brain.

There are two key types of touch receptors: Rapidly Adapting (RA) and Slowly Adapting (SA). RA receptors respond to displacement of skin and hair in the moment it happens (and also register the immediate pleasure of touch), but SA receptors continue to fire as long as they are being stimulated, are particularly sensitive to petting, and are mostly responsible for that "I've had enough!" reaction. Some SA units are more common on the lower part of the body, where most cats are particularly sensitive to petting.

As predator and prey, the Raw Cat needs to be sensitive. But for his alter ego, the housecat, that survival tool can become a nuisance. We ask cats to handle a lot of touch because we enjoy petting them. Does this mean that your cat shouldn't ever be petted? Of course not! Armed with this info about how and why cats respond to touch, you should realize that more times than not, that "Don't touch me!" vibe is a product of physiology, not a choice—which is to say, see it as an "aha!" moment and not a "my cat hates me" moment!

WORDS MATTER

Thus far, we've talked a lot about body language, and the particulars of how you might greet or interact with your cat physically. Now, let's turn our attention to what's going on between the lines and beyond the physical realm. What are you saying about your cat, both in front of him and otherwise? What words do you use to describe him and his actions?

The words we use are labels that shape how we see the world. They can also be like loaded weapons. When we use words like "attack," "aggression," "random," "mean," and "vicious," we're assigning intention and/or deeper meaning, inaccurate or exaggerated as it may be, to a behavior or action.

Speaking from my experience, specifically with "problem" cats in their homes, I'd say close to 90 percent of the time I'm at least partially dealing with a problem of perception, and the language used around that perception: "My cat is *attacking* me *viciously*" or "*randomly*." I'm not saying that the description isn't sometimes accurate, but by and large, it's just chatter. What may seem to my clients to be just words are, to me, poisoning the well of their relationship with their cat as well as being poison *to the cat*. These kinds of words suggest that your cat is a stranger to you, creating a wall between you. But I've heard them used over and over again for minor offenses like ankle nipping, even in cases where skin isn't broken . . . and even when no direct contact has been made, for that matter!

But the poison doesn't end there. When you nonchalantly say things like "he hates me" or "he's the devil incarnate," it paints your cat in a way that can't be unpainted. When you name your cat "Devil Kitty," "Bastard Cat," or "Satan," please, do us all a favor—especially your cat—and change his name to something more dignified . . . or at least a name you would bestow upon a human. Whatever your justification might be, it's not a valid reason for such a negative label. It's an unnecessary form of devaluing him that will conspire, on one level or another, to weaken your relationship.

Remember . . . if you say he viciously attacks, then that's what he does. If you say he's a bastard, that's what he is. Labels can hurt, and tone can crush. Cats may not understand English, but they certainly understand tone. The words we use reflect and influence the way we feel about something, but they also convey feeling and nuance—often hurtful—to our loved ones, even when we are not aware of it. This applies ten times as much to your cat. So, if you want to keep your home environment Mojofied at all times, you must remain mindful of the words you use around your cat—both spoken and unspoken.

The Kitty Curse Jar Concept

If you've gotten in the habit of directing ugly language at your cat, here's a solution: establish a designated "kitty curse jar." Then, every time you or someone else calls your cat something like "evil," "devil," or "bastard"—put a dollar in it. Do it for a few weeks, and you'll quickly become aware of how you talk about your cat and see how it can all add up.

Cat Daddy Tip: Oh, and what do you do with the money? Buy your cat a new toy, of course!

PROJECTION

Say you're having a rough day: You wake up and immediately get into a fight with your significant other; you get a speeding ticket on your way to work; your boss yells at you; then you drop your lunch in your lap. Finally, you get home, exhausted, humiliated, and with salad-dressing pants—and the first thing you see is your cat sitting there, just staring at you. All of a sudden, that frantic inner dialogue kicks in and you're like: "What? What did I do? What is wrong with you? I put a roof over your head and cuddle you and this is what I get in return? Well, screw you."

The problem is, you are attempting to make an objective judgment call about what your cat is thinking from an extremely nonobjective place. We call this **Projection**. In psychology, the term is used to describe the tendency to take our own feelings, insecurities, impulses, or anger and ascribe them to others. In the above story, you were projecting your own negative feelings onto your cat, who you think suddenly hates you.

Cats, in particular, are ripe for human projection, because people often find them "hard to read." For this reason, they become a blank canvas for us to scribble our manic ramblings on . . . untrue as they may be. That feline tabula rasa becomes a litany of revenge-seeking, masterminding plots on all imagined human wrongdoings. And projection doesn't even have to come from a place of anger or frustration. Sometimes we think that because *we* want something—like privacy when we're going to the bathroom—that our cats must want it, too. Again, not true.

As a result of projection, you can circle down this drain fast and often, and it is purely a result of not understanding cat life, body language, or Mojo. If you keep going down that drain, however, you will continue to unnecessarily degrade your relationship with your cat. Let's not go there.

As we approach the end of this section, I'm hopeful that the Cat Mojo Toolbox system has addressed almost any question or challenge you might have imagined—from the ground up. Moving forward, you'll need a system in place to maintain the Mojo, so that you can resolve any issues either before they happen or just after they do. This leads us to . . .

CAT DETECTIVISM

Part of the reason I've been successful at walking into someone's home and solving cat problems for them is because I don't live there. I'm like a detective; I come in, observant and impartial, and I assess a problem. I'm not entwined in the story line, or any drama, projections, or heavy emotions thereof.

Example: Your cat has been peeing in your new boyfriend's gym bag every night he stays over. You presume your cat is saying "I. Hate. *Him.*" But to me, pee anywhere is your cat saying "I'm anxious about my territory." As impossible as it may seem in the moment, there's no need to take it personally or create a big scene around it. That's called *living in the story.* Instead, we investigate the particulars of the how, why, where, and when, and try to resolve the issue. As Joe Friday in *Dragnet* would always say, "Just the facts, ma'am." I call this Cat Detectivism.

The art of detached observation will get you through a lifetime of living with your cat successfully. As humans, we don't have a decent frame of reference for what it is like to be a cat. We can't pretend we do. I'm not saying you have to be completely detached from a being you love and have a relationship with, but, for their sake, you can damn well do your best.

This is the cardinal rule of Cat Detectivism: you take the *actual* temperature in the room, not the exaggerated version. If you walk into the house and see a spot of pee, I need you to recognize it as urine—nothing more—then clean it up, forgive, and move on. This will enable you to notice, manage, and diagnose any issue much quicker. Just remember to forgive and move on. Take heightened emotions out of the equation. *Forgive and move on.* It's a hell of a lot easier to hot-wire a car when it's not already running. (Not that I would know.)

With the cardinal rule understood, here are a few more guidelines for Cat Detectivism:

1. Simply describe or write down what happened in the "just the facts" style that a reporter might: "It was four o'clock in the morning, I woke up, he was sitting on my chest, I did this, he did that. . . ."

2. If you are talking about urine issues, your best friend is a UV flashlight, otherwise known as a black light. You've probably seen it in detective TV shows like *CSI* as an invaluable tool to illuminate blood at crime scenes—not only to pinpoint placement, but the actual spatter, the shape of the stain. This tool is just as invaluable when dealing with urine as with blood. Simply wait till sundown when you can darken the space, and go for it. In many cases, sorry to say, you will probably find more stains than you thought existed. For the sake of Detectivism, record that shape. For instance, little drops can signify a urinary tract infection, while marks that start vertically on furniture or the wall and pool down at the floor tell you most likely it is territorial marking (more on this in section 4).

   Also, consider the color of the stain under the light. The darker the stain, the fresher it is. As it fades, it signifies that you've either attempted to clean it before, or it is just older. Time breaks down the protein strands of the urine, and with that comes a lighter color. Unfortunately, since cat urine is, in part, designed to permanently mark a surface even after it is completely cleaned, there will be a white "stain" under the black light (and only under the black light, not perceptible to the naked eye) since it broke down the color strands of the rug as well.

3. When describing the incident, remove any part that has a qualitative element. If you say he "viciously attacked you" when, in reality, he lightly bit or scratched in response to something like overstimulation, well, now we have some shoddy reporting gumming up the works. I've even heard the word "attack" ascribed to perceived intent; the guardian felt that an attack was about to happen. This level of interpretation clearly has no part to play in Detectivism. As we covered earlier, cats don't behave out of spite (or at least not our anthropomorphized definition of it). And as we covered earlier—words matter. Step away from heightened, sensationalized, or conclusive language. Remember, we're still just gathering facts here.

4. Knowing everything you now know about the Raw Cat, prepare a checklist of anything that could be Mojo threatening. The checklist should address these questions: What raised your cat's anxiety? What is threatening your cat's Mojo? Was there fighting? Did you run out of her favorite food? Is the carrier out? Your suitcases? Were there visitors, or outside cats?

5. Prepare yourself to be patient. Trust the process, because rushing things usually backfires. There are no deadlines or schedules—it just doesn't work that way. *No matter how hard you try to control the clock, cat problems run on cat time, not human time.*

Try to be informed by the behaviors you observe. Think in terms of stress and anxiety, and log behaviors, look for patterns, and write down details. Nothing is random and nothing is personal. All problematic behaviors are rooted in fear, anxiety, and pain, or some combination thereof.

Superdeluxe Cat Detectivism: The Anti-Treasure Map

Cat Detectivism is a great place to use the **Mojo Map** I introduced in chapter 8. The Mojo Map now becomes the **Anti-Treasure Map,** where Xs mark the spot where any incidences of unwanted behavior occurred. Whether we are talking about litterbox issues, aggression, or what have you, just slap an "X" on the exact location where it happened. And when I say exact, I mean it: which side of the couch, in front or behind, on the left or right of the front right leg. . . . For a good detective, the devil is in the details.

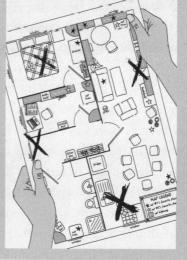

Also, add a key, of sorts, to your Mojo Map: for each incident, assign the X (or colored star sticker) a number. On the side of the map, record "Just the facts, ma'am." Time and date, any behaviors you observed before or after, and how close it was to mealtime or any other energy spikes of your home. Using all of the techniques I listed in this section, observe and record. Stick with detached observation, put it down on your map, and build your case. If you have ruled out medical causes for the behavior, I can almost guarantee that if you just gather the Xs for a number of days or weeks, remain detached and just gather information, the Anti-Treasure Map will emerge as Xs mark not just the spots but the patterns. You will see that random acts are anything but.

PREEMPTIVE CAT DETECTIVISM

If I went on TV screaming like the ShamWow guy that there were indelible tip-offs, little shortcuts I could give you in body language—gait, ear position, sleeping or eating patterns—that could predict destructive incidents of peeing or aggression in your cat . . . you might be tempted to grab the bait. After all, most folks see their cat as a collection of symptoms, a four-legged math equation that has a universal solution. Too bad such is not the case. You now know that, through the *art* of detachment, and the *science* of observation, you can begin to really understand the unique how, why, where, and when behind what makes your cat do what he sometimes does.

Earlier on, I made it a point that a good detective isn't entwined in the story line that he enters into. It's crucial to understand, however, that *the story* matters only insofar as it furthers your ability to tell *the real story*. Nothing, in the context of your case, happens in a vacuum; that is to say, use what you know in terms of the story of your cat as only you know it— her physical history, her life before she got to live with you (if you're fortunate enough to have that information), and the story of traumas she's endured and how she moved through that trauma. With that information, you can apply it to the present moment in the same way a detective could be interviewing either victim, suspect, or witness, and notice that as the person is telling a story he is tapping his foot and starting to sweat. Your unique perspective on your cat's life with and before you gives you incredible insights on her present, unusual behavior.

Finally, the next level to aspire to—and much of what we'll be covering in the final chapters—is the preemptive side of Cat Detectivism. This has to do with what we can do to circumvent or avoid certain anti-Mojo behaviors or actions. The thing is, it's actually much easier to bring a heightened sense of awareness to the behavior that a cat would exhibit *before she acts out.* This is an essential mindfulness tool to have on board, because sometimes Cat Detectivism isn't about saving your carpet from urine—it's about saving your cat's life.

A CRY FOR HELP: THE CAT DADDY RED FLAGS

The Raw Cat is *always* on guard—that's life smack in the middle of the food chain. There's always a hunt to be had and always a chance that she may be hunted. For this reason, the very last thing cats can do is show pain. Pain equals vulnerability, and predators can smell what they perceive to be weakness.

Your cat carries that stoic nature with her, along with most of the rest of her ancestor's survival tactics. That's why we have to keep an eagle eye out for behavioral changes that may signify physical challenges emerging.

The following list of behavioral red flags is by no means comprehensive, but most have presented themselves to me either in the context of my work or with my own cats. When approaching litterbox issues, for example, I often talk about the concept of cats "raising the yellow flag." What I'm reminding you of there is that while we are running around, postulating, theorizing, and throwing all kinds of behavioral spaghetti against the wall, seeing what will stick, the cat is actually saying "OUCH!" The upshot is, if you see something out of place, either visually, behaviorally, or just on a gut level, go to the vet.

Living on the fridge or under the bed: This is a sign that something in the environment is threatening. As I mentioned, the Raw Cat, feeling vulnerable because of pain or illness, would also choose to hide or withdraw.

Urinating or defecating outside of the litterbox: There are lots of possible medical reasons, including cystitis, crystals, infection, kidney disease, digestive problems, diabetes, and the list goes on. Two clues to look for that usually signify a physical component: eliminating directly outside the litterbox, sometimes by inches, and very small amounts of pee spread out by a matter of steps.

Chewing on things that aren't food: See chapter 17 for more on *Pica*, or the eating of nonfood items.

Changes in behavior, such as sudden-onset aggression: If a person in your life suddenly had a radical change in personality, you would be concerned. If your cat is suddenly lashing out—either toward human or animal family members—there's a solid chance that, just like us, he's got a shorter fuse because he's dealing with pain or discomfort of some sort.

Nighttime activity or an increase in vocalizations: Hyperthyroidism is a common medical condition in older cats that can increase activity and vocalization. Older cats who are experiencing worsening vision, hearing, or the onset of dementia may also become loud or disoriented at night when the lights go out.

Itching, scratching, self-biting, or grooming to the point of baldness or irritation: We've already discussed the incredibly sensitive skin of our cats. The potential causes of these symptoms can be frustratingly wide: allergies (food, inhalant, environmental), a skin problem or a flea infestation, or even escalating stress in the home that manifests in overgrooming.

Excessive sleeping: You now know that cats don't just sleep all the time. If your cat has become completely withdrawn or lost interest in all of the things, people, or activities that once gave her joy, that is a cry for help—just as it would be for a human.

12

Whose Line Is It Anyway?

Cat Parenting and the Human Challenge Line

IT'S ALMOST A cliché at this point to sum up our relationship with our animal companions by calling them our best friends. As a matter of fact, it's pretty hard to sum up the relationship in words, period. This brings to mind one of the most asked questions I receive about cats: "Why does my cat bring me half-eaten prey? Is it a gift of some sort? If so, by the way, can I bring it back?" Of course, just like any other most-asked question, there are multiple explanations and theories why—but that's not the point. I've always been fascinated by the gesture because I see it as being distinctly, yet frustratingly, double-headed.

First, yes, it seems like a "gift," almost like a child presenting you with a macaroni-and-glue portrait he made of you in his second-grade art class. But there's another side, based on what we know about cats: it can also be a meal. Mama cat returning to her litter with "test food" to encourage her young away from the nipple, and to get a taste of what they should be doing on their own. In other words, that simple gesture is both child-to-parent and parent-to-child. Which is to say, relationships are complicated, and each party may have multiple roles. Even in giving them meaning beneath their labels—best friend, guardian, parent—the label you choose matters less than the effort, sacrifice, and vulnerability shown to put your money where your relational mouth is.

Here's the thing—in the examples we detail throughout this chapter, it will become obvious that your cats don't always need a best friend; they need a parent. And you have to be cool with the knowledge that many times, the parent will not be the most popular person in the room.

I've spent much time asking you to follow me into the deeper waters of the heart, to take personal risk for the sake of building real relationships, to leave the concept of cat ownership behind and embrace the risk and reward of cat parenting. So here we are in the aforementioned deeper waters facing a problem—us. It's one thing to live the greeting card *ideal* of cat parenting, and another to live the Mojo-inspiring *life* of a cat parent. In this chapter, I hope to guide you more fully to the side where the Mojo waters run the deepest.

In chapter 9, we talked about our role in helping our cats cross key Challenge Lines, so they can enjoy a better quality of life. And we likened this experience to helping our human children across Challenge Lines by "making" them do things (like go to school, even if they're initially afraid to), all in the name of their personal growth. Now *it's time for us humans to cross a few Challenge Lines*, particularly when our personal apprehensions overshadow the best interests of our beloved cat children.

Besides, it's just the right thing to do. Perhaps you've never figured out how to get your cat into a carrier because you think she hates it so much. But what if you had a real emergency go down tomorrow and had to get her out of your home in a hurry? Or maybe the idea of medicating your cat freaks you out because you think it would freak her out to have you slip a pill down her throat every day. But if that pill ultimately meant the difference between health and sickness, or maybe even life or death, you would have to get it done, wouldn't you?

Instead of avoiding those things that cats don't like, and, by extension, we don't like, let's find a way to deal with them anyway. And I'm not just talking about the how-to mechanics of the dreaded activity. It's also about how you approach these procedures in order not to create bad associations for both you and your cat. And if this seems too daunting, take heart: even under these most trying conditions, there are ways to "mitigate the misery and maximize the Mojo."

LOVING TOO MUCH: BEATING OBESITY

One of the challenges with feline obesity is that we contribute to it. So many of us grew up in "food equals love" homes, so it's understandable that we would pass that feeling on. It pains us to deny our animal companions excessive amounts of junk food treats we know they love, so we put it squarely in our "unpleasantries" category. But if this food is destroying their health, denying them these excessive amounts is exactly what we must do.

Companion animal obesity even parallels the human obesity crisis, with recent data suggesting similar increases in the prevalence of obesity and type 2 diabetes in children, cats, and dogs. If that fact gives you pause, consider the following:

- As of the writing of this book, over 58 percent of cats are overweight, with some 15 percent of cats qualifying as obese. That means, according to the Association of Pet Obesity Prevention, that "80 million U.S. dogs and cats are at increased risk for weight-related disorders such as diabetes, osteoarthritis, hypertension, and many cancers."
- The number of overweight to obese cats and dogs has roughly doubled in the past twenty years.
- Obesity causes wear and tear on a cat's joints, which can lead to pain, irritability, and stiffness. I've seen a direct and repeated correlation between obesity and behavior problems like litterbox avoidance. Because carrying all that extra weight is so uncomfortable, and squatting in or getting in or out of the box hurts, these cats have a negative association with the location. Likewise, obesity leads to a reduction in prey-based exercise because it is just too painful an operation. This inactivity continues a vicious cycle of weight gain, unless we interrupt that pattern.
- Overweight cats have difficulty grooming themselves, which is unpleasant for cat and human alike.

As you can see, folks, feline obesity is an all-out epidemic, but it doesn't have to be that way. Here's what you can do to help:

1) Stop free feeding your cats, and stop feeding your cats junk, especially dry food. They should be eating scheduled, bio-appropriate meat-based meals (that means a raw diet or at least a grain-free wet diet).

2) Use slow feeding bowls and/or food puzzles to prevent them from scarfing. Just like humans, cats need a minute to register that they are full, and that can only happen if they are eating at a reasonable pace.

3) Don't forget about HCKE. Play, in conjunction with the tips above, will absolutely help get your cats to that optimal weight. They'll be happier, and because they are healthier and around longer, you'll be happier, too.

And as for the notion that you might fall out of favor with your cat once you put the kibosh on all of the junk food, consider this: A recent study surveyed guardians who had placed their cats on a sensible eating plan. Almost all of the cats lost weight, and most cats became *more* affectionate to their guardians, getting in their laps more, and purring more. So lest you think that restricting your cat's food will make him upset with you, it turns out the opposite is true.

DON'T FRET THE VET

Cat guardians generally take their cats to the vet *half as much as dog guardians*. Not only does it end up costing them more, but there are so many diseases that can be taken care of if found early: kidney disease, diabetes, dental disease, eyesight loss, hyperthyroidism, and heart problems. These are all treatable or manageable, but the earlier you know, the easier it will be. At the very least, you should be running a senior blood panel once a year in your healthy adult cat.

Sounds logical, right? So if you're not doing this, what's the holdup? Probably it's because the whole process of going to the vet is an ordeal for both you and your cat—on every level. I've known an unbelievable number of cats throughout the years who had never been to the vet, period. Not once. And we are talking ten-year-old cats! Basically, it's not until I call the guardians on their folly that these cats finally see the inside of a vet clinic for the first time since they were spayed or neutered—yet another example of how the "unpleasantries" can take avoidance to a new level. So how can you get on the other side of this?

First, consider the destination: your vet's office. Knowing what might set your cat off in terms of his or her surroundings, certain offices might be more stressful by nature. So go and visit a few in your area. Is the environment there loud or calm? What kind of ratio of dogs vs. cats do they generally have? Are there separate entrances for dogs and cats? A true litmus test is when you bring up concerns about your cat's anxiety to the staff. Are they responsive? Do they seem as if they genuinely care? I've had the pleasure of working with many a vet who, knowing that my cat is nervous, hustles us through the waiting room and into an exam room to avoid the stimulation. The point is, you don't have to settle. You have lots of options these days, so do your due diligence.

So we've talked about the destination. Next, we have one of the most dreaded elements of vet visits, the double whammy of the journey: getting your cat there, and getting her into a carrier.

CARRIERS CAN BE A CAT'S BEST FRIEND

Over half of all cats aren't making it to the vet for a yearly exam. And over a third of cat guardians get stressed out just *thinking* about taking their cat

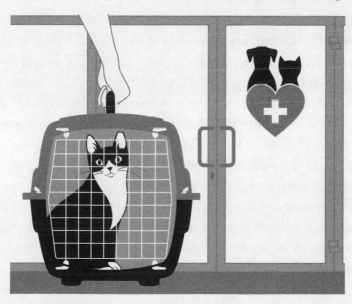

to the vet. The main reason your cat doesn't like the cat carrier is because every association they have had with that box has been negative. Think about it this way: What if, as a child, you had two cars in the garage. One car, a red convertible, was used every day to take you to school, friends' houses, the movies, etc., while the other car, a yellow station wagon, was used only to take you to the dentist. After this had happened to you enough times, you made the association. So, all your mom had to do was grab the keys for the station wagon and WHAM—racing pulse, sweaty palms, and a deep sense of foreboding took over you. To put it gently, you would do anything in your power to keep your butt out of the backseat of that damned yellow death sentence. This is how many if not most cats perceive their carrier. So what do we do? We change the station wagon into the convertible, of course!

First, we need to change the carrier from a place of dread and fear to a destination, a portable base camp.

1. Start by taking the carrier apart. Part of what will help undo the association is if it no longer resembles the yellow station wagon. Use the bottom part as a starting point, and turn the carrier into a cocoon. Make it cozy with some bedding that contains the scent of both your cat and you.

2. Use treats to make that cocoon even more inviting. Give your cat a treat for any curiosity around the carrier, even if she just gives it a sniff. Remember the concept of the "Jackpot!" Treats? Now is that time. While training your cat to love her new den, break out the Jackpots. Break them out *only* around the carrier. Even better, get your cat eating her meals in the carrier. It may take a few times, moving the bowl closer and closer to her new favorite place, so have patience and push that Challenge Line every day!

3. Once there is a sense of predictability in terms of your cat using the carrier not just to eat treats but to hang out, even for small periods, it's time to begin the reconstruction. First the top—use the same techniques to reinforce the continued positive association. Then the door. Then close the door for short periods. Many cats are triggered simply by the sound of the latch closing. In that case, start

with the latch taped open and then gradually desensitize. If you can get to the point where you can feed dinner with the door closed, the yellow station wagon is officially a red convertible!

4. Again, staying consistent with the association techniques that have worked best for you, pick up the carrier with the door closed (and of course the cat inside!). Don't even go to the car the first time. Close the carrier with your cat inside, and go outside for thirty seconds. Then go back in, open the carrier, put some treats inside, and let your cat try to figure out what the heck just happened. Hint: good stuff!

5. The next step would be a short car ride, just around the block. Rinse and repeat. Make sure every trip—whether short or long, whether a purely positive experience or somewhat challenging— ends with Jackpot!

What are we doing? We are showing your cat that being in the carrier doesn't always mean something monumentally bad happens. Being in the car doesn't always mean getting a shot or sharing a lobby with a growing number of other cats and dogs. The carrier is not the enemy. And if your cat gets in a carrier fifty times, but only one of those times he goes to the vet—not bad.

THE MARY POPPINS ASPIRATION

Whether we are discussing topics like bringing your cat to the vet, putting him in a carrier, giving him medication, trimming his nails, leaving him when you go to work, feeding him meals instead of free feeding, etc., they all have an emotional connective tissue—guilt. And this guilt is centered on the unbearable notion that WE are the reason our cat is miserable, that we are causing him pain (even if that pain is momentary).

Even if our avoidance of these "unpleasantries" would eventually spell increased misery for our cats, subconsciously we still sweep it under the rug. The Challenge Line suddenly emerging in this moment is *yours*. The paralyzing guilt that accompanies these tasks becomes the line you must cross if you want to be the most Mojo-rific cat parent you can be. (Hey, this is a judgment-free zone! Believe me, if I'm shining a light on something here, it's because *I've* had to cross this line, too.)

How do we cross our own Challenge Line and simultaneously get our cats to accept the nail trimming, vet visiting, pill taking, and every other "unpleasantry?" As Mary Poppins would say, "A spoonful of sugar helps the medicine go down."

Why the Mary Poppins reference? As it turns out, she represents both the calming persona and the skilled nanny. She knows all about the intricacies of getting done *what* has to be done, but is also mindful about the *way* she does it. This is an excellent model for every cat parent to follow.

"A Spoonful of Sugar . . ."

The guilt that we feel permeates both the tone of our voice and the words that we choose when trying to get through these various activities. As we just discussed in the last chapter, words matter; in truth, so does the rest of it, from tone to physiology. If you treat it like a big deal, it *becomes* a big deal. If you are in the midst of doing one of these uncomfortable things with your cat—like giving him a pill, for example—and your inner monologue is "my cat is miserable, I'm making him miserable, I'm a bad parent," you will most likely manifest a tone, an anxious energy that your cat will feel. Now you find yourself tiptoeing toward your cat, fists clenched around the medicine bottle or nail trimmers, every muscle from your shoulders to your jaw tightened as you verbalize, "Okay, baby, this is not going to be a big deal *at all.* . . ."

That's where Mary Poppins comes in. "A Spoonful of Sugar" is the idea that we let go of the angst and consciously bring *the sweetness* to a stressful situation. We do things "in the most delightful way." This is how we mitigate the misery.

". . . Helps the Medicine Go Down"

I can't know what the big red button inside you is that brings you to your Challenge Line. We took you through methods for dealing with various challenges, such as getting your cat to the vet, for instance. But when it comes to your specific sweat-inducing task, it's a pretty individual thing. Is it nail trimming? Pill giving? Simply leaving the house for ten hours? Switching food? Whatever it is, your goal is a true sense of ease in establishing an everyday context for the task. And here is where the "skilled nanny" element comes into play. This is all about getting more competent and confident about the mechanics of a given task, particularly those where you feel resistance.

The way to do this:

1. Define your Challenge Line moments.
2. Research methods to turn these moments into step-by-step tasks. Your due diligence, of course, includes online research. But don't forget to mine the knowledge and experience of your local pet professionals. Your vet, vet tech, groomer, or pet sitter can either demonstrate, or offer valuable info, about the how-tos.
3. There are many methods: find the one that resonates for you. For example, there are more animal nail trimmers on the market than I can possibly count. In the meantime, using ordinary human nail clippers works so comfortably for me that when I grab them, because I know what to do with them, my anxiety is immediately lowered.
4. Use the concept of the Fire Drill I laid out in chapter 10. If, before you even approach your cat, you have gone through the process so many times in your head—thinking about how you would react if things went sideways, so that there aren't many surprises that can happen in the actual moment—you'll be more able to release the stress you feel.
5. Take a moment before you approach your cat to ground yourself. Go through your fire drill, take a few breaths, consciously do a quick body check to become aware of where you are holding your physical stress, and release it.

When you combine both of these Poppins attributes—the *what* you do and the *how* you do it—you transform what was once a necessary but dreaded activity into yet another Mojo-fied interaction you experience with your cat, another slice of life, this time set to your musical mantra: *A Spoonful of Sugar Helps the Medicine Go Down.* Now, you can just be walking by your cat, bend down as if you're petting her to say "hi," and give her a pill. A flash of magic.

She won't know what hit her.

To Treat or Not?

Another very individualized component of this process is the reward. Could you offer a Jackpot! Treat after giving a pill? Of course, and that's a part of your fire drill. Whatever it takes to get you to feel absolutely nonchalant about the process. How many times have I personally done that? None. For these objectively small tasks, the reward portion of the proceedings actually made me more stressed because it heightened the significance of the event. In my experience, the better I got at the steps I outlined above, the more my fire drill became muscle memory, and the less I wanted to make it into a rewardable action.

In my view, there is a connection between the tension-fueled "It's okay, baby; this is SO not a big deal . . ." vibe before the action and making a big deal about how great she is for doing this, and how beautiful it is after the fact. The bigger the reward you give her for this action, the more you're also setting it up as a big operation. A small, matter-of-fact operation calls for small, matter-of-fact appreciation.

That said, it is *your* Challenge Line, which makes it *your* process. The key to figuring out your strategy is mindfulness and preparation. Whatever falls between those lines that works for both you and your cat works for me, too.

Lifelong Mojo: A Spoonful of Sugar for Kittens

If you have a kitten, all of these "unpleasant" activities we have to do for our cats are opportunities. Set up a lifelong dynamic now, because if they need a pill today, they are probably going to need a pill later. If you burrito them, scruff them, or sit on top of them, you are making it so there is going to be a boomerang effect; every time you go through the action of giving them a pill, they are going to struggle harder. Therefore, you are best served to find a way within yourself to stay centered. When people do something that they perceive their cats don't like, they tend to overdo it, or don't do it at all. Either way, you are not doing anybody any favors.

KEEPING CATS INDOORS

 If there's one topic that causes fights to break out (and I mean of the human variety), it's whether or not cats should be allowed outdoors. The indoor/outdoor debate centers on the concept of quality versus quantity—the idea that cats' lives are of a better Mojo quality when given access to their original stomping grounds, and that cats love being outside and it goes against nature to restrict their movements. At the same time, if they are given that free access, dangers abound and their lifespan can be shortened.

To be fair, both sides of the fence here make very strong arguments. Are cats innately "happier" when allowed access to the outdoors? I believe so. Are there problem-solving opportunities and challenges from both their environment and through practicing the Raw Cat HCKE that are difficult to replicate? Again, yes. Some say cats need to be outside, and by denying that, we're making their lives miserable. In the same breath, people acknowledge that the threats outside are numerous and can be fatal. Between the transmission of diseases like FIV that come from the inevitable fights with other community cats, and the usual suspects of cars, people, and predators from both air and ground . . . it's rough out there.

Where do I fall in the debate? I believe that cats should be kept indoors. I don't believe that we should even be getting into the debate about quality versus quantity of life. We can replace the perceived loss of quality by involving ourselves in our cats' lives more. My personal model of parenting dictates that I want my animal children around for the full natural duration of their lives. Do they love being out there? No debate. But I loved riding the subway around New York City as a teenager. I still had a curfew.

That said . . . it's a personal choice whether you're going to let your cat be indoor/outdoor. But if you do fall on the outdoor side of things, consider at the least these additions to you and your cats' lives, which will give them access to the outdoors but keep them safe at the same time:

Catio: This is a real game changer. A catio is basically a space that you can make for cats (which of course you can share with them) by enclosing your existing patio or creating an enclosure. There, you can offer great vertical spaces, wooden objects that they can scratch on, different grasses including catnip that you can plant and they can enjoy—even hunting that can happen when critters make their way inside.

Harness Training: Enjoying the great outdoors via a leash isn't just a "dog" thing. If your cat demonstrates that he really, *really* wants to get outside (not just because you think he should get out there), he can be trained to a harness and leash, and you can spend quality time every day cruising around the neighborhood with your cat.

Window Boxes: Sometimes you can't even take them outside because of your schedule or your apartment lifestyle, or you determined that they didn't want to go out badly enough to train to a harness. Or perhaps once they were trained, the outdoors just wasn't for them. There are kits that fit in your window just like an air conditioner that allow your cats to enjoy the view. Getting in the window box can become a wonderful hangout spot with a front-row seat to Cat TV.

Fencing in Backyard: There are several companies offering different versions of the existing, fairly foolproof method of fencing in your backyard. You can attach toppers to your existing fences or purchase a freestanding system. Either way, your cats won't get out, and just as important, nobody else can get in.

Still want to let them out? At least make sure your bases are covered just in case. Consider the following:

Letting Cats Outside Responsibly

- Please make sure your cats are microchipped and have their ID tag and a breakaway collar.
- Make sure they're up on their vaccines.
- Let your cat out only when you are home, so if your cat needs you, he can find you.
- When the sun goes down, your cat comes in.
- Stop free feeding. Have mealtimes so your cats will come home at certain times, and, again, you retain a measure of control about when they are out and when they are in.
- Take the most amazing pictures of your cats, in color, black and white, all angles. If they get lost, you will want those pictures for the flyers you hand out around your neighborhood.

- Be aware of how your cat might affect other cats. If your neighbors have a Napoleon cat who's indoors only, and your cat poops in their yard, that can drive that Napoleon so berserk that he will paint their house with pee. In that case, if you want to be a good neighbor, take your cat out on a harness or keep your cat indoors.

THE LAST STOP:
SAYING GOOD-BYE WITH LOVE AND GRACE

I was doing a speaking engagement in Milwaukee a few years back. It was at the Pabst Theater, an absolutely magical place. The night itself is one I will never forget for a few reasons. It was a full house and the vibe was, for lack of a better word, ecstatic. Most performers can point to a few times in their lives when they felt such an intense connection with their audience that the line between them just melted away. For me, that night in Milwaukee was that moment. Bonding over a love for cats, celebrating that relationship together, made it into a 2-hour, 1,200-person family reunion.

Riding this natural high of give-and-take from audience to stage and back again, I launched into my traditional end-of-night Q&A. A microphone was set up in the center aisle of the theater with a single spotlight on it. A line quickly formed that went from the center of the theater all the way down the aisle to the doors. After answering a few questions (mostly about pee and poop, naturally!), I saw that at the mic was a little girl who seemed to me to be about ten years old, small enough that she was partially obscured from view by the mic stand. She was clearly shy, uncomfortable to be standing in front of all these people. I remember thinking that whatever she had to ask me must be important because her body language was telling me she'd rather be anyplace but in front of that mic, under that spotlight, looking through the darkness up to me on the stage.

I also remember that the previous question and answer had left the place a little raucous, laughter lingering from the exchange between me and the person who'd asked the question. But when she stepped up, I felt a quiet overtake the place as though a small wind had gathered everyone's words from their lips and blown them all out the windows to scatter with the light snow on East Wells Street.

She shuffled her feet and started asking her question, but it was completely indecipherable. I asked her to speak up. Then she said:

"Jackson, I have a cat at home. I've known her since I was born—she's fifteen years old, she's my best friend, and she's really not well. I know she's unhappy and kind of scared. When's the right time to let her go?"

And then the room got really, *really* quiet. The courage of that little girl staggered me. Talk about walking the walk! It was so important for her to know how to help her friend (and herself) through the hardest time of both of their lives that she put herself on the line for me, a stranger, in front of 1,200 other strangers. Her innate sense of generosity toward her friend made me want to cry. I didn't—she needed a strong presence and I wanted to be what she needed. For the next ten minutes, it was just me and her, and what I felt like I owed her—the truth.

YOU KNEW WE had to go here together, right? For all of us who have shared our lives with animals, we know what it feels like to be that girl, standing in a void, throwing that question up to the universe: "When is it time?"

When is it time to say good-bye to a companion animal?

This question cuts to the heart of our end of the deal when it comes to the unconditional love that animals show to us. We have the ability to show them mercy at a time when they may be asking for that mercy. We have to remember that the spirit of euthanasia is probably best defined by its literal translation from the Greek: a kind death.

In the spirit of full disclosure, my views on the subject are, like everyone else's, built on my experiences. I worked at an animal shelter for almost ten years. I continue to keep my feet as rooted in the world of animal welfare as I possibly can, so the concept and experience of euthanasia is very much a part of my process.

At my shelter, we performed euthanasia as a service to guardians. Some would choose not to be present, but the majority did what we highly encouraged, which was to be there with and for their companion. In the course of my years there, I came across more unfortunate reminders of the human Challenge Line than I even care to remember. I don't think it's necessary to spell it out in graphic detail, except to tell you that my job— comforting an animal at the end of life, as well as assisting in the passing— sometimes left a bitter taste in my mouth. Guardians who loved their animals so much, and were so afraid of losing them, found themselves paralyzed and unable to see their friends suffering in front of their eyes. Sometimes this mother of all Challenge Lines, left uncrossed, caused a guardian to keep her companion alive too long, which resulted in an inability to be present for the last moments. But every time, the result was the same: a stranger had to step in to show mercy and be a loving presence because the guardian simply could not.

The irony of that situation playing out time and again solidified my approach to that night in Milwaukee, and gave me an unflinching answer to the courageous girl at the mic:

Never on their worst day.

It's a fine line and a loaded statement, for sure, but it has served me well over years of loving and losing animal companions and counseling many people through their process. It's not meant to be literally dissected; it's a way of keeping yourself in check while trying to stay completely present so that you can, in a clearheaded way, make one of the most difficult decisions you may ever have to make.

I keep the phrase in my mind to help bring me back to the moment, like snapping a rubber band that I keep around my wrist:

SNAP—It's not about me.

SNAP—It's not about my pain or suffering.

SNAP—It's not about how I will fall apart in the days and weeks after losing my best friend.

It's about them.

One of the things that makes this final decision so hard is not necessarily the finality of it all—rather, it's the concept that "their worst day" is actually a little more subjective than it might seem. To me, it's not just about their declining physical state, the collapse of the body. Beyond that, there's an essential dialogue that is always struggling to take place, desires that want to be heard, as long as you are in a space where you can be available to it. Does this mean that your cat will "tell you" when it's time? In my experience—yes. It just may not look or sound like what you'd expect. As with any very close familial relationship, you've developed a language together. During times like this, however, the communication can be very quiet, and the gestures minute.

Again, it's all about presence. And presence can only happen when your mind, your needs, and your fears are all safely on the back burner.

Part of my personal process is rooted in my belief that we are all transient, we are all spirit taking a pit stop in physical form. The process of letting go of an animal companion is, in part, about shepherding him to the next place. When I think about "never on their worst day," I am also thinking about their transition into another form. I want their last memories of this particular time around to be of love and light, not pain and suffering. I also believe that, unless they feel a bit of emotional detachment on your part when tuning into this sacred bond, they won't feel "permission" to make that transition. If they feel like you're still holding on, they might hold on longer than is good for them. Yes, that means that crying happens in another room, along with any other display that doesn't serve them in that particular moment.

I'm not in any way saying that there isn't a place for science or medicine, that there shouldn't be a measure of fight to help save their lives. That said, no doctor, no friend, no family member can know your animal's inner emotional and physical life better than you can. It is often a solitary decision. *You* are their protector from fear and from suffering. That's the deal you made with that animal the day you became his guardian, and in return he gave you his unconditional love. That love comes with a price, and this is it.

Obviously, there is no clean yes or no answer to one of the most complex, heart-shattering scenarios we will have with our cat companions. But remember that what we've built through the course of this book together is a toolbox, a heart-shaped container for all of the tools that are contained here. Use the tools and stay mindful of your empathetic center, and you will be guided to steer clear of the endless, tortuous inner conversations (or arguments) about whether it's too early or too late. You will also be guided toward that final bonding moment of peace and light.

I KNOW THAT was a tough subject to tackle, but part of what we are doing here is stopping to examine and question all that we thought we knew about our animal companions. In this section, we looked at our own

Challenge Lines and fearlessly put one brave foot in front of the other so that we might transcend those lines. Now that we've taken a deep breath, reaffirmed our relationship, and checked the stability of our toolbox and the tools that live inside, we are truly ready to put all that we have to the test as we solve the most common cat problems known to us.

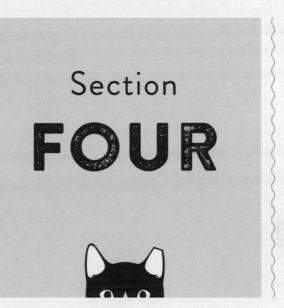

Section

FOUR

The Cat Mojo Cookbook—
Cat Daddy Solutions for
Industrial Strength Issues

13

When Excessive Scratching Becomes an Issue

MOJO SCRATCH MASTER

The Problem:

The corner of your sofa has become a cat-art display of shredded fabric; one side of your expensive mattress looks like it's been dragged down a gravel road at 90 mph; the legs of your favorite coffee table are beginning to look like dinosaur toothpicks . . . and it's all driving you out of your mind! In short, your cat is scratching everywhere but on his beautiful scratching post, which remains in pristine condition in the corner of your family room.

The Reality:

You can't make these impulses go away. As discussed in section 2, scratching is an innate activity that cats *must* partake in. Furthermore, you actually *want* them to do it—not just because it's a physical need, but because of the Mojo-fied choice the cat is making. Scratching is a confident exercise, one that marks territory in a self-assured way. Unconfident marking would mean peeing on the corner of the couch instead of scratching there. You can, however, reshape and redirect these impulses so that they are more acceptable to you and your shared household.

Cat Daddy Solutions:

Scratching problems are generally resolved through use of my No/Yes tool (as introduced in chapter 9). In this case, we're saying "no" to scratching the furniture, but "yes" to scratching the *right* type of scratching post. Here's my recommended process:

1. **Do Your Detective Work and Observe Their Scratching Style:** First, we have to make sure that the scratching post we use will accommodate the specific way your cat scratches. Surface preference is often at least one reason why they refuse to use the scratching post you might already have on hand, and could explain why the couch suits their needs better. So let's say it's your couch that's getting the worst of it.

   ◆ Observe the sturdiness of the couch. When your cat reaches way up, then pulls down, stretching out their pec muscles, removing those sheaths of nail, and doing all the things that are natural exercise to a cat, that couch is not going anywhere. So sturdiness would be a primary reason why your cat prefers the couch over the scratching post.

   ◆ Notice the texture of the couch and the fabric that it's made of. Is it notably different from what's on the existing scratching post? Or, if you're planning on bringing in a new scratching post, take note of the texture so you can find a suitable replica.

2. **Discourage the Scratching:** Since the basic principle of the No/Yes is that you have to give them a "no" before you give them a "yes," it's okay to tell your cat you don't want her to scratch your couch. One of the things I really love about this approach is that it's the environment itself, not you, that tells her "no" by making the locations unpleasant to scratch. There is double-sided tape you can use that's

designed to deter cats from furniture, but tin foil, plastic office runners, or silky fabric
furniture coverings also work
just fine as *temporary* deterrents. I think one of the main
reasons I get the "Oh, hell no!"

look when I suggest this solution, is that it is perceived as the end
product as opposed to a part of the process. The "no" is a learning
tool; it is meant to be temporary as long as the "yes" is equally
strong. When you have established a good pattern of "yes!" on the
scratching post, you can *slowly* start removing the "no!"

3. **Consider the Placement/Location of the Post:** Bring the "yes"
(scratching post) to the immediate vicinity of the "no" (the furniture
they've been scratching). It will no doubt be in proximity to where
you, the human, spend a lot of time. That's why your couch and your
bed are the number one and two most popular scratching targets—
because your scent is so strong in both. Scratching is a way of complementing your scent with theirs; it's a way of marking, in a visual
and olfactory sense, a piece of furniture that is equally owned by
both of you.

4. **Bring in the Appropriate Scratching Post:** Now for the "yes"—the
actual post. As mentioned, the type and style will be contingent on
where/how they've been scratching. So let's start with our couch-
scratching example:

   ♦ You will need a scratching post that is tall enough, and with a
   base wide enough, to accommodate the way your cat scratches
   the couch (think sturdy, similar texture, etc.). One serious com-
   plaint I have with many of the stand-alone scratching posts on
   the market is that they are almost built to wobble, and are barely
   tall enough for a kitten. When shopping, imagine your cat
   stretching as far up as he can go, then add six to ten inches, and
   a base that's at least twenty inches square.

   ♦ If the bottom of your couch has a low clearance, you can wedge the base of the scratching post under the couch itself, or under one of the feet of the couch, so that the post doesn't wiggle when it's scratched. Now you've created something that serves the purpose of proximity, and also provides the right scratching tool.

5. **Encourage Use:** You can encourage your cat into the "scratching position" by dragging a toy along the scratching post or using catnip or a treat to lure him to it. Whatever you do, don't force the issue. Carrying your cat to the post and moving his paws against the surface is a surefire way to annoy him!

Here's another hint that has worked for me in attracting cats to the scratching post: While rubbing catnip on the post is a common "trick," I think it is a bit hit or miss. But rubbing anything with your scent on it—i.e., a worn shirt or used towel—has worked much more often for me since it helps to accomplish the desired result for your cat, which is a mingling of scents.

6. **Positive Reinforcement:** To help lock in the new scratching protocol, give your cat praise and treats when she uses the post. Remember to save Jackpot! Treats only for these times of initial training so the association is unmistakable.

Notes from the Chef

A. Check out chapter 8 for an even more thorough explanation on scratching and post options.

B. If you're really struggling with the aesthetics of a scratching post and how it interfaces with your home environment, get creative and find something that speaks to your aesthetic. No excuses! (For inspiration, check out my book *Catify to Satisfy*. There you will find an abundance of cool scratching post ideas, inspired by fellow cat guardians like you.)

C. Always keep your cat's nails trimmed.

A FEW MORE odds and ends:

What about discouraging kneading as well?

I'm not a fan of stopping cats from kneading. It's a sign of love and trust that comes from a very deep place. Kneading, also known as "making biscuits" and "smurgling," among other terms, is a behavior that starts very soon after birth. The kneading action, when performed on Mom, stimulates the delivery of milk through her mammaries. Talk about a Raw Cat ritual! Of course, if it's an issue, you can keep a soft blanket on your lap to prevent your cat's nails from digging into your legs.

How about the use of SoftPaws/nail caps?

I consider nail caps a last resort; you really shouldn't do it unless you have to. You still need to trim your cat's nails, the caps can be tricky to size, and they pop off when the nail grows, so you need to reapply them. I prefer you accommodate the Raw Cat with scratching options, and let her assert herself territorially rather than trying to stop her from scratching.

What about having my cat declawed as a solution for all of this scratching?

Absolutely not, no, never ever, under any circumstances! Read on for more info on declawing. . . .

Declawing: Don't Do It!

We love our cats. We share our beds with them, we keep their photos on our phones, we cry when they are sick, and mourn like nothing else when they die. But in the United States, an estimated 25 percent of cat guardians still elect to have their cats declawed. In case you're not exactly sure what declawing is, let me make it crystal clear. Declawing is the amputation (either via guillotine, laser, or scalpel) of the ends of a cat's toes, up to the first joint. Don't do it!

- When cats are declawed, they experience incredible pain, both immediately after the surgery (which is often used as a procedure to test pain medication) and due to long-term phantom pain.

- Declawed cats are deprived of natural behaviors—they can't mark their territory in an appropriate way, they can't stretch their back muscles, they can't climb trees to escape predators, and painful paws are not going to make kneading during a loving moment very enjoyable.

- When cats' toes are amputated, you are changing how they walk, because cats naturally walk on their toes. Declawed cats pay the price later on with arthritis (imagine having to walk hunched over for your entire lifetime).

- A recent study out of Tufts University published in the *Journal of Feline Medicine and Surgery* illuminated some of the complications that arise when cats are declawed. Over half of the 139 declawed cats in the study suffered from a shoddy surgery—where fragments of bone were left behind in their paws, no doubt causing a permanent and painful "pebble in the shoe" sensation for those cats. Furthermore, declawed cats were more likely to suffer from back pain, to pee or poop outside of the litterbox, and to exhibit aggressive behaviors than a matched control group of cats with claws.

- The fact is, declawing is something that is done simply for human convenience—to essentially mutilate a living being to protect a couch. That is just crazy to me. Some compromise is needed for living with an animal. Yet many cats are declawed before even being given a chance to scratch an appropriate scratching post in the first place.

No cat would ever elect to be declawed. Cats need and use their claws for so many things: stretching, exercising, marking their territory, playing, protection, and hunting—all those things that boost Mojo!

If the Deed Has Been Done . . .

Perhaps some of you have declawed your cats in the past; I get it—it's unfortunately easy and in some places even encouraged. I can forgive those who work to educate themselves and never do this to another kitty they live with. This is your chance to join the fight to make declawing a procedure of the past. Let your friends, family, and neighbors know what declawing really is; and let your vet know how you feel about it, too!

14

When Your Cats Don't Get Along

WHEN IT COMES to violence between cats, I think one of the most detrimental mistakes that guardians make is the "let them work it out" approach, giving the warring parties access to one another, even when you're not home. Talk about letting inmates run the asylum! Let's stop fooling ourselves; if the cats were going to work out their differences, they would have done it by now. Instead, we are facing a relationship that, with every passing day, is becoming less and less "fixable." We have to take control of the situation, deal with the needs of both cats, and make the world safe and territorially "ownable" for both.

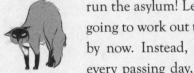

CAT DADDY RECIPE NO. 2—

THE RELATIONSHIP MENDER

The Problem:

If you have opened this book and flipped directly to this chapter, my guess is that you're finding some degree of pee, poop, fur, and possibly even blood in unexpected places around your house, and that you are separating your cats for fear that they're going to kill one another in your absence.

The Reality:

Anybody who has been in the position of dealing with cats who don't get along knows the incredible amount of stress it causes, both for human and animal family members. In my experience, the increasingly erratic and destructive behavior becomes a downward spiral for all of the animals in the home. The animal chaos raises your anxiety (and blood pressure), and that downward spiral becomes a category five tornado, taking out everything in its path. If I'm capturing the scenario in your home to a T, that's because I've lived it—and I get it.

The following recipe has brought resolution to the majority of cases I've dealt with through the years. There are certain variables involved in the most common scenarios, and we'll address those in a moment. But for now, this should get things with our feline family feuders back on track.

The Steps:

1. **Site Swapping (see page 172):** When Chinese philosopher Lao Tze said, "The journey of 1,000 miles begins with a single step," he probably wasn't thinking about resolving hard-core cat problems— but it definitely applies here. The first step is for you, the human, to reclaim ownership by taking a definitive stance in the name of control; in other words, it's time to separate. These cats should not have access to one another until we get to the end of this recipe. For now, they don't even make eye contact. There will only be swapping— co-ownership of space at separate, safe times.

2. **The "Other Side of the Door" Feeding Ritual (see page 199):** This idea is centered on setting Challenge Lines on opposite sides of a door. The only time the combatants smell each other, they smell dinner; the only time they smell food, they smell their "enemy." Peace is being forged through positive associations, and at a determined pace—dictated by you and your cats' ability to cross Challenge Lines peaceably.

3. **Eat Play Love (see page 200):** Once we have the cats at the end of the opposite-side-of-the-door introduction rainbow, it's time to intro-

duce Eat Play Love. The idea is simple but crucial. We are now giving the warring parties enough rope to be in the same room at the same time, not separated by a gate, door, or barricade of any kind. We are depending on our ability to entertain and compel them both in separate activities. Eat Play Love gives you many valuable tools in terms of predicting and avoiding troublesome scenarios. It's always best to do with someone helping, since it's easier to manage both cats this way.

While doing steps 1, 2, and 3, work on the following:

A. **Separated HCKE (Hunt, Catch, Kill, Eat) Sessions.** We want each cat to fully embrace his Raw Cat Mojo, without distraction. Remember, the "E" in HCKE stands for EAT. That means we do these sessions around mealtime, so we can segue into our mealtime door sessions. Also, don't forget—different cats have different play needs. While you practice Boil and Simmer, your cat might be so energetically charged after dinner that the final round of play needs to happen then. Knowing this will pave the way for a peaceful reintroduction since you can ensure a relatively drained Energetic Balloon when they finally see one another.

B. **Catification: Increase the peace by increasing the space:** Make sure there are escape routes and secure passageways. Be sure to take away death traps by blocking off the Unders and getting rid of ambush zones. Be aware that clutter can make one cat an easy target for the other. Once we reintegrate, we want there to be plenty of space for both cats to coexist comfortably.

The Mojo Moment

Our Mojo moment when it comes to reintroduction is technically a place where journey meets destination. Eat Play Love sessions, at first maybe lasting a few minutes before ending on a high note and packing it in till tomorrow, get longer and longer. Then, the night will come, the cats will eat their dinner in a shared territory, watch the other move about the space with no incidents (or even the threat of one), and you decide that maybe it's time that *you* eat dinner as well. And, suddenly, it's not an exercise; it's life. Congratulations—you have arrived at the moment of group Mojo.

Notes from the Chef

Recipe Timeline: For each of these steps, the timeline can vary widely. Part of your job is to keep an eye on the Challenge Lines for the individual cats and the community at large. Each step can take days or weeks depending upon the willingness of the participants and how entrenched the problem has become. The key is not to move on to the next step until you have predictable results at the current step.

Dealing with Setbacks: Whether it's as minor as a hissing war across the door at dinner, or as major as a fight breaking out during Eat Play Love, all you need to do is reverse engineer the process back to the last successful Challenge Line. In other words, simply back it up to the last "mile marker" instead of backtracking to the first step of the thousand-mile journey. The key to all of this? Get back on the horse! Do not let the paralytic trauma of a single event define the future of your home. Take a minute if you must to lick your wounds (emotional or physical), and get back to it!

Positive Associations: Both cats have to be shown over and over again that the other cat is not a threat—either physically or territorially. As long as we keep the good vibes flowing throughout the session, and those vibes continue to the next session . . . vibes become communal Mojo, and we are golden.

Always End Sessions on a High Note: If we're trying to "rewire" the feuding cats with good vibes toward one another, then the last thing we want is for a last impression from being together to be a bad one.

Even if nothing particularly earth-shattering has happened during the session, that *is* a high note. It's a tough call sometimes, but trust your gut. Although daily challenge is the name of the game, so is daily peace.

Avoid Fighting: As described on page 200, one of the key challenges and most critical objectives of the Eat Play Love session is to avoid fighting. One of the best ways to initially circumvent this is through distraction, and we can do this by interrupting eye contact (with Yes/No). In other words, stop the staredowns, which will prevent throwdowns and beatdowns. Momentary eye contact between cats gives them information, but the moment movement ceases and staring takes over, danger is not far behind. **If you can predict it, you can redirect it.** All you need to perfect is being able to get Napoleon to turn her head. From there, she knows something with higher value awaits, and we get to show our victim that the bully can be in his presence without an ass-kicking being the inevitable end.

WHEN TO USE THE RELATIONSHIP MENDER

Here are four of the most common—and most fixable—scenarios I encounter when it comes to cats not getting along. See which one hits closest to home for you, then check out the additional notes.

1) Bullies and Victims: When One Cat Is Picking on Another

The Problem: You have a bully in your house and she's constantly picking on at least one other cat.

The Reality: Whether the motivation is play or territorial, a cat who runs is a cat who will be chased. Not to blame the victim, of course, but it's not particularly productive to hang the black hat on the aggressor, either. We often focus on changing the behavior of the Napoleon (the bully), which is, of course, essential to show him that there is no reason to overown. But the reality in the world of the Raw Cat is *if you* *act like prey, you will be treated like prey.* And while there are things we can do to affect change in the Napoleon, one thing is for sure in their world as well as ours: bullies think twice about attacking once they sense confidence in their victims.

Key Points:

1. HCKE is a vital part of the solution in bully/victim cases. In separate sessions, we use HCKE to drain the aggressor's (bully's) energy and, through repetition, to raise the victim cat's self-esteem. Over time, the "victim" becomes more confident, and when the bully sees her full of Mojo, he'll stop treating that victim like prey.

2. Crucial Catification: We're now familiar with how hunters use Cat Chess (see page 166) to predict the moves of their prey. So let's raise the victim's self-esteem, and remove the need for the Napoleon to overown, by creating infinitely more territory. We can best do this by being aware of how the victim sees the world. Timid cats need to find their Mojo, and for some cats, the Confident Where is being up high. Shelving, for example, allows them to be elevated while the other cat plays on the floor. This vantage point, which works just as well, as we saw in chapter 8, allows detached observation where the victim can see their one-time tormentor in a completely different light as just an individual—eating, playing, simply *being*, without the component of an attack at any moment.

3. Preventative Measures: Although we are expecting our recipe to do the trick, here are a couple more "just in case" ideas you can try:

   ◆ Put a Bell on Aggressor's Collar: This will serve as an early warning system to prevent sneak attacks.

   ◆ Wallflower "Scissorhands": I'm not adverse to the concept of keeping the nails of a Wallflower (or victim) long. We work very hard to get Wallflowers to stand up for themselves. Why not slip a pair of brass knuckles onto their paws? Your Napoleon's going to be a little more hesitant the next time around.

What's in a Name?

Napoleon vs. Bully vs. Corrections Officer vs. Alpha Cat

 On page 68, I discussed the "Corrections Officer," often mistakenly perceived as an "alpha cat" (which doesn't exist in my book). A true bully is pretty much always going to be a Napoleon Cat—overbearing about overowning his territory, puffing his ego out because underneath is a deeply un-Mojo-fied being. On the other hand, the Corrections Officer is a Mojito Cat and a leader. He has a firm hand, but rarely uses it. For example, by walking up to a favored sunning spot at 3:37 p.m., when someone else might be there, and placing a nose on the backside of the reclining cat, he is demonstrating a look at his pocket watch, saying "Time to move along." With this gesture, time-sharing is enforced, and the multicat world continues, well oiled. The Corrections Officer leads with the least amount of effort necessary, and this judicious use of power is what separates him from a Napoleon Cat. A multicat home with a Corrections Officer stands an infinitely better chance of being a home with happier endings.

Recognize the Signs

Besides an actual fight, there are a few clues that tell you there might be discord or bullying going on between cats in your home:

Avoidance: This is a behavior seen in what I call the cabinet cats, the fridge cats, the closet cats, or the under-the-bed cats. These Wallflowers are often not Wallflowers by choice, but by circumstance, in response to being stalked. Constant stalking—even without the result of blood or hair being thrown around or various Tasmanian devil–looking results—is still psychological torture, and will lead many times to physical illness, or at the very least, a pretty stressful existence. Using the tools here, learn the difference between a favored hangout place and a cry for help.

Pee or Poop in a Vertical Place: When I'm doing my own cat detective work, a symptom that always provides me with an "aha!" moment is pee or poop on the counter, on the stove, on a table, even on the top of the fridge. More often than not, this pattern is a result of bullying. In one scenario, the victim had been chased and cornered in that place and—in the heat of running away from the aggressor—*had the pee or poop literally scared out of him.* In another scenario, the victim didn't feel safe enough to leave that vertical nest; getting to the litterbox felt like a trip through the valley of the shadow of death. The only choice, whether because she was being proactive or because an aggressor was sitting on the floor waiting for her to move, was to pee or poop up in her only safe place.

Competition for the Most Socially Significant Places in Your House: In chapter 5, I catalogued the archetypes of cats. If the concept of the Napoleon Cat resonates with you, and you're seeing aggression in your house, you've probably seen evidence of bullying. The biggest telltale sign is a cat who, for no apparent reason, has abandoned hanging out in socially significant areas. These are the places that are just as important to the humans as they are to the cats (i.e., your bed and the couch, where your scent is just as strong as the cats' scents), as well as places that are ownership hotspots (places where there are resources like food, advantageous Cat Chess locations, or spots along the Sundial).

2) New Kid in Town: When the New Cat Isn't Getting Along with the Resident Cat (or Cats)

The Problem: You recently adopted a new cat. You followed the introduction protocol in chapter 10 and you are still having issues. Or perhaps you didn't follow the protocol, and now you're in a pickle.

The Reality: Some cats need a slower introduction than others to be integrated. That could mean weeks or even months. In the vast majority of cat adoptions, we know much less about our new family member's life before she came to us than we would like. What kind of abuse did she suffer? Did she have to compete for resources either on the street or in a home with too many other animals? Was she taken from Mom and siblings too early, affecting her ability to communicate and coexist peacefully with others? And let's not forget that this individual is trying to find her way into a rhythm that was already established before she ever showed up. It's like territorial double-dutch—and we shake our heads trying to figure out why they just can't work it out? Silly human.

Key Points:

The key here is specificity. This is not one of those recipes where we add salt "to taste." The steps must be followed as written and until the cats prove that they have earned the next step. Is your new adoptee one who just shouldn't be with other cats? Perhaps, but you want to be absolutely sure of that before considering a rehome, since that tag will be on that cat as he searches for a new family. Regardless of his final destination, the information gained about his personality and preferences is another reason why you must be mindful every step of this process.

3) Who Are You?—When Cats Who Used to Get Along Now Fight

The Problem: Your cats used to be the best of friends, or at least they tolerated each other. Now they're fighting around the clock.

The Reality: There's usually a good reason why cats who used to get along don't anymore. Two of the most common ones are nonrecognition aggression and redirected aggression.

- **Nonrecognition aggression** often breaks out when a cat comes home from the vet or a boarding situation—or after spending a day or two lost in the neighborhood—and smells distinctly different. Cats use scent to identify friend or foe. The confusion of seeing friend but smelling foe can easily lead to a Raw Cat false alarm of epic proportions.

- **Redirected aggression** typically happens when a sudden stimulus either surprises a cat into action, or that sudden stimulus happens in the midst of a simmering, stressful situation. An example: two of your cats are sitting side by side in a window, just watching the day go by. Suddenly, a community cat who was hidden from sight pops into view. At that moment, the Raw Cat comes screaming to the forefront, fight or flight, live or die. The house cat ceases to make decisions; his body, his finely honed Raw Cat instincts, take over. He wants to get at the target, but the target is inaccessible. So that fight-or-flight energy gets taken out on whoever is nearby. In this case, it's your other cat.

Key Points:

1. If you feel like it could be a case of redirected aggression due to outside cats, see "When Outside Cats Cause Trouble for Inside Cats" (chapter 18), while applying Recipe No. 2 from the beginning of this chapter.

2. No matter the root cause, the major problem is that if the relationship is damaged in that moment, it can be permanently damaged unless you take immediate action. In fact, one of the most difficult cases I've ever worked was exactly the above redirected scenario—and the participants were seven-year-old littermates!

I'm sure you can relate: Imagine you're sitting at dinner with your significant other or a family member. The smoke alarm gets triggered by said dinner, and whomever you imagined in this scenario then attacks you, punching you in the face repeatedly. Let's face it, you are going to have some significant trust issues moving forward, because there's something inside you that has decided you just don't know who that person is anymore.

All of this is to say: don't underestimate the damage done to a relationship in moments. It goes a long way toward understanding that using this recipe involves threading a tricky needle—reintroducing and building positive associations as if they had never met.

4) I Hate Your Face: When Cats Just Refuse to Coexist

The Problem: No matter what you do, you can't get your cats to get along.

The Reality: Some cats will never accept an intruder into their territory, and some personalities will never mesh. I have worked with so many multiple-cat homes where we did *everything* to make positive associations between the two animals. But no matter what, as soon as they had access to one another, they were at it, rolling around on the ground, Tasmanian devil–style, fur flying, someone peeing on himself, sometimes headed for the hospital. In this case, it must be acknowledged that a cat can look at another cat and just say, "I hate your face."

It's important for us to try to equate their experiences to our own to better understand the crossroads at which everyone stands. Think about that college roommate, or the work associate you had to share an office with. You just couldn't put your finger on it—the roommate paid his bills on time and cleaned up the kitchen; the work associate never left early, saddling you with his or her workload. But there was something about the way they laughed, or ate their food—you just couldn't stand them. You hated their face and HAD to get away from them. The difference between us and our cats? We could make that choice to move out or change offices. Our cats can't.

Key Points:

1. Nobody likes talking about rehoming a cat . . . me as little as anybody else. But I also want to make sure that we're keeping their needs on par with ours. When is that time to start thinking about rehoming? When there are constant fights and *you have been trying to reintroduce the cats for months and months?* Quite possibly. But first . . .

2. **The Site-Swap Solution:** If you are okay with that site-swapping arrangement you've implemented during the bulk of any reintroduction process, and can manage your own expectations to accept that it may never work out, and you understand that you may be living in a system of gates and doors (which many people have done successfully)—well, then, that's the way that you can keep the cats together in the home. Otherwise, it's time to switch your frame of reference from guardian to foster parent, and start finding what you consider to be the perfect home for one of these cats.

I'M NOT SAYING, by any stretch of the imagination, that we should jump to conclusions or rush to judgment. Options need to be exhausted before taking action or even getting into that ultimate conversation about rehoming a cat (there are some more ideas and tools below). In the course of my long history working with cats and their relationships, it's cases like these that I dread the most, where my ego can so easily take control—*my desire and determination* to make this square cat fit into the round hole. My ultimate job, remember, is to act as cat ambassador first and foremost. If one or both of the cats in a scenario like this says to me, "Jackson, I hate that guy's face," despite all of the negotiations and positive association building . . . that exclamation has got to be respected. Now you might be read-

ing this, shaking your head and saying that no matter what, you would *never* rehome a family member. Believe me, I get it. But that family member also needs a say.

"NOTHING IS WORKING!"— A FEW MORE THINGS TO TRY

You've gone through the full Introduction (or Reintroduction) process and it's still looking like WWIII between your feuding felines. Before you decide it's a match made in hell, consider the following:

Reintroduction Reflection: So you've gone through the Introduction process at least once, right? Before drawing conclusions, take a critical eye to your own process, looking for signs of "skipping or skimping." Did you follow the steps to the letter, or did you "improvise" here and there? Did you decide that a certain step didn't apply to your cat or your particular situation? Did you get frustrated at the glacial pace of success and gloss over the finer details? Sound familiar? If so, considering what's at stake with the outcome of this process, take another shot at a thorough reintroduction. Make sure that you are setting concrete goals for each step, and that you're not moving ahead until that goal is met. Also, be sure to take note of exactly where it all broke down last time, so you can give those phases of the process extra attention this time.

Catification Reflection: Another place in the process that tends toward skipping and skimping is Catification. Catifying, if done in a thoughtful and complete way, will almost always bring down the territorial tension in the home, since what you are doing is creating more resources. Competition over these resources, as well as plain old square footage, will no doubt be dampened when there's more than enough of it to go around.

Behavioral Medication: This could be a book unto itself. As such, there are certain things I'd like you to consider. I don't recommend this step lightly, and when I do, it is first and foremost to alleviate suffering in the cat we are considering it for. I've also recommended it in certain cat-on-cat situations, where both parties could benefit from a short-term course in order to get them to adjust their frame of reference and release either their aggressive or extremely fearful responses to normal stimuli. There is no black-and-white in this part of our world. I consider behavioral meds incredibly effective, but they are by no means magic. I also just as readily recommend natural solutions (I have, for years, made my own brand of flower essence remedies), or modalities like acupuncture or cranial-sacral work. In conjunction with the techniques I've laid out, the meds can really help break through deep-seated problems and help forge a solution.

One thing you will never see me do is recommend a lifetime of medication for a cat who doesn't personally need it in order to relieve suffering. If we have to rely on meds just so two cats can tolerate one another, then, in my opinion, we've gone too far.

Also, you will obviously want to consult with your vet to see if one or both of your warring felines are candidates, and if they are physically okay enough to handle the medication. Please, though—do not let your vet, or me, or any one person make this decision for your cat and you. Do your due diligence on this matter. Research it fully, ask why one medication was prescribed over another, etc. The truth is that advances are being made every day when it comes to medical assistance with animal behavior, and one professional may not have the same level of expertise as the next. The only way for you to feel good about a decision like this one? Be your own expert and your cat's advocate. Research the behavior AND the medical options so that you can ask the right questions and make the right move.

15

When Your Cat Is Biting or Scratching Humans

BLOODLETTING, IN THE course of your life together with a cat or cats, happens. Most of the time, it happens by accident—a scratch during play, toes that move under the blanket, a swipe at an insect that misses its target. Of course, there are times when cat-on-human aggression is not so innocent—but in either case, it's not your skin that pays the ultimate price. If the context of the aggression is not properly identified and approached, your relationship takes the biggest hit. Hurt feelings leave a bigger scar than a bite or scratch. Let's nip that one in the bud!

CAT DADDY RECIPE NO. 3—

TAKING THE EDGE OFF

The Problem:

You or a loved one have been feeling the wrath of claws, teeth, or both, and probably have the war wounds to show for it. You've even started to distance yourself from your cat as friends and family have started calling him names like *the cat from hell* (my bad, sorry). His actions could best be described as "out of the blue," "unpredictable," or "random," and something must be done about this before your relationship—and the trust that goes with it—completely comes undone.

The Reality:

As we've discussed, cats don't "attack" without a reason, even if that reason is apparent to nobody but them. Whether it's due to play aggression, redirected aggression, overstimulation, chemical or territorial fear, anxiety, or pain, we have to quickly assess the issue as we take a step-by-step run through this recipe.

The Steps:

1. **Rule Out the Medical:** If you feel that your cat's aggression could be stemming from a physical ailment (for example, when she suddenly bites or scratches when she's picked up a certain way), a vet exam should be part of your immediate future. Also, if the aggressiveness seems especially random or irrational (a judgment to be made *after* your detective work in item 4), there could be a chemical imbalance or other neurological issue that should be addressed with a medical professional as well.

2. **Ascertain Your Cat's Natural Body Rhythm (a.k.a. circadian rhythm):** Detectivist homework no. 1: Chronicle each attack, including what time they happen. If they're demonstrating aggression first thing in the morning when you wake up, or later in the day when you come home from work—these are considered high energy times of the day (see more about Detectivism in step 4). And the good news is, it tells you that your cat's body clock is synced up with yours: he's sleeping at night, and that's a natural body rhythm you can work with. If not, don't despair—you can get him there. (This gets back to the Three Rs we've been talking about—see chapter 7.)

3. **Play, in the world of a cat, is not a luxury—it's a necessity:** If you have a dog, and you don't have a leash and a collar, people are going to call you crazy. Because if you don't walk dogs every day, if you don't fulfill that innate need they have, then undesirable things will happen. That energy must go somewhere. Now replace the word "dog" with "cat," and the words "leash and collar" with "interactive toys." That's how strongly I feel about cats and play. The one

6 **Your Part in the Pain:** There are those times when we are just asking for it. Here are a few of these times:

♦ **Roughhousing:** When it comes to roughhousing, it is a big mistake to assume that cats enjoy play in the same way that dogs do. Remember, cats are prey players, and fun for them is hunting, catching, killing, and eating—not the kind of rough interaction that dogs might enjoy more. Yes, cats respond to the stimulus of roughhousing, but not in the way that you might expect, especially if you're used to playing roughly with dogs. With cats, it will likely trigger defensiveness and fear, or at the very least dangerous play like the on-their-back, all-four-paw wraparound. And you definitely won't like the way that feels.

♦ **Overstimulation:** This is a form of aggression that is typically induced by either petting a certain way and/or for a certain duration of time. This is another one that's "on you" if it happens. See chapter 11 for more info.

♦ **"Putting your hands in the blender":** It is ill advised to use your hands to break up a fight, or try to comfort, pick up, or move a cat who is clearly upset. Instead, try to guide them to a quiet location for a time-out. (For more on time-outs, see page 136.)

♦ **Keep those nails trimmed:** A little trimming can go a long way, should you happen to encounter the "Scissorhands" in passing or otherwise.

Hands Are Not Toys

If you already have a cat who has learned that hands are toys, he's probably also become very sensitive to hands approaching him. There are ways to change that reaction.

1. Teach your cat that hands are only used gently by being aware about *when* you bring your hands to your cat. If you approach your cat with your hands during a time when she is already in a hyped-up state, then you're asking for it. Only approach your cat for petting when there's a sleepy late-night vibe, as opposed to when she is ramped up and ready to play.

2. If your cat is now hand-shy (meaning that every time your hands come to her, she shrinks away), then you'll want to approach slowly, build positive associations by holding treats, and come at her from a low angle, as opposed to above her head.

When we humans are afraid of cats, we try to pet them by taking our hands and gingerly going over the top of their head. That is an invitation for disaster with a fight-or-flight animal because it could be perceived as a threat. Again, try to approach your cat with your hands from a low position and, if possible, use the Michelangelo technique (see chapter 11, pages 232–33).

When you're trying to recondition this behavior, *everyone in your home must buy in*. If everyone is adhering to the exercises and rules we've laid out here except for one person, who is still roughhousing and using hand-play, it will undo everyone else's hard work. Just as with any exercise we present in this book, consistency and group buy-in from the humans are key.

The Mojo Moment:

More than anything, our Mojo Moment includes randomness being replaced by predictability. Understanding your cat is the first step toward helping him. Helping him means that your relationship is back on track. You can now predict his rhythms and head off any aggressive behavior at the pass, and if the problem was physical in nature, your cat is definitely *feeling better*—and that's a huge bonus.

Notes from the Chef

Stay Calm and Carry On: If and when your cat might exhibit some aggression, don't have a big reaction—such as screaming, yelling, or pushing your cat—as this will escalate things. This can also explain why cats may prey more on certain people in the home; they tend to "pick on" those who are fearful and have a huge reaction to their bites and scratches.

Avoid Being a Threat: Cats will bite when cornered or threatened. This may be circumstantial, or it may be because you have a Wallflower.

A House of Plenty: Keep a Napoleon at bay by making sure your home has plenty of vertical space, scent soakers, and signposts.

Stranger Danger: Help your cat have good associations with visitors. See "Getting Comfortable with Visitors," page 327.

Forget Punishment: This will not work. As discussed, your cat will not understand what you're doing and it will ultimately only serve to undermine your relationship.

16

When Your Cat
Exhibits Annoying,
Attention-Seeking Behaviors

HANDS DOWN, IF I have a job, it's due to three things: litterbox
issues, aggression, or the huge pile of aggravation contained in
this chapter. However, these issues are the ones that routinely
drive guardians to the brink faster than the other two. I guess irritating
rings that bell faster than despairing. I know clients who have swept peeing problems under the rug (sometimes literally) for years. Waking you up
in the middle of the night? That's what gives you the impetus to track me
down in the cereal aisle of the supermarket (and for those who have, yes, I
still like Cap'n Crunch—don't judge).

CAT DADDY RECIPE NO. 4—

THE ANNOY-ILATOR

The Problem:

From clawing up the curtains to climbing the
walls, swinging from the chandeliers (both metaphorically and literally), scratching artwork, knocking things over, and being what some might call a
"pain in the ass," or what the Internet has dubbed

"Asshole Cat," your cat is driving you crazy with his annoying behavior. And worse yet, he seems to be fully aware that it's driving you crazy.

The Reality:

If my last point hits home, let's start by stepping away from the crazy. In many cases, unwanted nuisance behavior is something we bring on ourselves, because there's something in it for the cat. If your cat meows incessantly, wakes you up in the middle of the night, sits in front of your computer monitor or in your lap while you read the newspaper, or scratches or bites you as a way of trying your patience, there's always a payoff. When you're annoyed by a behavior, you give it weight by showing your dissatisfaction in some way (usually by yelling), or by appeasing your cat by rewarding the behavior. Either way, to your cat, all attention is reward.

I'm going to give you suggestions that will address the "big picture"—which is why your cat is being annoying in the first place. Then I'll talk about the most common nuisance behaviors and some specific remedies to restore your relationship with your "asshole cat."

The Steps:

1. **Battle Boredom:** This means we step up our play routine, making sure that it is routine, a ritual, and a part of our daily rhythm. Your cats need their energy drained in a constructive way each day. Remember our mantra: Play = Prey. Engage your cats in play during high-energy times of the day.
2. **Back to the Three Rs:** If you think about it, your cats will be knocking things off the shelves during predictable times of the day. They'll be counter surfing at predictable times of the day. Usually, it's when you're there, and the energy in the whole home has risen—when everybody's getting up in the morning, when everybody has come home from work, or when everyone's getting ready to go to bed at night. So make sure that you're being proactive about *when* you play, as much as you're stepping up the amount of time that you play with your cat.

3. **Catification:** Your cat might knock over things on the mantel, when she's just trying to get to her window perch. He might be on the counter, surfing to get to a window. Try to think about where the layout of the home is leading your cat. Your cat sees every ounce of territory as a potential piece of Superhighway and a potential destination. If you don't want her going from Point A to Point B, it's up to you to Catify, and to lead her from Point A to Point C instead. Create a satisfying Superhighway for your cat that avoids delicate areas, whether they be counters, mantels, or any place where your cat could break something or hurt himself.

4. **Cat-Proofing:** If there are things you don't want your cat to knock over or play with, consider the concept of cat-proofing (it's a lot like childproofing). Let's face it—you live in a cat's home now. If that piece of fine china sitting on your mantel is important for you to have out, then do what we do with everything in California: earthquake-proof it. Museum putty is a great start. Securing your belongings to the place where they live is always a good idea, because it doesn't necessarily have to be your cat poking at it until it falls, just to see what happens. Tie up those curtains and bundle computer cords. Take the potential toy out of all of those household objects!

5. **The No/Yes:** If you're going to say "no" to your cat, there's got to be a "yes" nearby. Go back to chapter 9 and review the No/Yes technique (page 147) and consider how it might apply to what your cat is doing.

6. **Rewarding the Silence (or the Good Behavior):** Remember the child who was crying for ice cream back in chapter 9? Make sure that you are giving your cat praise or treats when he's being quiet and calm, and behaving in a way that makes you think, "More of this please!"

CAT DADDY RECIPE NO. 5—

THE COUNTER SURFER

The Problem:

Your cat is getting his dirty paws all over your kitchen counter. Maybe he's stealing food or just getting in your way when you're trying to cook. Regardless, it's annoying at best, and unsanitary at worst.

The Reality:

Your cat might love to be up high, or he might be really food motivated and is hoping to snatch a snack while he is counter surfing. Perhaps you've been gone all day and he's just really happy to have some quality time with you.

The Steps:

1. **The No:** Say no to your cat by taking double-sided tape, affixing it to a plastic placemat, and putting the placemat up on the counter. Every time your cat jumps up onto the counter, she is inevitably going to get sticky, and she'll stop jumping to that area. In chapter 9, I also suggested using a motion-sensitive compressed air canister, which can be very effective. It's nothing that's going to hurt the cats, but it's something that will show them that this is not the kind of place they want to hang out. Remember, consistency is the key when you're doing any kind of training, and consistency in this kind of work is basically impossible to do yourself since you can't be there to dissuade your cat 24/7. This is part of the reason why just yelling at your cat to "get off!" is useless. All she learns is to come back when you're not around.

2. **The Yes:** Now that you've found ways to say "no" to your cat, how do you say "yes"? One of the best ways is providing him a perch that is a "yes." Put a cat tree in the dining room, in an area by the kitchen, so that your cat can be up high and part of the action, and you can actually reward him for being in that spot. Train your cat to jump up onto the cat tree and, once he gets there, give him a treat.

Then he'll come down again. Then lead him back up with a treat. Every time he gets to that perch, he gets that treat. The payoff from the perch becomes bigger than that from the counter. That is, of course, if you don't leave food out on that counter. What cat is going to say no to a free buffet?

Notes from the Chef

Meal Matching: Set up your ritual of feeding your cats to match the humans' food times, and in the same proximity, and now you've got a proper No/Yes going on.

Keep It Clean: For sanitary purposes, you might not want your cat in the same place where you're prepping food for humans. While you're training, keep sanitizing wipes handy.

Stoves and Safety: The other thing is the danger of stoves and cats. If your cats are determined to walk across the stove to get to their favorite perch, you'd want to make that area a "no" with the tools that I've just discussed. But just to be safe, childproof the stove and cabinets: there should be childproofing covers on the burners and knobs, and baby latches to keep your cats out of the cabinets. Finally, don't set them up for failure: if the only predictable route to a desired area is across that counter, it's on you. Create a new pathway if you want the behavior to stop.

The Mojo Moment:

Our Mojo Moment happens somewhere in the intersection of when we stop being annoyed at our cat for bothering us, and when our cat stops being annoyed at life for not giving her more to do. As with all of our "annoying" recipes, a true win/win is compromise, and that gives us the Mojo Moment.

THE BACK-ENDED COMPLIMENT

CAT DADDY RECIPE NO. 6—

PILLOW TROTTING:
WHY YOUR CAT KEEPS YOU UP ALL NIGHT

The Problem:

Your cat is waking you up at some obscene hour while you are trying to sleep. She might be walking on your face, running across your bed, meowing for food, scratching at your door—the list goes on. Sleep deprivation is taking its toll. Which is why most people will do anything to try to keep their cat quiet at night.

You may have tried confining your cat in the bathroom, yelling at him, throwing pillows, using a squirt bottle, feeding, cuddling him, locking him out of your bedroom (and then he probably scratched and meowed at your door for another hour). Yet the very next night your cat is meowing at 3:00 a.m. again.

I've even had clients who slept in their car to get a good night's sleep.

The Reality:

If you are asking "How can I sleep through the night without strangling my cat?" you need to be aware that the idea that cats are nocturnal animals is a fallacy. People just think this is the price you pay for having a cat. But your cat being up all night is a symptom of your failure to provide Routine, Ritual, and Rhythm.

Cats actually aren't nocturnal. They live on a crepuscular rhythm, and naturally want to get up at dusk and dawn when their prey is most active. But we can reset their body clocks. If you want to know how you can sleep through the night, this ritual is IT. It's all about getting your cat on the rhythm of your household.

The Steps:

1. First, **Stop Free Feeding:** See "Feeding for Mojo" (page 91). Feed in conjunction with play. If you go to bed at 11:00, feed your last meal at around 9:30. Right before that last meal, engage in HCK. Bring your cat to a boil (see "Boil and Simmer," page" 88), get him pooped out, then go for that second wind; now it will take less time for him to get completely worn out. Then he eats, grooms, and sleeps, and then you go to sleep.

2. **Match Their Energy with Yours:** Keep them active when the family is active. Again, it's all about the Three Rs.

3. **The Hard Part:** It's 3:00 a.m., and your cat is waking you up. Your cat should be down for the count, but she is not. This is tough, but you have to IGNORE HER. COMPLETELY. You definitely don't get up, feed, play, get up and go to the bathroom, etc. But completely means don't say her name, don't chuck a pillow—play dead. Yes, it will absolutely suck—but any attention whatsoever, negative or positive, is the payoff for her. If you tell her through your inaction night after night that nothing will happen after that behavior, she WILL stop. It might be tough for ten days to two weeks. But then you'll be good.

See the **"extinction burst"** (page 149) for more on why those two weeks will be rough.

Can You Lock Them Out of the Bedroom?

Look, the bedroom is the most scent-heavy room in your house. It's a socially critical area, so I recommend that your cats be allowed in. I'm generally not okay with rooms being off-limits.

Especially if your cats are used to sleeping with you, locking them out of the room sets up another battle zone—your bedroom door. Instead, remember the No/Yes: Why not place cat beds on nightstands or nearby furniture, with a heated pad to encourage their use? You can gradually move those heated beds to other rooms if you want, but you've created a desirable destination, which should help diminish her insistence.

Cat Daddy Tip: Meowing for Food

If your cat is really persistent about meowing at you for food, you can use an automatic timed feeder—by having a meal simply appear at exact timed intervals, the environment becomes the provider and the human is taken right out of the feeding equation. Of course this isn't my optimal choice—there are many advantages to the giving of food being a part of your relationship—but desperate times call for desperate measures.

The Mojo Moment:

The Mojo Moment might be when your alarm clock wakes you up, and you realize you made it all the way to the alarm without hearing a single meow. You get out of your bed and your cat says . . . "You know what? I'm good. I'm gonna snooze another fifteen minutes."

CAT DADDY RECIPE NO. 7—

THE DOOR DASHER

The Problem:

You open the door. Your hands are full of bags of groceries. Your cat zooms out.

You've got a door dasher.

The Reality:

Many door dashers get outside and then they just stand there, like, "Okay, NOW what?" They don't usually race down the street. But for some cats, door dashing can be downright dangerous. Especially if your cat is indoors-only, door dashing is a fast track to getting themselves lost.

The Steps:

1. **The No/Yes:** If there's a low, bush-dwelling place, like a coffee table, by the front door, that's going to be a prime door-dashing place. **The No**—Block off some of those routes that lead your cat from an Under to the outside. **The Yes**—Create destinations that are in the opposite direction of the door. Place cat trees in a safer place. Guide them to other bush-dwelling places in the main living space away from the door. Give them cocoons where they can be their bush-dwelling selves, so they stop thinking about going outside.

2. **Go Vertical:** Because most door dashers are also bush dwellers, try bringing them up into the vertical world. Most door dashers will not jump from a high place to get out the door. They usually need to be on the floor first. If you give them an observation post four or five feet off the floor that is also near the door, they'll usually sit there watching the traffic go in and out the door, because the activity is what fascinates them.

3. **Interactive Playtime:** Train them to go to those new destinations by using interactive playtime and keeping those destinations in mind. Think of it as you would train with a toy for an agility course,

leading them to those vertical spaces or cocoons. Put treats in those locations to end the play.

4. **Bring the Outside In:** Think about what it is that they want outside. Perhaps you can meet this need by having a planter in the house, with cat grass or catnip in it. Give them an alternative that fulfills that desire for them to get outside and roll around in some dirt.

5. **The "Ultimate" Solution:** A catio with perches and grass for them to chew on and roll around in is the ultimate No/Yes to the door-dashing question. A catio solves all your problems.

6. **Harness Training:** Finally, if your cat is one of those guys who just needs to go outside, you can do that safely by training him to a harness. (See chapter 12, page 258.)

The Mojo Moment:

When you get home from work, your cats greet YOU, not the opportunity for escape. Whether they're at face level on their tree that you've placed near the front door, or in their cocoon on the other side of the house, you feel assured that they aren't making a run for it any time that door is opened.

A Note from the Chef

Pick Your Battles: I was just in a house yesterday where I asked the guardian, "What can I do for you?" She said, "Well, I don't want my cat walking on the counter, on the dining room table, on my desk, or on my head while I'm sleeping at night." I had to ask, "Well, what do you want your cat *to do*? And have you considered a goldfish instead of a cat?"

You have to choose your battles. Now, absolutely, if we're talking about cats not being on the counter—especially where food prep is done—that's a good battle to pick. But the other ones? You may want to think long and hard about saying no to your cat too many times.

Many of these behaviors, like being an "asshole cat," are clear examples of boredom. I'm giving you activities to keep your cat from being bored, and you need to take that bull by the horns.

Again, I can't overstate it: pick your battles. And when you do pick your battles, remember: Cat TV, Catification, HCKE, the No/Yes, and clicker training. All of these things can make sure that your cat's not an asshole, and that you're not overreacting.

17

When Your Cat Exhibits "Anxiety-Related" Behaviors

IN THE NAME of transparency, each and every time I come up against certain behaviors, even if I can tell the guardian what they are looking at, I panic a little bit because there will inevitably come a moment when they look to me for an answer and they don't get one. The conditions described in this chapter are rife with question marks about their origins, their symptoms, and their "cures" (if there are any). What all of these behaviors have in common are that: (a) they have (or *appear to have*) anxiety as a primary symptom, and (b) they send guardians past frustration into concern and often into panic. Sometimes having a name for a condition gets you somewhere, but not all the way to the finish line. Hopefully my experience with, and empathy for, my clients provides relief—and a way forward.

CAT DADDY RECIPE NO. 8—

THE SEPARATION ANXIETY RELIEVER

The Problem:

You've got a suspicion that your cat *really* doesn't like it when you're gone. Perhaps you're coming home to destruction or poop on your bed, or to find that your cat has licked himself bald in your absence. Maybe your neighbor has complained that your cat meows nonstop as soon as you leave for work. Bottom line? Even if you run to the store and come back, chaos happens.

The Reality:

The "textbook" manifestation of separation anxiety in an animal is signs of distress *only* in the absence of their humans. You will find endless resources online about separation anxiety in dogs, but as far as cats are concerned, there's still a scarcity of information. Part of the reason is because of the misconception (still even in the medical community) that cats are socially aloof; since they don't really have a connection to humans in the first place, how could they have separation anxiety?

Adding to the challenge is the fact that cats are rarely destructive in the ways that dogs are; you usually won't come home to chewed up window sills or broken doors, meaning a cat's cries for help are often left unanswered. That said, some signs of separation anxiety are similar for cats and dogs: vocalization, predeparture distress, overgrooming, and continually following their human from room to room. In cats, you often see behaviors like marking items that are heavily scented, like you.

Although there are genetic predispositions toward this condition (Siamese and others considered Oriental breeds are more prone), it is possible that early weaning or other experiences may influence how overattached a cat might be. The thing that universally connects the separation anxiety experience, whether you're talking about a cat or a dog, is a lack of confidence.

The Steps:

1. **Journaling:** Documenting your cat's behavior and your interactions with your cat is a great place to start. For separation anxiety in particular, it will be important to note how long you are gone before she starts to exhibit symptoms. Also, remote viewing cams are another great opportunity to gather info and potential symptoms in regard to what your cat is doing when you're not home, since many separation-related behaviors happen only in your absence.

2. **HCKE:** Make sure to have an HCKE session every morning. I know making time for this can be a challenge but even a short session will help dramatically. The advantages are twofold: (a) we know the Mojo-inspiring benefits of play for a cat lacking confidence is a gimme in this case, and (b) the feeding part that happens right before you leave makes it so she's occupied while you exit stage left. That said, don't forget the next step . . .

3. **Change It Up:** Avoid predictable cues that you are leaving. Instead, switch up your routine. Right now, your cat knows that you putting on your coat = leaving. The jingle of your keys = leaving. You putting on the radio every day before you leave = leaving. So . . . pick your keys up when you wake up, then stick around, or go outside for a moment, then come back inside.

4. **No Big Deal:** The hardest thing for my clients to do is take my advice and just walk out of the house. Don't even say good-bye, just leave. Go back to the section on your Challenge Line (page 150). The habit of soothing your cats before you leave the house feeds into their anxiety—they don't catch the English, they catch the tone of guilt and dread, and now they are expecting the sky to fall. Now you have inadvertently encouraged separation anxiety because of your fear that they will have separation anxiety.

5. **Cat TV:** Enrich their world while you're gone. Move a cat tree next to a window so your cat can look out, or add a bird feeder and all the trimmings right outside the window to keep your cat engaged during the day. Heated beds can be helpful for some clingy cats. Last, don't forget to pay attention to the Sundial!

6. **Other Alternatives:** If you can afford it or have a friend who can help, you might want a cat sitter to check in on your cat at the midway point of your absence, perhaps a lunchtime check-in while you are at work. There are also numerous pharmaceutical approaches that have proven to be effective to help treat separation anxiety, and if your cat's symptoms are persistent and severe, it is an option well worth considering.

The Mojo Moment:

In this case, you come home from an especially long workday, and your cat is sleeping in the last remaining sliver of sun on her window perch. She sleepily notices your arrival and gives you a "Hey, how ya doin'?" nod. As you check mail and head into the kitchen, she stretches and yawns, jumps down, and walks over to get a pet or two and wait for dinner to be served. You feel like you were missed, but you don't feel guilty about your absence. And all, in this moment, is Mojo.

CAT DADDY RECIPE NO. 9—

GETTING CHEWED OUT

The Problem:

Your cat is eating basically anything that's not nailed down. He's chewing on corners of books, pencils, plastic, paper towels, chair corners, and cabinets, and turning your favorite sweaters and blankets into Swiss cheese. You're beginning to think that just because he might be bored, or might want attention (or might just be hell-bent on annoying you), he's going to destroy everything you hold dear.

The Reality:

What to many cat guardians looks like a maddening effort on their cat's part to annoy is a compulsive condition called **Pica**. The definition of Pica is the ingesting of non-food items, and if you thought the behavior itself was frustrating, the diagnosis is even more so. Whether it is a condition that has a genetic component; is present, in part, because of inadequate weaning or early social experiences; is a response to stress; or is a mix of all of the above, Pica is still a huge question mark in the scientific community. We know that some breeds (namely Siamese, and other closely related breeds) are more prone to wool-sucking behavior. The debate, however, is secondary to this: Pica is to a large degree mysterious; there is no known cure, and it can be very dangerous. Ingesting fabrics or other objects can be a life-or-death

situation—and involve an expensive and risky surgery if materials become lodged or twisted somewhere in the digestive tract. Despite the lack of a cure, though, we must do our damnedest to manage it.

Cat Nerd Corner

Paper or Plastic?

A 2016 study found a relationship between cats with Pica and frequent vomiting. Pica cats tended to *ingest* shoelaces, thread, plastic, and fabric, while all other cats seemed to enjoy *chewing* on plastic and paper the most. Almost 70 percent of the control (non-Pica) cats in the study chewed on nonfood items (although they didn't ingest them). Meaning: chewing is common in ALL cats, not just cats with Pica.

The Steps:

1. **Do Your Cat Detective Work:**
   - When does the behavior happen? Is it when you are present or gone?
   - Look at chewing locations and mark them on your Mojo Map. These might be areas of high stress or frustration.
   - What are the preferred targets? Certain objects, such as photo emulsion or plastic bags, might be attractive to your cat because they are rendered with animal fat.
   - What textures or types of objects does your cat try to chew or ingest?
2. **Protect Your Pica Cat:** Always start with a thorough vet check including blood work and make sure a dental or vitamin-deficiency or digestion problem aren't contributing. Also, the self-soothing behavior that your cat is demonstrating can be because she is in consistent pain or discomfort. Finally, your vet may prescribe mood-stabilizing

medication. Some medications have been moderately effective in reducing Pica.

3. **Commit to Daily HCKE** ritualized around food and energetic spikes.

4. **Catify** the areas you highlighted on your Mojo Map. If an area presents stress, tried-and-true Catification techniques can help neutralize that stress.

5. **Encourage Acceptable Chewing Options:** Try high-quality, high-protein treats and cat grasses, placing them in areas identified as hot spots on your Mojo Map. Crunching on something else may be helpful. Also, dog toys tend to be more durable than cat toys—hard rubber puzzle toys, which can be stuffed with some type of food that motivates your cat will keep his mouth busy on something that can't kill him. Of course, also consider the dangers of toys with hanging doodads made out of string, ribbon, or anything that can get wrapped around intestines, etc., is obviously a trip to the ER waiting to happen.

6. **Pica-Proofing:** Put stuff away—you have to cat-proof if you have a chewer!

7. **Reward the Silence:** Sometimes humans forget to attend to the cat when they are doing anything *besides* chewing. Go back to chapter 9 and think about ways you can give your cat attention without reinforcing the chewing behavior.

The Mojo Moment in this case is really about having done due diligence and knowing everything you can about Pica, so that nothing takes you by surprise. Going through the steps has helped keep the things in your home safe from your cat, and you've incorporated all of the steps to the point that you've seen a decrease in chewing and an increase in your cat's confidence. For Pica guardians, the Mojo Moment is looking up from your book as you unwind, and seeing your cat sitting in between a duvet and a puzzle ball and choosing the latter. Well done!

Cord Chewing: A Special Case

Cord chewing can be dangerous because your cat could get electrocuted or start a fire. Get cord wraps—make sure they are solid, really hard plastic. Motion-sensitive air canisters can help; every time your cat approaches these computer cords, the air blast happens and tells him, "There's no reason to keep going there." But you need a "yes" for that "no," so lead your cat to a destination with cat grass or other chewable treats.

Notes from the Chef

My personal approach to Pica is to take into consideration what we know and what we don't. For instance, Pica, like many OCD-type behaviors, appears to contain a component of self-soothing mechanisms, like a human reaching for a cigarette or a drink, "stress eating," or nail-biting. Of course, the well-balanced human would turn to exercise or meditation, but my experience is that we gravitate back toward quick and easy ways to bring down the fever of radical discomfort. In certain cats, chewing helps make the stress go away. Self-soothing behaviors start early in life—when kittens are still on the milk line—and tendencies toward Pica often appear when a cat is young. Of course, another component of obsessive behaviors is that they take on a life of their own—so while reducing stress is helpful, it's not everything. Like I said, frustrating, for sure, but these steps have definitely provided some relief.

That said, where there is mystery, there is opportunity. There is also support somewhere in the Web-o-sphere. Due diligence and reaching out, taking what you learn here, and remembering that you know your cat better than anyone else—these are the ingredients for being an advocate for your cat. Established science will help us get a grip on conditions like Pica, but so will you. Whatever you do and whatever you learn, please pass it on; remember that there are so many other Pica households out there suffering the same frustrations—and potential losses—that you have.

CAT DADDY RECIPE NO. 10—

UNHAPPY TAILS TO YOU

The Problem:

Your cat hates his tail. He may hiss and growl at it or even attack it. Perhaps during these moments, he actually redirects that aggression onto you. Out of the blue, and multiple times a day, he just turns into a skin-spasming, growling, howling animal—he becomes someone you don't recognize. He may even be ripping the hair off his tail until he bleeds. Maybe you've used the terms bipolar, unpredictable, "Dr. Jekyll and Mr. Hyde," or just scary to describe him. Either way, you feel horrible for him and scared for his—and your—safety.

The Reality:

This insidious—and largely mysterious—problem is called FHS (Feline Hyperesthesia Syndrome), sometimes referred to as "twitchy cat disease." The back lightning, or skin rippling, is particularly pronounced, and you may see muscle spasms throughout cats' bodies. Cats with FHS behave like a ghost is chasing them. They can be loving with you, and then it's like a light switch is flicked, and they can, all of a sudden, turn and attack.

Hyperesthesia makes cats feel like their body is attacking them. They may even be experiencing hallucinations. These cats might enjoy some petting, but their sensitivity is usually off the charts. Sometimes we can link FHS to a previous injury, and it's important to remember that the tail is an extension of the spine. It's already incredibly sensitive. But here's the deal. There is basically zero research on this. There may be multiple causes, including: genes, stress, anxiety, sensory processing issues, trauma, skin problems, neurological problems.

Basically, we don't know the underlying cause(s) or how to fix FHS, but some cats do improve on a trial of painkillers or antiseizure medi-

thing that I can tell you is that if you commit not only to playing every day (that's a given), but *investing in the play* and draining hunter energy out of your cat during play, you're going to be thwarting a tremendous amount of bad behavior—not just play aggression. It goes far beyond that. But, hey, nobody wants to bleed, and this is a great way of making that stop. Your work in step 1 informs your work here: if you ascertain a time pattern to the aggression, step that time back by thirty minutes and institute your HCKE ritual.

4. **Cat Detectivism:** One of the reasons I have all my clients create a very detailed journal is to remove yourself from the story line and just write about actions, timing, and patterns that you start to notice in your cat's behavior. Once you look at the information you've gathered, it's a good bet that if your cat is engaging in play aggression, he's probably doing it around the same time every day. So if that's the case, then you have the capability to be proactive. It means that if you take a look at your journal and say, "I get up for work at six a.m. and I'm out the door by eight a.m. In between those times is when my ankles get attacked," then—well, I know you're not going to want to hear this because you've got lots to do in the morning, but that means that playing with your cat for at least a couple of minutes is really important in the morning. *The key is not to wait for the behavior. Be proactive!*

5. **It's not just about the when—it's about the where:** Use your Mojo Map! Aggression that happens by windows indicates that you might have outdoor cats triggering aggressive behavior in your indoor cats, and that could be causing a form of **redirected aggression**. See "Barbarians at the Gate" in chapter 18 for some solutions.

   If your cat tends to do that ankle attack from under a table, that tells you you've got a bush dweller; that's where he gains his hunting mojo. If that's the case, then play with him under the table. Use your feather toy and start bringing it to that floor level; commit to ground prey instead of just flying the bird in the air. Hunting-wise, he'd probably be more inclined—at least when it comes to starting that hunter motor—to start on the ground.

cation. It's the kind of thing that may require a lot of testing—X-rays, a visit to the neurologist—and lots of advocacy on your part.

The Steps:

1. **Log Episodes:** Put on your detective hat and chronicle every attack—you need baseline observations. Note the symptoms and triggers: Where and when do attacks happen? What was going on in the house at the time?
2. **Vid for Vet:** Take your cat to the vet and bring video so they can see what the behavior looks like. Discuss the right pharmaceutical assistance for your cat.
3. **Control the Energy:** Energy spikes can trigger episodes, so be aware of the activity in the household and manage triggers whenever possible (the Three Rs, etc.)
4. **Encourage Relaxation:** Make sure there are cocoons and other safe places to retreat.
5. **Catification, Cat TV, and HCKE:** Utilize some of the Total Cat Mojo staples to give your cat other things to think about besides his tail!

The Mojo Moment:

Hyperesthesia isn't about a cure; it's really about management. As with Pica, your Mojo Moment is one of peace in knowing what you're dealing with. You've done the research and you've met others dealing with the same issue in online forums. But the moment arrives when your cat has realized that the tail, while still possibly slightly annoying, is not the enemy. Even if you've succeeded in reducing but not eliminating the attacks, each of these moments is a Mojo-fied one.

THE OVERGROOMING SOLUTION

The Problem:

Your cat has taken her grooming regimen to a whole new level, and not in a good way. You notice that patches of fur are missing from her legs, or that she has a completely "naked belly," all due to her incessant overgrooming.

The Reality:

It's normal and important for cats to groom themselves, but some cats take it too far. Sometimes it starts with a flea allergy, a food sensitivity, or other skin condition. That licking that starts off as a way to relieve itching becomes habitual. In other cases, overgrooming could be a response to anxiety. For some cats, it can be a self-soothing behavior, like nail-biting in humans.

There are possible clues to the cause: A cat who is licking all over is usually itchy. A cat who is licking in one particular area is more likely to be experiencing pain. For example, some cats with painful bladders will lick their bellies raw.

The Steps:

1. **Vet Time:** Take your cat to the vet and rule out a dermatological or other medical problem. In some cases, cats who overgroom just need meds, plain and simple, to help support your other treatments.
2. **Identify Stressors:** Address any stressors in the environment, be it a threat from within (such as conflict between companion animals) or a threat from without (see "Barbarians at the Gate," page 317). Self-soothing mechanisms like overgrooming wouldn't be needed if the cat felt like she could deal with the stressors of everyday life.
3. **Bump Up Your Catification and HCKE:** Finding an interactive toy that your cat loves is key. Not only can you just drain energy out

of the Energetic Balloon every day, which will make your cat a little less likely to stop and groom, but the proper toy can help lead your cat away from targeting her own body. Notice the giveaway signs that she is beginning to lick herself, and redirect her into a small moment of play. Many times that's all it will take to end a grooming session before it begins.

4. **Lock in the House Rhythm:** Don't forget about the Three Rs—any cat with anxiety will get security from routine.

5. **Food!** Another reason a cat will overgroom is due to an allergy. A systematic food allergy trial will absolutely help, but it's a commitment. Starting with a limited-ingredient diet, and with a commitment from you AND your family and friends not to sneak treats, an allergy trial has often led to amazing results.

The Mojo Moment:

This is an easy one, folks: your cat still has her fur; even if it's thin, new growth, it's a sign that a corner has been turned and you have gained control of a very tricky problem.

18

When Outside Cats Cause Trouble for Inside Cats

HERE ARE MOMENTS of twin surprise that happen all the time between my clients and me. One of those moments is when I inform them that, because of the patterns of urination I see around the perimeter of their home, there must be outdoor cats, maybe ferals, that are causing serious stress. A look of shock comes over them, either because they knew there was a colony nearby but didn't know they had anything to do with the problem, or because they had no idea there were any cats in the neighborhood (which, most of the time, they'll find out once I assign some Detectivism homework). My surprise hits because to me, it's a Mojo basic, and I assume everyone knows that neighborhood cats can be territorial poison to indoor house cats. And then I think to myself, "I should write a book. . . ."

CAT DADDY RECIPE NO. 12

BARBARIANS AT THE GATE

The Problem:

A neighborhood community cat or four has taken an interest in your home turf and is creating territorial anxiety for your cat. They could be feral or free roaming; it doesn't matter. When this cat is around on the outside, bad things happen on the inside.

The Reality:

Imagine that neighborhood cats are sneaking into your house, eating your cat's food, using his litterbox (or the wall around it), and walking out again. Considering all we know about Cat Mojo and the sanctity of territory, we know that would be pretty catastrophic for your cat. Truth is, there's not much difference between that and cats circling the perimeter of your home. Cats don't recognize walls as boundaries in the same way that humans do. As long as they can smell the neighborhood cats, and as long as they can see them, they're just as much a present threat.

The Steps:

1. **Cat Detectivism:** Historically, one of the hardest parts of this equation has been figuring out where these cats are coming from and knowing the angles they take into your yard, because you have to set up deterrents where they can actually be triggered. Setting up a motion-activated camera can remove all doubt as to where these cats are coming from, and allows you to set up traps so you can TNR (trap-neuter-return) and/or place your deterrents and make changes or repairs to your fence to increase security. The technology of these cameras over the past few years has gotten so much more advanced that "tricks" that were considered high-tech and virtually unaffordable for most of us just a few years ago are completely within reach now. Some of these cameras, apart from just being motion activated, have night vision, even ways to time stamp an event and save it in a separate file. They are also completely portable, needing only an outlet, and they hook into your Wi-Fi. Man, do I wish this stuff had been available to me in the early days of my practice! Detectivism has never been easier.

While you're working on Step #1, continue with the rest of these steps:

2. **TNR Power:** One thing that requires more work on your part, but will save you years of aggravation, is TNR. If they are feral cats, get them TNR'd. If you're uninitiated to the process, finding a neighborhood group that does TNR and can help guide you through the process is a great first step. Either way, this is hands down the best way to eliminate the problem. Because as long as these cats are propagating, you'll always have a problem, and keeping them away becomes harder and harder. Also, TNR is, very simply, the right thing

to do. For more information about TNR and how you can make a world safe for your community cat friends, check out: www.jackson galaxyfoundation.org.

If the cats are walking around with collars and tags, it's okay to go to your neighbors and let them know the incredible damage that their cats are wreaking on your home. I've had that discussion with many a neighbor over the years. And as long as you don't go to their house waving your fists with veins bulging out of your neck, there's common ground to be found.

3. **A Room Without a View:** Although by no means a cure-all, sight blockers, such as cardboard, paper, or window films designed for privacy can be placed in the windows where your cat can see the other cats. However, just because your cats can't see something, it in no way means that they don't know that those guys are out there. If your windows are open, your cats can smell them a mile away.

4. **Remove Any Allure to Your Territory:** Why are those cats coming around? Usually, it's food or shelter. If you're leaving food outside your house, then you're setting up a buffet for the invaders. And as much as this pains me, and as much as it likely pains you, your territory has to be free of other cats if you're experiencing these symptoms of aggression inside your home. If you take care of ferals, move your feeding stations to beyond your property's lines, or at least to an area that is completely nondisruptive to your indoor cats.

5. **Deterrents:** Cayenne, orange peels, and eggshells aren't going to cut it. There are many products on the market that remotely squirt water, blast air, sound an alarm, or flash lights when movement breaks your cats' sight line. These are great tools, but they're not meant to be permanent. Think of them as training devices. The cats coming into your territory need to be reminded only so many times that every time they come in here, they get wet. As long as it happens every single time they come in, it shouldn't take that long to guide them to greener pastures.

Of course, there's the downside. The common complaints are that these things go off every time someone walks by; you get wet, your neighbors get wet, or the UPS guy gets hit. We've actually had traffic setting off the alarms in the middle of the night. But, in my experience, it's well worth it. It's not permanent, and it usually helps get the job done.

6. **Scent Unsoaking:** Wait for the sun to go down, take your black light around the outside perimeter of your house, and clean sprayed areas as you would clean any stain in your house. As you're ridding yourself of the outside threat, you can also tell if there are holes in your "fence." You can go back and double-check any repair work with a clean slate. By doing that, you find out what areas have been hit more than others, what resources the cats might be claiming and guarding—and that is where you reposition your deterrents.

7. **Vertical Territory:** Depending on who your cat is, putting vertical territory in the windows that he tends to get all crazy about can be a good thing. Oftentimes you'll see the aggression happen when your cat is on the floor, and he's face-to-face with the enemy. Having a crow's nest is a strategic boon for any cat. Being able to survey their domain completely keeps them a step ahead of their enemy.

8. **A Signpost to Boost Mojo:** A litterbox in those territorially vulnerable places can ease the territorial stress of a Napoleon. Signposts can forestall graffiti or redirected aggression, giving him that sense that, hey, I've got this area locked up.

The Mojo Moment:

Your backyard is now just that, and not a collection of battle lines. Your one-time Napoleon might be interested in Cat TV but not vigilant, running from window to window on high alert, building his moat. You might see cats pass through your yard occasionally, but you know them and their tendencies, they are neutered, and there's no reason for them to linger since their feeding station is at a safe distance. Your indoor cats are secure Mojitos who aren't bothered to take up arms to protect what is theirs.

An Outdoor Sanctuary

As I mentioned in chapter 12, there is a growing number of guardians who are fencing in their backyards with new and very cool designs that keep their cats in the yard and other critters, including other cats, out. If you've followed my recipe but the territorial frustration is still running in the red, think about this solution. Your cats get to go outside, feeling more secure about what they own, and at the same time expanding what is theirs exponentially. In the meantime, boundaries can be better enforced. As the old saying goes, "Tall fences make for good neighbors."

19

When Your Cat Is a Wallflower

VERY EARLY ON in my emerging career with cats, I began gravitating toward the Wallflowers. Especially in a shelter environment, the suffering I identified was unbearable to watch. Extreme fear in shelters was then, and in many cases today remains, a killable offense. I developed many of my techniques just to help get these guys off the ropes so that they could not only survive the process of moving through intake, evaluation, and adoption, but could do it while discovering their Mojito-ness  at the same time. I was determined that they would leave with more confidence than when we met. That rule stands to this day—whether in a shelter, a foster home, or a forever home.

Of course, I'm not in any way unique—we all, to a certain degree, identify with, and root for, the Undercat. Where we might differ is whether we cater to the fear by cloaking it in sympathy, or whether we dare them to step into a different light. This recipe is about embracing the latter.

THE BLOOMING

The Problem:

Your cat is demonstrating one or many of the classic fearful Wall-flower behaviors (as outlined in chapter 5, page 61). She may be spending most, if not all, of her time invisible—in hiding spots like closets, cabinets, on top of appliances, under the bed, or even inside the box spring of your bed. Wallflowers head for the hills whenever strangers enter the territory, or even when somebody they know moves too fast. For a constellation of reasons, yours may not feel safe coming out into the open until everyone is asleep. If you do see her, the one thing she never demonstrates is *confidence*.

Part of the problem that needs to be addressed here is human collusion. It's a combination of sympathetic intentions and, let's face it, the fact that Wallflowers are the least squeaky wheel in your home, and so the problem tends to disappear with the cat. Many guardians tend to normalize the scaredy-cat behavior of their Wallflower: "This is her favorite spot, her hidey-hole." "She's just more comfortable in the closet." "It's okay—he uses the litterbox, but only after everyone goes to bed." To be clear, hiding all the time is NOT normal, and shouldn't be dismissed as being okay. In order to address the problem, it has to be recognized *as* a problem.

The Reality:

Cats may be Wallflowers due to their genetics, a lack of early socialization, threats in the environment, or a combination of these and other factors, although being a Wallflower is often perceived to be "their personality." The goal is to allow your Wallflower to be the best version of himself, but first, we need to remember that there is no cookie-cutter result in terms of what his greater self looks like or how long it will take to get there; this is much more about natural change that will occur in the time it should when you apply the steps and are unflinchingly honest with both your cat and yourself. Your job is to provide love and comfort, but not in the hiding spots. You have to challenge your cats. If it's left to them, Wallflowers will spend the rest of their life disappearing, because it works for them. At some point, you're going to have to say, "This isn't going to work for you anymore." And in reality, it never did.

The Steps:

1. **Mark your Mojo Map:** When you take a hard look at where your cat spends his time, that will tell you just how small his world might be by identifying his Unconfident Wheres. It will also help you determine what some of the causes of small living might be—in some cases, Wallflowers are forced into a life of seclusion due to conflict with other animals in the home. At the same time, look for small indications of Dwelling Spots, of Confident Wheres. Then you will create destinations as you help him cross his Challenge Lines. Your job here is Detectivism—the map, at this point, helps you keep to "just the facts, ma'am."

2. **Identify Your Wallflower's Challenge Line:** Now it's time to start applying the facts that you are gathering. Look at your map and look at your cat. For instance, if your cat has one specific hiding place, use painter's tape to mark your cat's Challenge Line—where you see your cat hesitate, beyond which he will just not venture. Put a bowl of food right at that line; tomorrow, you'll move that bowl a few inches out. Then you reset the line by tiny amounts day by day. Find his Jackpot! Treat and hold it back at all other times *except* when his Challenge Line is being pushed. Your cat will welcome the challenge because on the other side of the challenge is this great reward.

3. **Revisit Your Challenge Line:** In chapter 9, we talked about your Challenge Line and the importance of always putting the best interests of your cat first—even as you feel those pangs of guilt when you watch your Wallflower experience a few growing pains. Stay the course here. Think about the rewards and what is on the other side for him: a better life.

4. **Stop Living in the Under-World:** Applying lessons learned about your Challenge Line, start getting serious about theirs. As an exam-

ple, please don't feed your cat under the bed. You can give your cat love and comfort but just not there. To help your Wallflower, you have to lay down a series of gentle but actual challenges, including closing off the spaces that represent caving.

Blocking off the Unders, however, is a gradual process (see page 110). Don't remove everything all at once. Say you start with blocking off under the bed. Chances are that if your Wallflower caves under the bed, she goes all the way back under the headboard. That's where you start blocking—at the heart of the cave, gradually moving out until the bed is no longer a caving destination.

Research tells us that it is critical that cats have safe spaces in which to spend time. While blocking off those Unders, you can give your cat cocoons that allow him that same sense of safety, without the ego-deflating choice of life under a bed.

5. **Expand Their Territory (Bit by Bit):** One of the most useful tools we have for our Wallflowers is base camp. Set up base camp like I outlined in chapter 8 (page 102)—make that room as pleasant as possible, using scent soakers, cocoons, perches, tunnels, and, of course, items that share your scent. While challenging your cat to come out from caving, you are presenting a closed environment that she will find safe and will marinate with her scent/Mojo. Then, using Base Camp Expansion (see page 103), you enlarge the world but keep it just as safe as before. Basically, you want to expand her turf bit by bit, spreading her scent throughout the home as if it were a new territory.

6. **Catification:** Allow the territory to become your Wallflower's friend. Both when setting up base camp and beyond, add features that allow your cat to move around in those "comfort zones," while you gently push his Challenge Line. Get your cat into the vertical world with a Superhighway using the basic teaching techniques outlined in chapter 8, demonstrating to him that he can move from that place of fear into a more confident world.

7. **HCKE:** Play therapy is critical for Wallflowers. The math is simple—when they pounce on that toy, they own that spot. Ownership of territory = Cat Mojo supreme. Unleash the Mojo! Encourage your

Wallflower to play, paying special attention to providing small, quiet, interactive toys if that's what he likes best.

The Mojo Moment:

With Wallflowers, it's really about the journey and not about the destination. For me, with my cat Velouria, it was a big deal the first time I came home and she was sleeping on the bed instead of in one of her cocoons. That was when she was about six years old. That may seem like a long time, but as I developed my approach with her (yes, she is the original Wallflower), I noticed improvements that kept me going. For each Wallflower, it's really about being the most Mojo-fied version of herself possible. She might always be shy, but you'll find her having more and more Mojo moments—and that cocoon has allowed your cat to truly transform into a butterfly.

Getting Comfortable with Visitors

Progress with Wallflowers requires consistency and daily work to gain their trust.

1. Have people call instead of ringing the doorbell; many cats learn that the doorbell is a precursor to something scary. Instead, go out and walk back in with your visitors, and give your cat a Jackpot! Treat. You can also use basic desensitization techniques like the one I outlined in "Cats and Kids," chapter 11 (page 204).

2. Visitors should not attempt to interact with Wallflowers on their first visit; they can just come in and do nothing. A gentle approach is important: revisit the **Three-Step Handshake** and **the Slow Blink.**

3. Another helpful technique is what I call the **Santa Claus Effect.** Every single time a human comes to the cat's home, he must bring the cat a Christmas gift. Have people other than you feed your Wallflower dinner and play with her; every time somebody comes over, it's Christmas.

Cat Daddy Dictionary: The Handoff

When cats are afraid of strangers, or seem to swipe at everyone except their guardian, you can use the guardian's "insider status" with the cat to help widen the cat's circle of trust. Being fearfully defensive toward people can shrink a cat's world, because other humans will just stay away. That creates a vicious cycle of isolation, and that can lead a cat to become overly attached to the one person they trust.

THE HANDOFF TECHNIQUE can help break that cycle. It starts with that trusted human (guardian) teaching other people how to touch his cat. As the guardian pets the cat, the new human should slowly and quietly get closer while the cat is in a relaxed state, eventually replacing the guardian's hand with hers. This widens the cat's circle of trust, but keeps the cat feeling safe because the guardian is right there.

The Social Bridge

Some Wallflowers benefit from having a social bridge: a Mojito Cat who can act as a bridge between that shy cat and other cats or humans in the home.

Wallflowers will "follow the leader" when they see another cat demonstrate play and confident behavior, and may start testing out some of those relaxed behaviors themselves!

20

When Your Cat Is Thinking
Outside the (Litter)Box

I F YOU'VE OPENED the book to this page, you're probably hoping for a
chapter that takes all litterbox problems, bundles them up in a cat
daddy cookbook, and gives you recipes that you can flip to in moments
of need—like this one. And, at least in my opinion, that unicorn doesn't
exist. Wait! Don't close the book! Let me explain. . . .

No matter who you are and where you find me—whether it's on social
media, during a Q&A session, in line at the supermarket—it doesn't matter. If you say, "Jackson, I have a problem with my cats and their litterbox,"
I can guarantee that fifteen minutes later, you'll *still* be explaining the
problem. Then I'll be answering for another thirty, after which I'll shrug
my shoulders and ask you to take me to your home.

If I had a nickel for every time I was approached to write a "quick how-
to" or a "top five reasons your cat won't use his litterbox," I'd be a dead
millionaire (because I'd shoot myself).

If I've done my job right in this book, you have in front of you all the
tools you'll need to successfully address the fifteen-minute question you
were about to ask me. You should also understand by now that no matter
how deep the toolbox and how many tools are in it, we are talking about
your cat. In *your home*. Among *your family*, both human and animal, and the
cat's cradle of relationships that links it all together.

In other words, when it comes to litterbox issues, there are simply no stock, one-size-fits-all solutions that I can pull out of my magic bag and hand to you. If there were, I would use them myself—every time.

Instead, I show up for work. Using the same toolbox I gave you (well, guitar case for me), the same tools, and the fine Total Cat Mojo tradition of cat Detectivism, I still have to work through the "process of elimination" to try to piece together clues at the scene of the crime. After twenty years of doing this, it remains a challenge, and I still have to return to the proverbial drawing board sometimes, reassess the data, and try, try again.

Of course, the good news is that there is help to be had. Solutions are there for you. THE most important part of this chapter—and the fine art of litterbox issue resolution as a whole—is not the fix itself. The most important part is taking the journey with your cat family that I take every day of my life—the journey from question mark to period. It begins with discovering unhappy surprises in the form of pee, poop, or both— somewhere besides where they are supposed to be—and coming completely unglued, suddenly drowning in frustration and helplessness. And it ends with knowing *why*.

Now, bear with me. . . . I believe that if I gave you one magical direction and it worked, you'd be worse off. It's like how I, along with probably 50 percent of the male species, fix any household thing that breaks with duct tape. So now my sink doesn't leak anymore. Despite my boasting to the contrary, I didn't *fix* anything. I now just have a broken sink wrapped in duct tape.

So, as we go through this chapter, even though you will actually have ample opportunity, I'm asking you to step away from the duct tape. Show up for your cat and yourself by doing the actual work. Remember, the pee (or poop, or both) isn't the problem—it's a symptom. Holding the root of the dis-ease in the palm of your hand is the goal. Then you'll address the symptoms, and you'll gain the key to the Cat Mojo kingdom along the way.

THE PROCESS OF ELIMINATION

I want to stay as true to my actual process as I can with you. If I came to your home and the only information at my disposal was that there was a litterbox issue, this is where we would begin. It's safe to say that you have a very real sense of urgency about the situation—after all, you called in a professional to help, and to some degree or another, your home and your family's sanity are both taking a hit. My sense of urgency comes from the fact that, as I mentioned earlier, *any* extracurricular litterbox incident is a symptom of a cat's dis-ease; there is some suffering going down, and resolving it ASAP is the goal. So the process here is to start in the shallowest part of the investigative waters and begin to wade in.

The goal is to strike pay dirt in the shallows, which is to say, find solutions in the place where Detectivism is done with broad strokes. In many cases, we can not only wrap up the issue pretty quickly but also prevent it from returning because it was an open-and-shut case. It may be, however, that the problem doesn't fit neatly into a category, or it's more deeply entrenched, or both. In that case, we just go into deeper waters. Then the only thing you'll need in that case is patience, because the deep water tools will be here for you as well.

But let's not get ahead of ourselves. The Process of Elimination always begins with the "Why?"

LITTERBOX PROBLEMS: THE BIG WHY

I group litterbox issues into three primary umbrella categories. They are:

1. **Territorial Stress:** In Mojo-centric thinking, it  would stand to reason that most litterbox issues have a territorial component to them. Whether the threat is real or perceived matters little; as we've seen with so many other problems that we've addressed, *if the Mojo is missing, there will be some pissing.*

   Included under this category would be:

A) Threats from within: Broken or nonexistent relationships (either with other animals or humans) as well as changes in the established rhythm of the territory or the territory itself will threaten the Mojo balance.

B) Threats from without: A feeling that the threat is causing the territory to shrink from the outside in.

2. **Litterbox Aversion:** Here, the choice is not to eliminate in strategic places outside of the box, but rather, to eliminate anyplace else *but* the litterbox. Physical issues, trauma of various shapes and sizes, preference in design or substrate, or issues with other inhabitants of the territory can all contribute.

3. **Medical Issues:** There can be a number of physical maladies that trigger eliminating outside the litterbox. Left untreated, many of these can lead to, or serve as an indication of, more serious health risks. (Of course, I should point out here that I always recommend a visit to the vet—without fail—at the first sign of any litterbox issues. More on this in a moment.)

With these three issues in mind, let's now proceed to the fastest path to resolution.

STARTING WITH THE "WHERE"

The fastest track I know to take an educated shot at a solution is to consider location first.

Perimeter

Where it is: Against exterior walls, under windows, around doors that lead outside (including the door that leads to the garage).

Why it's likely happening: *Territorial Stress.* If your cat is "perimeter marking"—that is, targeting the perimeter of the house—this typically indicates territorial stress, a Napoleonic response to a perceived threat. Something is coming at him from outside, usually other cats: "*This is my castle, so I'm building a moat.*"

How to fix it: Barbarians at the Gate—See chapter 18 (page 317) on identifying the exterior threat and what to do to restore balance.

Other info: In most cases, it would be spraying, as opposed to peeing. The key distinction is that peeing is what you're used to seeing, and spraying (or marking) is when they back up to a vertical surface and blast away.

Middle of the Room

Where it is: On the floor but away from the walls, either in the open or under a table or chair.

Why it's likely happening: *Territorial Stress.* It's likely that your cat is living in fear of somebody in the house and is being bullied. Being under the table, for example, gives him a 360-degree view of the entire room. He can pee someplace where he knows that in Cat Chess terms, he won't get checkmated while he's trying to pee.

How to fix it: Check out Bullies and Victims in chapter 14 (page 276).

Catification tips: Make sure litterboxes have multiple exits, and don't give your cats a covered box with the only opening facing the wall. In other words, avoid dead ends and ambush zones!

Bathroom

Where it is: In the bathtub or sink.

Why it's likely happening: *Litterbox Aversion.* Most often, it has something to do with the substrate itself. Bottom line is that the tub and sink are cool, smooth surfaces. The litter does not feel good on their paws, so they go for something smoother. Of course, this may lead to *Medical Issues.* This is a behavior I so often see in declawed cats because they are experiencing an associative/phantom pain, or because they're older and arthritis has set in either in or around their paws.

How to fix it: For this situation, or any time a cat has formed a negative association with a litterbox, it's possible for a new relationship to be built. See "Reintroduction to the Litterbox" later in this chapter.

Personal Belongings

Where it is: On the personal belongings of someone in the household, like clothing, a purse, shower mat, or even a baby crib.

Why it's likely happening: *Territorial Stress.* This is often the result of what I call Critical Mass. Most often seen in multianimal homes, your cat's inner Napoleon comes out as the family grows by one more being—animal or human. Whether it's a foster, an adoption, the birth of a baby, or a new boyfriend or girlfriend who starts spending the night, he decides enough is enough. He feels territorially threatened and claustrophobic and has to make a land grab. And he does it by planting a flag made of pee in belongings with the new being's scent strongly in them.

How to fix it: This is a territorial cry for help, as many of these extreme behaviors are. First things first: decrease the pee by increasing the space; go back and read chapter 8 on Catification. Also, read up on the nature of your Napoleon Cat (page 58). Finally, in chapter 19, we talked about the **Santa Claus Effect** (page 327), which is basically all about getting the "targeted person" back in the good graces of the peeing cat, so that a positive new association can be made. Conversely, now is the time to step away from the perceived emotions of the story line. In other words, it is at times like this that we decide the cat hates (fill in the blank). But in reality, it's what he feels insecure and anxious about, not who he hates, is jealous of, etc.

Doorways

Where it is: In or near doorways within the house, connecting rooms to hallways, etc.

Why it's likely happening: *Territorial Stress.* As I've always said about Catification, if you don't have enough in the way of signposts, the insecure cats will compensate with graffiti, literally "tagging" places with urine to signify that they own the area or the area past the doorway (and yes, in true tagging fashion, this will be done via spraying instead of just urinating on the floor, but there are always exceptions).

How to fix it: Catification, first and foremost. Make sure there are enough signposts throughout these areas, not just in the doorways but in the area through the doors that apparently is significant for the cat to overown. Also, this may call for heavy-duty scent soakers instead of just beds, etc. Putting a scratching post near the pee spot, or ideally a litterbox, will help matters. Don't forget, tagging is a symptom of anti-Mojo. Detectivism is called for to get to the root of the problem, beyond the quick fix.

Major Furniture Pieces

Where it is: Beds, couches, chairs: major human scent soakers.

Why it's likely happening: *Territorial Stress.* Most often misinterpreted as "He hates me since he pees on my side of the bed!" Think of this as the backhanded compliment. When home, like it or not, we will be in or around two scent soakers more than any others—the couch and our bed. Your cat peeing in those spots is the opposite side of the Mojo coin from a Mojito's gesture of rubbing up against you or your belongings, leaving his scent on it. This does the job also, but from a completely insecure place. As opposed to "I love and own you," this says "I love you and I'm desperate to own you (because someone else does or I'm afraid they are going to). Similarly, we will see land grabs like this when there is intercat animosity afoot.

How to fix it: Go back and reread the section on Napoleon Cats (page 58) to see which aspect resonates with your cat in your home, and use the tools to build up that Mojo. Catification *always* helps diffuse situations like this. Also, use the No/Yes technique from page 147 with the "no" being that piece of furniture and "yes" being scent soakers next to it, like beds, cat trees, and scratchers.

Additional note: Just remember that with objects of a distinct texture, there could always be elements of *Medical Issues* and/or *Litterbox Aversion*. If a quick pass through this fix doesn't take, explore the other paths before moving on.

Cat Furniture

Where it is: Major cat scent soakers, i.e., cat beds, towers, perches, and scratching posts.

Why it's likely happening: *Territorial Stress.* This is classic anti-Mojo graffiti. There is usually competition, or the perception of it, on the part of the culprit. This competition could be with other cats or dogs (and sometimes kids). Besides just being an expression of ove-rownership, a classic Napoleon maneuver, it can also be a desperate Wallflower move as she perceives that every other valuable piece of property has been taken or kept from her.

How to fix it: Go back to chapter 5 and read up on our cat archetypes. Fixing the problem begins and ends with knowing where the anxiety originates, not just which cat is doing it.

More high-value scent soakers can also help. Clearly the target has value either because of its location, texture, or popularity. Let the cats know that there are plenty of similar pieces they can own as well. If there is aggression between animals in the home, also consider the re-introduction technique outlined in chapter 14.

Vertical Surfaces

Where it is: Tables, stoves, countertops, etc.

Why it's likely happening: *Territorial Stress.* As with any of these locations, there can be many factors at play, but in this case, it usually happens in a classic bully/victim scenario. Either the victim doesn't feel safe on the floor and/or in the litterbox because she is constantly getting ambushed and chased, or she is on the losing side of Cat Chess checkmate. The victim/Wallflower goes vertical to get a better lay of the land so she can finally go in peace . . . OR she is chased vertically and pees/poops because, in part, it was scared out of her.

How to fix it: Clearly a 911. Separate the warring parties and begin the complete reintroduction technique from chapter 14.

Extra note: Other signs of territorial stress that don't necessarily have to do with the verticality of the location: (a) when the pee or poop happens in a trail and not just in one place; as the victim is being chased (or is running because she was ambushed and assumed she was being chased), she will just release her bladder or bowels or both as she runs; (b) a mix of hair with the excrement tells us that a fight was happening and bladder and/or bowels were voided during it.

Near Litterbox

Where it is: Within two feet of the litterbox.

Why it's likely happening: *Litterbox Aversion* or *Medical Issue.* Again, this is one of those things that as soon as I see it, I know what's going on. Of course, I've been wrong, but with this one, not so often. When there is a negative association with the box itself (most often because there is a pain issue involved with eliminating), the cat in question doesn't think to himself, "Damn, it hurts when I pee." He thinks, "This *place* hurts me." And with that logic, why go back? He knows that's where he should go, so he gets as close as possible. This also goes for cats who have started the habit of eliminating while standing so close to the edge of the box that the poop or pee winds up on the floor. Same avoidance.

How to fix it: See the Back to Basics section up next for the surface preference part of the equation. Also, this is a reminder once again to get to the vet to make sure that while we are working a behavioral track, your cat is not "raising the yellow flag." Once a diagnosis is made, then see litterbox reintroduction tips later in this chapter (page 343) as well.

BACK TO BASICS

If you didn't have much resolution from starting with the "Where," no worries. This is a process, after all, so we forge ahead. Next stop? The basics. First, review our Ten Litterbox Commandments and make sure you're on board with the lot of them. I've seen litterbox issues go away immediately just from the implementation of one of these suggestions.

Cat Daddy's Ten Litterbox Commandments—Quick View

(See the full explanations of the commandments in chapter 8, page 124.)

Thou Shalt Have One Box Per Cat + 1

There should be one litterbox for every cat in the house—plus one extra. For example, if you have two cats, you'll want three litterboxes, etc.

Thou Shalt Have Multiple, Well-Placed Stations

The boxes should be located where they work best for your cat, not you.

Thou Shalt Not Camouflage the King of Scent Soakers

I only recommend unscented litter, with no deodorizers in the litter, and no air fresheners right next to the box. Same thing goes for other forms of camouflaging—that is, disguising your box as a potted plant, etc.

Thou Shalt Observe the Law of Litter Common Sense

When keeping Raw Cat preferences in mind, litter common sense calls for the simplest choice. The fancier the substrate, the more that can go wrong.

Thou Shalt Not Mindlessly Fill the Box

Overfilling the box is a common problem simply because we think that more of a good thing will just make it a better thing. Not true. Try starting with just an inch or two of litter and adjust from there.

Thou Shalt Honor the Right Box

The box should be attractive and convenient—in other words, a friendly place that your cat won't think twice about getting into. The length of the litterbox should be at least 1.5 times the body length of your cat.

Thou Shalt Not Cover

Lids can lead to ambush zones and dead ends, especially in a home with dogs, kids, or other cats. Covers can get pretty nasty after repeated use and are hard to clean. Also, long-haired or larger cats can get a static shock from touching the sides of the hood as they enter or exit.

Thou Shalt Not Use a Liner

You might think that liners make your life a bit more convenient, but in reality, many cats don't like the texture of liners and can even get their claws stuck in them.

Thou Shalt Keep the Litterbox Clean

Cats unquestionably prefer a clean box to one that contains clumps of pee or poo logs.

Thou Shalt Allow Your Cat to Covet Another Box

The best way to find out what your cat likes in a litterbox is to give him choices (of size, style, location, types of litter), track what he uses, and adjust accordingly.

NEXT, REVIEW THESE:

Cat Daddy's Big Three for Litterbox Mojo

One of the first things I ask a client who's been dealing with litterbox issues is to go back in time to when the peeing outside the box first began and simply ask, "When did it start, and what could have possibly changed in our lives around that time?"

Changes with the Litterbox

An obvious place to start would be with the actual litterbox. Did you change any aspect of it, from the type of litter, to the location, to the box itself? If so, see if you can determine what your cat is missing about the old box and try to go back to what was working.

Changes in Routine

Did you get a new job or lose an old one? Did school start back up? Did you begin or end a major relationship? Basically, anything that would cause you to spend either more or less time at home will change the rhythm of the home . . . which gets back to the all-important Three Rs (see chapter 7). Reestablish a reliable rhythm!

Changes in Relationships (Comings and Goings)

New humans, new animals (cat or dog), a new infant . . . any of these additions could bring about a seismic shift in the home dynamic, especially if proper introductions or ongoing dynamics had been slighted. See chapter 10 for animal relations and chapter 11 for human relations (covering all ages). Relationship harmony on the home front could ease any territorial stress and get things "back in the box."

ADVANCED DETECTIVISM:
WHEN CASES ARE NOT OPEN AND SHUT

The examples I've given here are what I would consider the "broad stroke" solutions. Sometimes, the litterbox problems that are being experienced fit neatly into a category. Most of the time, however, they don't—at least not entirely. That's the folly of trying to write a handbook of sorts when it comes to complex behavior problems. While I firmly believe in all of the high-level Detectivism pieces in our process, there are an infinite number of variables involved once we plug these formulas into your home. It's not just about the cat who has "the problem"; it's also about the other players, human and animal; it's about the history of your family, the family's current dynamics, the complexities specific to your territory. . . .

So then, what if you have pee in a variety of our "Where" areas throughout the house, involving more than one "Why" category? Welcome to my world! Of course, just because you didn't get a complete answer to your cat's issues in the shallow waters is no reason to despair. I would say that at least 50 percent of the homes I've worked in, especially multianimal homes, contained a sort of "hybrid" diagnosis and resolution. This is where we have to take our Detectivism to the next level, get crafty with our powers of deductive reasoning, compile evidence from multiple vantage points, and truly engage the "process" of the Process of Elimination. And one of our best tools for "going deep" into the issue involves . . .

Bringing in the Mojo Map

As introduced in chapter 8, the Mojo Map is basically a blueprint of your house that details your cat's physical world: where things are placed in each room, where the litterboxes are, how traffic flows (for both humans and animals), and, as is relevant for our Cat Detectivism here, where fights and confrontations have broken out, and where "outside the box" activity has occurred.

The first step is to prepare the map exactly as you would have in the Catification section. Use different colors to represent where fights have occurred, where peeing/pooping has occurred, where your cats like to congregate, favorite resting spots, litterbox locations, food stations, and favorite locations to play.

Think back to the **Anti-Treasure Map** on page 243 and how the information was gathered. We will employ the map here just as we did then. The results take a little time to reveal themselves—remember, it does take time for our cat's actions to present a pattern. But that's the beautiful part of this way of working: my clients never fail to connect the dots as they go through a week or two of recording the comings and goings, so that a detailed macro view of the terrain emerges. It is then that we arrive at a critical point in our Advanced Detectivism process: things we initially saw as random occurrences, we now see as reliable patterns.

MORE CAT DADDY LITTERBOX MOJO

Yes, there is a whole lot of information when it comes to a cat's relationship to her litterbox (as I'm sure you've deduced by now). It is, after all, the primary scent soaker, and for her, a core component of her territory—and in turn, of her Mojo. The following tips, tricks, and techniques are absolutely key when it comes to rounding out your cat know-how and in turn, your Cat Mojo.

 ### Schedule an Appointment with the Vet

I don't mind being a broken record about this one. If you were to call and ask me to come to your home for a consult, I would schedule it far enough out that you would have time to go to the vet first. If I'm told that you had your cat's annual exam a few months ago and everything was fine, I would send you back, because a checkup isn't an exam with a purpose. An exam as part of my consultations is a true tip-to-tail. A CBC (complete blood count) with a thyroid level is important, as is a urinalysis (if dealing with a urine issue) or fecal exam (if it's a poop issue). Not to keep draining your bank account, but I may even send you back to the vet after our initial consult.

One thing your vet doesn't have the benefit of seeing is how your cat moves around the home territory—how he walks, uses stairs, gets in and out of the litterbox, etc. (Incidentally, this is one of the reasons I absolutely recommend trying to find a house-call vet in your area.) The blood panel will reveal signs of diabetes, renal issues, hyperthyroidism, even cancer—all things that can distinctly and suddenly affect behavior as it damages the body. In my years of work, I have seen an abscessed tooth cause extreme aggression and a broken tail or impacted anal glands cause months of litterbox avoidance. Cats hide pain—it's part of the Raw Cat makeup. We must make sure that while we are working a course of dedicated behavioral Detectivism, your cat isn't raising the yellow flag the whole time, saying "OW!" and not "I really hate your new boyfriend."

Common Signs of Medical Issues

- Vocalizing while in the litterbox
- The "poop and run" that often indicates pain or discomfort
- Small, marblelike poop nuggets, or conversely, soft stool that looks like pudding
- Really stinky poop
- Blood in the urine
- Dark, crystallized urine

Reintroduction to the Litterbox

A cat who has had a traumatic experience with a litterbox, whether the root of that trauma is medical, behavioral, or a combination of the two, cannot be expected to just "jump back in the saddle" once the problem is resolved. It makes sense. Let's say you take the subway to work every day.

Suddenly you hit a stretch where the train derails—not just once or twice, but six times in a row. I think it's a safe bet you'd start walking to work, and it would take quite a bit of effort to get you back on a subway.

The best way to reintroduce your cat to a litterbox is to present her with choices so that she can make the least scary one. Keep the old box for sure, but add a few more that look nothing like the original in terms of shape and feel. I've used everything from cookie sheets (with puppy pads on top) to round boxes, corner-shaped boxes, and Rubbermaid containers meant for storage—all with different shapes, different textures, different appearance, different height . . . just plain different. Try the same litter in the old box, but also a completely different one in the new boxes. Keep the consistency the same, but each brand has a unique feel to your cat. Steer away, as I always recommend, from scented litters, crystals, or, in my opinion, anything clay. There are now an absolute multitude of natural litters out there.

In general, I'm not a fan of boxes with lids on them or liners in them. As I said, keep the original box with all of the accoutrements you had with it, but in the new ones, stay simple. I also want you to offer other options in terms of location. This is one of those times that you may not like what I have to say, but it has worked for me so many times that I'd be loath to exclude it. Put the new boxes exactly where you wouldn't put them if it were up to you, like the center of the room, or in a room like your bedroom. Again, the idea is for her to have NO association with using the old litterbox—and we all habitually place our litterboxes in the same general area. With box reintroduction, the general rule of thumb is to make the diametrically opposite choice so that the experience won't trigger the trauma all over again.

Which Cat Is It?

I feel so old when I say this, but man, back when I started this work, if we had access to the kind of inexpensive surveillance cameras we have today, I would have been able to solve so many cases so much more quickly. With an ongoing litterbox issue, once you've narrowed down the most "hit" spots, you can have one of these cameras trained on the area. They are motion-activated, so only when one of your cats moves into the sightlines will it start to record. It's a brave new world out there, you youngsters with your hi-tech doodads!

There are many surprises that will crop up as you collect data. I think one of the larger mistakes my multicat clients make is thinking that only one cat is committing the crime. You're basically ignoring the rules of graffiti. So many times, cats will imitate street-gang turf warfare, "tagging" the same area over and over in a vain attempt to claim ownership. Even if initially it was one cat's misdeed, it's very easy for the other cats to misinterpret these signs. For example, let's say one cat is peeing outside the box because it's a physical issue; the other cats may take it as a territorial slight, and suddenly you've got a pissing war going on.

Another great benefit since surveillance technology became affordable to the cat masses is that we can blame the right cat. I can't even count how many homes I've worked in where the family had anywhere from three to six cats and were 100 percent convinced they knew who was doing all of the peeing or pooping around the house, even though they had not a shred of evidence. They were convinced, based on the personality of the cat they were pinning the blame on. In the past several years, I just leave one of my cams with the clients to actually get data, and the result has been, in at least a quarter of those cases, that they had blamed the wrong cat. The camera never lies!

CSI—Cat Scene Investigating: Black Light Tips

I honestly don't know where I would be if I didn't have a UV light (a.k.a. a "black light") to help me gather data and make interpretations when working cases that have a litterbox component to them. If you have a urination issue in your home, a black light is just an absolute must. Here are some tips, if you're a cat-pee black light newbie:

1. Use the black light in the dark, or get the room as dark as possible. Information becomes very unreliable with ambient light.

2. The colors that fluoresce will change over time, going from a deeper orange-yellow to a white as the proteins break down over time.

3. Swirl marks indicate a spot that you used a cleaner on at some point, like those rug shampooers. It might look like Spin Art. In a bad way.

4. Don't panic when, even though you cleaned it a million times, you still see the urine spots under a black light, because cat pee breaks down the dye in the carpet, so it will always fluoresce, no matter what (even when the smell and actual stain are imperceptible).

5. You can distinguish a fresh spot from a spot you've already cleaned. The fresh spot will fluoresce more brightly.

6. Make sure that each stain has a beginning and an end. Trace it, especially when you're looking around places like the baseboards.

Look at patterns:

- A circle on the floor signifies your cat letting go of his bladder.
- Spraying is usually on vertical surfaces, and the amount can vary.
- Little drops, most often in multiple spots, usually signifies a urinary tract problem.

AND FINALLY, FOR all I've been suggesting that you *do* to resolve litterbox issues, let's end the chapter with a few Do Nots:

THE DO NOTS

Nothing can fray your nerves faster than dealing in the moment with an ongoing litterbox issue. No matter how bad it gets, however, it's so important in those moments to step away from the cat! Remember, all you are doing is ramping up the anxiety, trying to punish when they have absolutely no idea why, all the while doing things in the name of "training" or "teaching a lesson." So remember:

- Do not pick up your cat and carry him to the litterbox.
- Do not rub his nose into his pee or poop.

- Do not put your cat into a time-out because she peed outside the box.
- Do not lock her in the bathroom with a litterbox and a dish for the next three days (or God forbid, three months).
- Do not yell at her.

Your cat will have zero idea, after about two seconds post-accident, *why* you are acting the way you are or doing to them what you are doing (or, through your "discipline," what lesson you are trying to teach). Literally, all you can do during this process is collect the data, clean up the mess, and move on. Armed with just a few frames of the movie, you're in no position to assess and in even less of a position to act upon what you see. Besides that, as we discussed in chapter 9, punishment just doesn't work, so just don't do it.

21

Eso Es Mojo

STANDING ON THAT stage in Buenos Aires a few years ago, slowly realizing that nobody knew what the hell I was talking about, I vaguely remember poking my head above the smog of my public speaking nightmare to think to myself, "I should write a book about Cat Mojo. That might keep me out of this kind of trouble, at least."

Whether it comes to *Saturday Night Fever* or your beloved Mojito Cat, hopefully you now got the mojo in you—and in your cat. I also hope that your number of "aha!" moments far outweigh the "WTF?!" moments. Along with that turnaround comes the banishment of words like "randomly," phrases like "out of nowhere" to describe your cat's behavior, and misguided anthropomorphisms about your cat hating you, your husband, wife, or kids.

When I was alone, usually late at night, in my old shelter stomping grounds, surrounded by scores of these . . . beings, I would often find myself frustratingly at the end of my human reasoning abilities. Cats, it seems, were taunting me with their inaccessibility; just like many of you, I found myself feeling resentful of the four-legged firewall staring back at me.

I had been a pretty lousy student at school. From beginning to end, my school years were pock-marked with wild inconsistencies. If the topic was purely theoretical, book-bound—forget about it. I was gone, daydreaming and clock-watching. If, however, the topic gave my creative side room to roam, that's when I was hooked . . . and happy.

In the case of cats, there were twin engines that roared to life, propelling me to the present moment—that creative side was fueled by learning about the Raw Cat. How absolutely miraculous it was that the ancestor was alive in front of me, parading their decidedly undomestic Mojo, trying with every passing day, every tick of the evolutionary clock, to fit into our world. It was a club that I didn't just want to observe—I wanted to belong to it, and to pass that fascination along to everyone I met. Secondly, there was another clock ticking; if I couldn't crack the code on a daily basis and help nudge the Raw Cat into the modern world of house cat, then he could die. I found myself, in spite of my best efforts, emotionally vulnerable as individual relationships were forged, realizing that these innocents were looking to me for their happiness and their very lives. That's when everything changed.

As I've said throughout this journey, the goal has never been about solutions, "fixing a hole where the rain gets in," as the song goes; it's about your desire to protect your family from the rain. The building and strengthening of your Mojo Toolbox has been a consistent solution. The success you've found in committing to empathy has given you the permission, so to speak, to explore cat guardianship as a two-way street—a relationship of value where compromise, not a sense of dominion, achieves harmony.

Maybe you've just flipped through the book, looking fervently for a solution to a problem that's been driving you mad. Of course that's why I've provided you with recipes—achieving sanity in the short-term is often the only way to keep this family unit intact during those end-of-your-rope periods. That said, I hope that you take my instruction as nothing more than a springboard from the world of Cats with a capital C, and dive into *your cat's world*. Recipes will get you only so far—if followed, they will keep you from starving (or at the very least from eating cold pizza and ramen for the rest of your life). But once you develop the intuition and imagination, you can build something that is *yours*, something that you can be proud of because you poured your heart into it. That's why I hope that at some point after the crisis passes, you'll take the time to explore all of the nooks and crannies of your cat's world; it's there that the one-time lousy student is waiting to share all of the juicy details that turned curiosity into fascination, appreciation into passion, and that ultimately turned him stark-raving cat almost twenty-five years ago.

Just as with any relationship, there will be head-scratching (or head-banging) moments when smooth sailing turns suddenly into choppy seas. For those times, here are a few Mojo mantras to keep in the back of your mind as your journey of Total Cat Mojo continues for years to come:

First, when in doubt, go straight back to the ABCs of what builds Raw Cat confidence: the Three Rs, the Confident Where, and HCKE. These tools will always unlock Mojo, no matter how old or young the cat is, the degree of trauma they may have had to endure, or any special needs that may inform their everyday life. And second, take a moment, as often as you can, to remember that you will never have it all figured out. Thinking that you have control over the outcome of any relationship will absolutely destroy it. Stay humble to, and remain a student of, the relationship itself. That was the hardest lesson I had to learn in the past, and the source of the most joy in my present.

As a last note, I'd be remiss if I didn't mention that as members of Team Cat Mojo, we all have the obligation to pay it forward. There are too many cats, millions of them, that would do anything just to have a family like yours and a base camp to call their own. There are also so many humans who say they don't like cats, are afraid of them, or are just "dog people." Quite simply, we need them *all*. While we can continue to take sides in the matter, the solution resides in our ability to compassionately educate, dispel myths, and in doing so, create a larger pool of adopters to give all of the homeless a home. Further, we need to spread the word even more aggressively about how spaying and neutering for house cats and TNR for feral cats can, for the first time, bring about a reality where we don't have to kill cats because there are just too many.

The human side of Cat Mojo is defined by those who realize that their guardianship extends well past the walls of their own home and into their community. Feral cats are our cats. Homeless cats are ours, also. And ultimately, so is the exponential joy we can feel and spread as we help shape a world that mirrors the love and familial protection we feel for *all cats*.

Now, go forth and Mojo-fy the world!

Illustration Credits

The letter d behind the number indicates it's a duplicate image found elsewhere in the book.

Osnat Feitelson: xvi, 3, 4, 5, 6, 8, 11, 12, 13d, 15, 22d, 23d, 26d, 27d, 28d, 29d, 33, 36, 37, 38d, 43d, 44, 46, 47, 48, 50d, 51, 53d, 55, 56, 58, 59, 61, 62, 64, 65, 66, 68, 69d, 78d, 80, 84d, 91d, 98, 100d, 104d, 106, 110d, 115, 123d, 130, 134, 137, 140, 148, 150, 153, 155, 158, 162, 163d, 164, 166d, 169, 171, 173d, 175d, 177, 181d, 184, 186, 187d, 189, 194, 195, 198, 203d, 206, 207, 208, 209, 215, 220d, 222, 227d, 228d, 231, 241, 244d, 251, 257d, 259, 267d, 269d, 270d, 273d, 277d, 280d, 286d, 287d, 289d, 291, 293d, 294d, 295, 297d, 299d, 302d, 303d, 304d, 305d, 312d, 315d, 316d, 322d, 323d, 328d, 330d, 331d, 333d, 336d, 341d, 342d, 345d, 347d, 348d, 351

Franzi Paetzold: 67, 76, 96, 102, 109, 114, 118, 135, 211, 243

Omaka Schultz (artist), Brandon Page (inker), Kyle Puttkammer (art director): 82, 87, 129, 143, 283, 292, 318

Emi Lenox: 40, 49, 121, 122, 131, 217, 219, 254, 274d, 300, 337d

Sayako Itoh: 6, 18d, 45d, 72, 89d, 233, 237d, 264d, 310d

Index